Chick Lit and Postfeminism ,

CULTURAL FRAMES, FRAMING CULTURE

Robert Newman, Editor

February 7, 2011
Dear Dover Public Library,
    Thanks a bunch for your support
and the opportunity to speak in a most
charming library! DPL is a local
treasure and has been a source of stimulation
                                    and delight
Stephanie Harzewski since my move
to Dover in August. With fond appreciation,
                                    Stephanie H.

Chick ❀ Lit ❀

and Postfeminism

University of Virginia Press

Charlottesville and London

University of Virginia Press
© 2011 by the Rector and Visitors of the University
of Virginia
All rights reserved
Printed in the United States of America on acid-free paper

First published 2011

9   8   7   6   5   4   3   2   1

Harzewski, Stephanie, 1974–
    Chick lit and postfeminism / Stephanie Harzewski.
        p. cm. — (Cultural frames, framing culture)
    Includes bibliographical references and index.
    ISBN 978-0-8139-3071-8 (cloth : alk. paper) —
ISBN 978-0-8139-3072-5 (pbk. : alk. paper) —
ISBN 978-0-8139-3075-6 (e-book)
    1. American fiction—Women authors—History
and criticism. 2. English fiction—Women authors—
History and criticism. 3. Chick lit—History and
criticism. 4. Women—Books and reading. 5. Single
women in literature. 6. Consumption (Economics)
in literature. 7. Man-woman relationships in
literature. 8. Popular culture in literature. 9. Social
values in literature. 10. Feminist theory. I. Title.
    PS374.W6H379 2011
    813'.6099287—dc22

                                                    2010018728

To Vincent Harzewski, my beloved father, who taught me how to read. This generous act lives on through my students. Our bond is forever.

She was almost the age that Balzac held so
dangerous—almost she was the Woman of Thirty—
yet she had not properly tasted of the apple of
knowledge. She had to wait until she met a young
man who was not her husband, was destined to tarry
until she was under the influence of a Southern
moonlight and the whispers of the Gulf and many
other passionate things, before there began in her
the first faint flushing of desire. So, at any rate, Kate
Chopin asked us to believe.
—Percival Pollard on *The Awakening*

When women stop reading, the novel will be dead.
—Ian McEwan

Contents

Acknowledgments

I WISH FIRST to thank the organizations and centers whose financial support enabled the writing of this study. This project was funded by an American Association of University Women Dissertation Fellowship, a Kosciuszko Foundation Tuition Scholarship, an Alice Paul Center for Research on Women and Gender Dissertation Fellowship from the University of Pennsylvania, a Woodrow Wilson Foundation Dissertation Grant in Women's Studies, and, after I completed my PhD, a Research Grant from Romance Writers of America. Vicki Mahaffey and Emily Steiner helped guide me through the beginning of this project in the summer of 2003 as leaders of the dissertation prospectus workshop. My colleagues Alexine Fleck, Kristina Baumli, and Stella Singer continued this support as members of a dissertation group. Their copyediting and content suggestions were met with the assistance of additional readers, my best friend, Jeffrey Lieber, and Paul Delnero. The University of Pennsylvania's Dissertation Bootcamp offered a quiet writing space, motivation, and sustenance during the summer of 2005 as I completed the first draft of the manuscript.

I am grateful to scholars Mallory Young, Suzanne Ferriss, and Lisa Johnson for their support of the project and astute editorial suggestions for earlier versions of this manuscript; Young and Ferris's volume *Chick Lit: The New Woman's Fiction* (2005) paved the way for my own study. Cris Mazza and Jeffrey DeShell generously shared valuable historical background in tracing chick lit's evolution from an avant-garde literary movement to a subset of popular fiction. Many members of Yahoo!'s Chick Lit listserv (now named "Fiction That Sells") offered thoughtful answers to questions sent to the list; the enthusiasm of this group helped sustain my energy level during the composition of the manuscript. Novelists Caren Lissner, Deanna Carlyle, Shanna Swendson, Melissa Senate, Candace Bushnell, Jennifer Weiner, and Alisa Valdes-Rodriguez graciously agreed to interviews or answered questions about this media phenomenon via e-mail. The Taylor and Francis Group and the Barnard Center for Research on Women granted permission to reprint sections of the introduction and chapters 1 and 3 that were published in earlier form. Excerpts from the introduction and chapter 1 were published in earlier versions in " 'Chick Lit' and the Urban Code Heroine: Interview Symposium with Caren Lissner, Melissa Senate, Alisa Valdes-Rodriguez, and Jennifer Weiner," in the anthology *American Voices*, edited by Laura Alonso Gallo, and are reprinted here with permission from the publisher, Aduana Vieja (Cádiz, Spain). The Philadelphia chapter of the Kosciuszko Foundation and the University of New Hampshire's Edmund G. Miller Fund for the Department of English generously subsidized the publication of this book.

I am grateful most to my dissertation advisor, Rita Barnard, and committee, Jim English, John Richetti, Wendy Steiner, and Kathy Peiss, for their world-class editorial assistance. My editor, Cathie Brettschneider, continued this support and encouraged me to see the project through the stages of the publishing process. Their professionalism and goodwill I aim to emulate throughout the duration of my career. My parents, Vincent and Kathleen, sister, Caroline, and late grandmother, Helen McNally, gave love, humor, and patience during the long haul of the PhD. It is a great comfort that my father lived to retire and see the completion of this manuscript. Finally, I thank the trees of West Philadelphia, and my dear cats, Princess Silk and Josie, for their gifts of beauty, mischief, and grace.

Chick Lit and Postfeminism

Introduction

Heels over Hemingway

> Popular romance, in whatever media it may come,
> is often an expression of a frivolous or silly social
> mythology, and a value judgment on the social
> mythology is likely to be more relevant to criticism
> than a value judgment on the literary merit.
>
> —Northrop Frye, *The Secular Scripture*

IN THE *Westminster Review* essay "Silly Novels by Lady Novelists" (1856), George Eliot surveys contemporary British romance fiction as a "genus with many species," including the "frothy," "prosy," "pious," and "pedantic," and condemns it all as witless. It is not the fact that women are writing novels that elicits anxiety for Eliot but that men—and women—may take sentimental or romance fiction to be definitive statements on women's prose craftsmanship. Eliot fears that whimsicality, part of these novels' infectious quality and commercial appeal, will be seized on by men to perpetuate negative gender stereotypes, specifically, that women are dreamy, artificial, and silly.

Eliot's apprehension is not unfounded when one considers the history

❀ I

of the novel since its rise in the eighteenth century and the counterdis-
course it has provoked at the crossroads of female sexuality, authorship,
and commerce. When a new class of women writers availed themselves
of improved printing technologies and an expanding middle-class reading
public, many achieved popular recognition and sizable capital and thereby
incurred the wrath of their male counterparts. This anxiety over women's
writing was expressed in vituperations against amatory fiction and, in latter
decades, domestic novels. For instance, in *The Dunciad* (1728), Alexander
Pope cast Eliza Haywood, the most prolific woman author of eighteenth-
century England, as a publishers' pissing contest trophy—partly because
this Danielle Steel of Pope's day was an adversary in the literary marketplace. William Dean Howells in 1871 classified women's nineteenth-century
popular domestic fiction under the rubric of "dubiosities," while Nathaniel
Hawthorne, in an 1895 letter to his publisher William Tickner, cursed the
"d——d mob of scribbling women," an invective surely motivated in part
by their enviable sales (Howells 383; Marks 14). With women's popular
fiction historically so denigrated, it is not surprising that the writer born
"Mary Ann Evans" would employ similar condescension to avoid the label
of silly lady novelist.

Nearly 150 years after Eliot's essay, a variant of romance fiction emerged
and was denounced soon after as being of superficial interest and merit.
The last decade of the twentieth century witnessed a resurgence of anti-
novel discourse directed at a new set of women prose writers. These authors have been classified by the neologism *chickerati*, scribblers of "chick
lit," their popular fiction characterized by its detractors as consisting of
"connect-the-dot plots" enclosed within "identikit covers" and titles in
loopy cursive script (Thomas). Established women writers have publicly
decried chick lit, perhaps to avoid association with commercial writing.
Dame Beryl Bainbridge judges this latest manifestation of the courtship
novel as "froth," while Doris Lessing deems it "instantly forgettable"
(Ezard). *New York Times* columnist Maureen Dowd, in an editorial from
which I take this introduction's title, lamented the genre as "all chick and
no lit"—the novel, once said to be a looking glass of its time, reduced to
"a makeup mirror" (15). These distinguished writers, as well as a growing
number of women journalists, are concerned that chick lit not only will be
taken as representative of "women's writing" but will disqualify aspiring
and younger women writers from critical recognition.[1] That chick lit is

showcased in bookstore displays titled "It's a Girl Thing" and a growing number of titles are pigeonholed into this classification can only increase the ire of women critics who, like Eliot, are fearful that frothiness might once again come to seem the hallmark of female literary expression.[2]

These controversial novels are the subject of my study. In vain I have struggled to mask the dumbing-down effect on sentences that is nearly instantaneous with the inclusion of the phrase "chick lit"; experimenting with substitute diction like "this popular reading" and "this corpus" casts me as prematurely geriatric or simply inflated. The phonemic proximity of "chick lit" to a brand of chewing gum impedes rigorous considerations from the get-go. Rhetorical impediments aside, this book seeks to understand the social conditions that gave rise to chick lit—a new incarnation of the courtship novel in the mid-1990s—and its continued popularity. Though not what Ralph Ellison might call "disguised sociology," these urban period pieces offer parodic commentary on significant demographic shifts in the United States and the United Kingdom. New social phenomena—the rise of serial cohabitation, the increasing age for first marriage, the phenomenon of the "starter marriage," and declining rates of remarriage—have led to the emergence of what chick lit authors call "singleton" lifestyles. (In 2005, married couples became a minority of all American households for the first time [Roberts].) Chick lit is both a commentary on and a product of the singles market, which expanded in the late 1990s from matchmaking services and Club Med to a large-scale commercial sector and e-business niche. Chick lit not only emplots the past two decades' upheaval in marriage and education patterns but dramatizes the plight of the increasing number of women who are hitting "the glass ceiling of relationship standards" despite the proliferation of new dating technologies (Napalkova).

The chick lit genre is best exemplified by HBO's *Sex and the City* series and Helen Fielding's *Bridget Jones's Diary*, both originally newspaper columns published in book form in 1996. It is propelled by and responds to what has been dubbed "The Bridget Jones Effect," a syndrome, some journalists maintain, afflicting especially thirtysomething women who become consumed with "dating panic" and strategies for meeting Mr. Right (Match. com Public Relations Team). In the past decade major publishers have launched imprints capitalizing on a particular kind of feminine angst, fictionally rendered humorous or, as some readers have claimed, archetypal.

The semiautobiographical adventures of their protagonists—typically a single, urban media professional—provide an ethnographic report on a new dating system and a shift in the climate of feminism. These novels, often set in the contemporary metropolis, reflect the consumerism and high energy of a world I once inhabited, having worked several years in the Manhattan publishing sector and lived in New York City for more than a quarter century. Though bearing strong ties to earlier courtship novels in their protagonists' quest for a husband, chick lit novels' representation of modern love is starkly different, as is their depiction of the single woman and her economic status.

Marrying elements of the popular romance with the satiric aspects of the novel of manners, chick lit extends Jane Austen's comedic legacy and brings elements of adventure fiction to the contemplative tradition of the novel of manners. Chick lit revisits the "class without money" conflict central to the novel of manners tradition. The predicament of having to satisfy couture tastes on a middle-class budget, analogous to Lily Bart's class-without-money predicament, is a standard plotline in the genre. Protagonists wrestle with a barrage of the city's material temptations, particularly fine apparel, and often succumb to hefty credit card debt. Not surprisingly, Manhattan and London, as publishing capitals and shopping meccas, figure prominently in both Anglo and American texts. With Edith Wharton and Austen as acknowledged precedents, chick lit chronicles heroines' fortunes on the marriage market and assesses contemporary courtship behavior, dress, and social motives. References to these authors also operate affectively: the female reader can indulge in perceiving herself as a modern-day version of a classic heroine, her situation cast in the light of a private epic.

The novel of manners focuses on society and culture, frequently satirically, with narrators and characters often reader-participants of class hierarchies, their maintenance, and their penetration. This usually lightly ironic subgenre has ties to the romance in its frequent marriage plot and may join subjects in marital union. Because an earnest endorsement of a protagonist's behavior is not requisite, the novel of manners often has a romantic plotline while being critical or reserved in its stance on a specific male-female union. These novels sometimes end with death, an unfruitful marriage plot, or both, the last the case, for example, in Henry James's *Daisy*

Miller (1878) and Wharton's *The House of Mirth* (1905). While somberness, isolation, or tragedy is a potential destination within these texts, the subgenre is more commonly infused with a comedic, entertaining current.

In his *The Sense of Society: A History of the American Novel of Manners* (1977), a survey of the works of Henry James to Louis Auchincloss, Gordon Milne highlights the "not-quite-belonging figure" whom authors of this fiction frequently select as a protagonist, with plot tension emanating from the conflict between the individual pursuit of self-fulfillment and social responsibility (12). This usually aesthetically sensitive figure is not central to chick lit, as it typically foregrounds a relatively average female, though she may confront marginality and experience anxiety, even desperation, because of her single status. While novels of manners have upper-middle- to upper-class protagonists and are more often than not authored by writers of the same class, the majority of chick lit concentrates on the middle and upper-middle classes, with protagonists often aspiring to greater material resources; to remain average is not the goal of a chick lit protagonist, though numerous novels reward an average protagonist with a more socially and economically superior man. The "balanced, chiseled, polished style" Milne identifies as an attribute of the novel of manners, one evoking the genre's upper-class world, is not characteristic of chick lit, with its impressionistic, colloquial, more journalistic narration (13). Whereas the novel of manners is traditionally written in the third person, chick lit typically uses first, with numerous texts self-classifying themselves as semifictional diaries. While witty, the novels lack the lengthy repartee we associate with Austen's Darcy and Elizabeth Bennet. The chick lit genre presents a new novel of manners, I argue, not in the presentation of an exaggerated version of its codes, but in its often parodic and intricate bricolage of diverse popular and literary forms.

An underanalyzed body of postmodern fiction, chick lit serves as an accessible portal into contemporary gender politics and questions of cultural value. Since the turn of this century, chick lit has been a lively topic of debate in American culture wars. The *Oxford English Dictionary* defines the genre in innocuous enough terms as "literature by, for, or about women; esp. a type of fiction, typically focusing on the social lives and relationships of women, and often aimed at readers with similar experiences" (*OED* 2007). It has been judged, however, as a pink menace to both established and debut women authors who perceive it as staging a coup upon literary seriousness and undoing the canonical status of earlier works from *Pride and Prejudice* to *The Bell Jar*. Chick lit's expansion from a marketing niche to a dominant presence on fiction tables has been noted by Dowd, who, with dejection, interpreted this takeover as a sign that American fiction is "undergoing a certain re-feminization" harking back to the popularity of domestic fiction of the nineteenth century ("Heels" 15). A medium of "women's culture," chick lit, for Lauren Berlant, serves as a "commodified genre of intimacy," one that operates by enacting a fantasy that a woman's life is not just her own but an experience understood by other women, even when it is not shared by many (or any); such insider self-help genres function as "a critical chorus that sees the expression of emotional response and conceptual recalibration as achievement enough" (x). Berlant, like Dowd, reads chick lit as a permutation of the sentimental novel, one that attempts to validate the reader's feelings as "normal" and part of a collective affect.

Some, such as novelist Jennifer Belle, maintain that authors and buyers of chick lit are deliberately "undermining the women's movement." Members of this camp view the chick lit label as literary branding at its most pernicious and have publicly distanced their writing from this categorization. For instance, Curtis Sittenfeld, author of *Prep* (2005), in a pan of *The Wonder Spot* (2005) by Melissa Bank, whose short story collection *The Girls' Guide to Hunting and Fishing* (1999) was pivotal in igniting the chick lit explosion in the United States, criticized Bank's novel in her *New York Times* review by labeling it chick lit and comparing this label to *slut*. In her words, "To suggest that another woman's ostensibly literary novel is chick lit feels catty, not unlike calling another woman a slut—doesn't the term basically bring down all of us? And yet, with *The Wonder Spot*, it's hard to resist."

Odium toward the chick lit label and its growing string of associations (slick covers, fast craftsmanship, and the pleasures of an easy plot) was made most empathic in the anthology *This Is Not Chick Lit: Original Stories by America's Best Women Writers* (2006), edited by Elizabeth Merrick and consisting of eighteen stories by marquee names like Francine Prose and Mary Gordon, as well as burgeoning distinctive voices. Merrick in her introduction presents a clear dichotomy between authors of chick lit and women writers of literary fiction:

Chick lit's formula numbs our senses. Literature, by contrast, grants us access to countless new cultures, places, and inner lives. Where chick lit reduces the complexity of the human experience, literature increases our awareness of other perspectives and paths. Literature employs carefully crafted language to expand our reality, instead of beating us over the head with clichés that promote a narrow worldview. Chick lit shuts down our consciousness. Literature expands our imagination. (ix)

Merrick, albeit in rhetoric reminiscent of an introduction to a high school English textbook, sets what she assesses as the anesthetizing, reductive world of chick lit against the expansiveness and vitality of literature. With cover lettering in chick lit's signature pink, superimposed over a black background of negation, the anthology features well-developed protagonists of various nationalities set in working- and lower-middle-class backgrounds, a demographic atypical of chick lit's predominantly white bourgeoisie characters. Besides an edgier, more multicultural scope, the anthology in its back matter stresses the legitimacy of the literariness of its authors: each author bio highlights fellowships, teaching positions, and prizes. These pedigrees, together with representations of terrorism, female elderliness, and the alienation of struggling immigrants, lend the volume a politically correct tone, with certain stories such as Chimamanda Ngozi Adichie's "The Thing Around Your Neck" fine choices for Introduction to Women's Studies syllabi.

Others, however, do not see chick lit as a privatized simulacrum of female sociality but find its comic treatment of high-class problems a breath of fresh air, perhaps an intermediary between the pure escapism of the Harlequin and the compulsory progressiveness of feminist polemics. A rejoinder to Merrick's collection, *This Is Chick-Lit*, edited by Lauren Baratz-Logsted and published almost simultaneously, has a red d'Orsay evening pump proudly gracing its front and back cover. This icon prefaces each of the eighteen short stories, with titles such as "The Infidelity Diet," "Nice Jewish Boy," "The Ring," and "Dead Friends and Other Dating Dilemmas." Baratz-Logsted's introduction stresses the entertainment purpose of chick lit and includes a discretionary caveat: "Please be advised: none of the stories solve the problem of what to do about Iraq or deliver a prescription for curing cancer" (4). The predominantly first-person, dialogue-driven stories are each preceded by a paragraph in which the author speaks to the chick lit label and its level of offensiveness. A short author bio follows each piece, and while, like those in *This Is Not Chick Lit*, they do not shy away from mentioning literary distinctions, the bios, in a more commercial gesture, contain references to authors' blogs and Web sites. An appendix features book recommendations by each author, with choices ranging from chick lit to the nonfiction feminist classic *Reading "Lolita" in Tehran*. Together, both anthologies defend competing agendas for the function of the woman writer and the purposes of fiction.

An analysis of chick lit would therefore be perfunctory without substantial attention to its mediation with feminism. While the market for the Harlequin romance exploded with the advent of second-wave feminism, chick lit emerged in what has been described as a postfeminism era, and it has been frequently pointed to as evidence, if not the cause, of feminism's debilitation. The most popular image on chick lit book covers—high-heeled shoes with "toe cleavage"—is an icon of postfeminism. Yvonne Tasker and Diane Negra's volume *Interrogating Postfeminism: Gender and the Politics of Popular Culture* (2007) bears such an image on its cover. From as early as the mid-1980s, feminist literary critics have ascribed the designation *postfeminist* to certain works of women-authored fiction, such as The Vampire Chronicles series (1976–) by Anne Rice, as well as to the vision of communities imagined by Margaret Atwood and the lesbian science fiction writer Nicola Griffith. (While commonly believed to have emerged at the end of the twentieth century, the term *postfeminist* dates from a women's literary group's manifesto of 1919, and its evolving meanings are taken up in greater depth in chapter 5.) Though literary critics have identified postfeminist attributes in contemporary fiction, their efforts are isolated in their treatment of individual, and sometimes not widely known, texts. While particular texts have been labeled as postfeminist, chick lit is the first genre of fiction that has been generally discussed in this fashion. Journalists and chick lit authors themselves have classified the novels as postfeminist, and Maureen Corrigan, the book critic for National Public Radio's *Fresh Air* program, has referred to chick lit as "the pinking of postfeminism." Chick lit is not the only existing type of postfeminist novel, but it is the most culturally visible form of postfeminist fiction.

Arguably the most overarching and holistic analysis of twenty-first-century postfeminism to date, *What a Girl Wants? Fantasizing the Reclamation of Self in Postfeminism*, by Diane Negra (2009), adroitly examines a diverse range of media forms—Hollywood romantic comedies, advertising and journalism, women-centered prime-time TV dramas and talk shows, reality TV programs, as well as female advice gurus and tastemakers such as Nigella Lawson and Rachel Ray—to reveal the pervasiveness of this discourse in the lives of teen girls and women of childbearing years. Postfeminist discourse does not confine itself to twenty- and thirty-something women, but, targeting a wider generational cluster, "accelerates the consumerist maturity of girls, carving out new demographic categories such as that of the 'tween,' " through phenomena such as princess-themed marketing (47). A confusion of girlhood and womanhood, with female adulthood represented as a state oscillating between pleasure and panic, is quintessentially postfeminist, and popular films such as *13 Going on 30* (2004) and *Enchanted* (2007) indicate that postfeminism seems to be "fundamentally uncomfortable with female adulthood itself, casting all women as girls to some extent" (12–14). By extension, postfeminism thrives on anxieties about physical aging while simultaneously extending the promise of age evasion through elite beauty products and Bliss Spa–type consumer subcultures (12).

Concentrating on the genres of film, television, and lifestyle magazines, rather than print fiction, Negra dexterously extracts tropes of postfeminism, several of which underlie the chick lit phenomenon. For example, postfeminism, for Negra, positions itself as "pleasingly moderated," a contrast to a notion of feminism as "rigid, serious, anti-sex and romance, difficult, and extremist," employing largely negative invocations of (often anonymous) feminists (2). Postfeminism frequently operates through the "stylistic alibi" of irony, its hip style masking conservative ideologies such as the rejection of feminist-inflected working-women career paradigms in an urban context, a glorification (and commodification) of pregnancy, and a retreat from the corporate workplace, tropes assisted by fundamentalist Christianity, though this last detail is not fully developed (62, 33). Chick lit does not match up with postfeminism's narrative motif of what Negra identifies as "the social fantasy of hometown," embodied in the scenario of a professional urban woman who returns to her hometown, a trope dramatized in the hit NBC television program *Providence* (1999–2003) or pop sociology documenting the "daughter track"—that is, the giving up of paid work to care for elderly or infirm parents. "The rediscovery of hometown via romance (and vice versa)," Negra contends, is a regular feature of chick lit, but she cites just two novels (15). I did not find overlap in my sample with the use of the New England or southern hometown as an idealized regional space in what Negra calls "retreatist media fiction." Again, *What a Girl Wants?* however multifaceted in its selection of primary media texts, does not purport to be a study of chick lit; the point instead is that while chick lit aligns itself with postfeminism on many facets, it is but one, though certainly a major, incarnation of this social moment, and works in tandem with other postfeminist media.

The most salient intersection with the media in Negra's sample and the genre of chick lit, however, is the importance accorded to consumption, particularly the ability to select the correct commodities to attain a lifestyle inspired by celebrity culture, such as luxury weddings, the mainstreaming of the nanny figure, and the routinization of cosmetic surgery and breast implants. Journalists skeptical of postfeminism's being anything more than a mentality conflating personal empowerment with narcissism code the term as a cross between a lifestyle available for purchase and a sophomoric dilution of earlier feminism and its idea of "choice." Michelle Goldberg's AlterNet editorial "Feminism for Sale" (2001), though not explicitly mentioning the term *postfeminism*, refers to chick lit, HBO's *Sex and the City*, and girl-power zines like *Bust*, *Maxi*, and *Lucky* as "shopping-and-fucking feminism," "easy-to-swallow feminism," and "user-friendly feminism." To classify chick lit as synonymous with similar descriptors such as "me-feminism" is, as I hope to demonstrate, somewhat simplistic. Nevertheless, chick lit's mélange of narrative traditions carries over to its stance on feminism, as it adopts an à la carte tendency that selectively appropriates aspects of feminism into a primarily consumerist model.

A microanalysis of chick lit and concurrent media phenomena such as the HBO *Sex and the City* series enables us to isolate a strand of postfeminism, one we can call "late heterosexuality." *Late heterosexuality* is an adaptation of *late capitalism*, a term that originated with the Frankfurt School but was reconceptualized by Fredric Jameson in *Postmodernism* (1991) as coincident and roughly synonymous with postmodernism. Late heterosexuality is symptomatic of the growing challenge of separating considerations of heterosexuality in Anglo-American culture from business-based diction and economic considerations. Jameson's definition of *postmodernism* as "the consumption of sheer commodification as process" dovetails with operating dynamics in chick lit; though *chick lit* denotes a genre, it is also practically an adjective for a lifestyle in which happiness, romance, and acquisition (whether of media recognition, capital, an image, an item, or a husband) chase each other, with the terms sometimes but not always conflating (x). I do not mean to imply that this stage of heterosexuality shares all of late capitalism's elements (which include an internationalization of business and computer automation), though it is an offshoot of postmodernism and an amplification of some of its characteristic facets.

To make global statements about postmodernism would be at odds with its scrutiny of master narratives and the idea of a "universal," so I wish instead to pose chick lit as a strain of postfeminism containing elements of postmodernism, the latter of which, for Jameson, is synonymous with "spectacle or image society" and "media capitalism" (xviii). Along these lines, many protagonists, like numerous chick lit authors, work in publishing and the media; in fact, publishing industry journalists have claimed the chick lit heroine as paradigmatic for the savvy acquisitions editor (Zeitchik). The media occupation of the characteristic chick lit protagonist adds a fitting frame to the genre's ethnography of sexual politics: the protagonist directly generates social observations on modern life. One of chick lit's contributions as a genre is the production of what we might call a sexual theory of late capitalism or a reflection of how the latter has filtered into and commercialized the most intimate arenas of everyday life.

Whereas Adrienne Rich's thesis in "Compulsory Heterosexuality and Lesbian Existence" (1985) is that heterosexuality operates as a nonchoice for women, functioning as an institution through which patriarchy is manifested and maintained, late heterosexuality ushers in a new stage of straight relations—post–compulsory heterosexuality—in which women are less gullible toward romantic myths and often remain celibate. Judgments about sexual orientation are frequently image appraisals rather than political issues. But late heterosexuality marries this supposed increased freedom to a new phase of capitalism—compulsory style—wherein men function as accessories or a means to them and courtship is described in the idiom of business. This phenomenon is explored further in chapter 3, but an introductory example can be found in the recent self-help book *How to Shop for a Husband: A Consumer Guide to Getting a Great Buy on a Guy* (2009) by Janice Lieberman and Bonnie Teller. A consumer reporter on NBC's *Today* for ten years, Lieberman wryly advises recessionistas to "nab a guy who is classic: a little black dress among men," with the back cover's macroconcept—"the most important purchase of your life: your spouse"—making literal the metaphor between husband-scouting and shopping. I can write soberly, without triumph, that the question among girlfriends on learning about another female's new beaux—"Is he good looking?"—has been supplanted by "What does he do?" or the flat-out "Does he have money?" The preoccupation with men in chick lit is frequently deceptive. This incarnation of postfeminism blurs the line between the desire for marital union and simply wanting more money, with titles like Lauren Weisberger's *Chasing Harry Winston* (2008) playfully placing luxury jewelry at the apex of the dating hierarchy. The reifying values of the marketplace and the sovereignty of style permeate how the chick lit protagonist perceives herself, her stratagems, and the judgments of her peers.

For example, a protagonist of Alisa Valdes-Rodriguez's *The Dirty Girls Social Club* (2003), the first Latina chick lit novel, describes an outfit worn on a vacation in Italy with her boyfriend with proud nods to designer names: "I choose a black and white Escada twin set with matching black pants. I add black and white Blahnik flats and a luxurious alpaca wool black Giuliana Teso cape (made in Italy, of course) and my sunglasses. I put on a pair of black leather gloves, and transfer my wallet and cell phone to a smooth leather Furla, in black and white" (120). It is not quite hyperbole to state that the chick lit protagonist can experience romance, desire, or self-esteem only through commodities, particularly small objects such as jewelry and handbags. There is something childlike (or simply silly) about this enthusiasm. At the same time, shoes and high-quality housewares function as a type of female porn. As consumption is never satisfied, the chick lit protagonist is, at worst, an addict. Additionally, the novels rarely acknowledge the deflation or self-loathing that can accompany the aftermath of an impulse purchase or heavy spending.

The protagonist of Kim Wong Keltner's *The Dim Sum of All Things* (2003), a twenty-five-year-old Chinese-American receptionist, has a cousin who names her son Armani but would have called the baby Prada if it had been a girl, both appellations we could wager would get Valdes-Rodriguez's character's attention. While commuting to her workplace, the San Francisco–based fictional magazine *Vegan Warrior*, the protagonist's breasts incite unwanted stares, which are more offensive because of her top's classic quality, and she uses a trendy accessory to deter nuisances of the cityscape: "She felt his eyes laser-cutting small holes like cigarette burns into the boob region of her white Banana Republic sweater. . . . Lindsey leaped to the sidewalk and swung at some hovering pigeons with her Gap bag, yanking the drawstring like a yo-yo just in time to avoid accidentally swatting the guy who sat in front of Walgreens combing his calico cat" (17). Shopping and subsidiary elements of the chick lit lifestyle may be a defensive mechanism for the stress of urban jungle. Its pace hinders adequate time for self-reflection, as the fashion-publicist protagonist of Kavita Daswani's *For Matrimonial Purposes* (2003) implies in a rare metacriticism of the genre:

> That had been my life—catwalks and cocktail parties and being able to say I had been in the same room as Angelina Jolie. It was fun and frivolous, but that was it. The other day, I had read some of the pages from my journal last year: "Yes! Got the last Kate Spade bag in the Barneys sale!" or "Why did I spend fifteen hundred dollars at Patagonia when I hate hiking?" or "Exhausted by power yoga, and not helped by the three Raspberry Stolis I had afterwards."
>
> There were no words about being moved in deeper ways, except for those occasions when I might have attended a meditation class and returned home vowing to change my life, become connected with the greater universe, find inner peace. But then *The West Wing* came on, and all was forgotten. Mine had been a life lived on the outside. . . . So, instead I'd buy a Cosmopolitan, buy a pair of shoes, whatever. It was, essentially, a biodegradable life, one that, if I let slip from my grip, would merge with the dirt and disappear, leaving nothing behind.[3] (44–45)

The protagonist's close reading of her diary plugs in the best-known stereotypes of chick lit, its detail of three Stolis immediately after power yoga a bit suspect (coming from someone who has experimented with both forms of muscle relaxation); yet the protagonist, who, two hundred pages later, adds another pair of Manolos to her shoe collection, offers the beginnings of a metacommentary on the role of commodities in chick lit. They mask a postlapsarian moment for romance in a world where networking trumps courtship; they attempt to console for, in some cases, the disintegration of the family unit; and they mitigate an anxiety-based restlessness, if not a deeper emotional frustration and malaise.

I aim, then, to analyze chick lit as a genre as well as an overlooked source

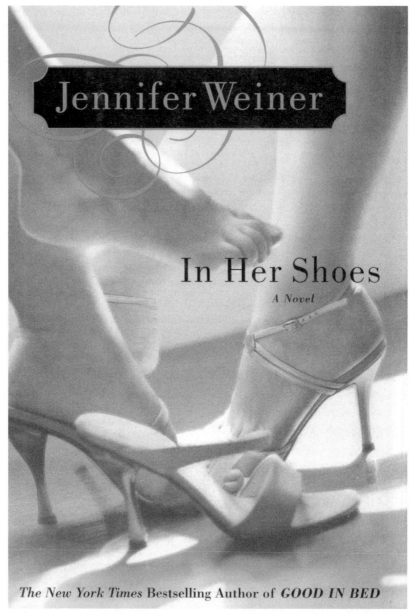

FIGURE 1. Front cover of *In Her Shoes* (2002) by Jennifer Weiner. (Courtesy of Honi Werner, cover artist.)

of sociocultural commentary. My inquiry will define the term *chick lit* with greater precision and will examine a highly layered genre: one that appropriates both literary and popular forms as well as media discourse. I hope to capture the playfulness of this new fiction and to challenge perceptions of chick lit as a homogenized category, a misconception perpetuated by the novels' nearly uniform covers. My purposes are thus twofold: (1) to set up a literary historical framework to examine chick lit's reworking of major narrative traditions such as the romance and bildungsroman and (2) in conjunction with that framework, to use chick lit and its reception as a lens through which to view gender relations in U.S. and British society since the late 1990s. I analyze chick lit as a formula in dialogue with other major narrative traditions and as a key to modern mythologies. For example, we cannot help speculating whether covers like that of the internationally bestselling *In Her Shoes* by Jennifer Weiner (figure 1) are partially responsible for a new trend in foot surgery, as a growing number of American women are having part of their toes lopped off solely to improve the appearance of the foot or to fit into Manolo Blahniks or Jimmy Choos (Harris). Conversely, fashion journalists have linked the comeback of flats—a trend taking off in spring 2004—with new episodes of *Sex and the City* concluding on HBO.

In each chapter I approach chick lit in a different way—as a realistic parody of Harlequin romance, as a female bildungsroman employing classic novels of manners as frequent intertexts, and as a counterparadigm, at times backlash, to feminism—in order to piece together different aspects of its origins and popularity. Each chapter looks at chick lit through a different genre or theoretical lens to provide a historical narrative of the conditions in publishing, consumer culture, and courtship that have coalesced to produce this genre of often veiled comic memoir. To achieve this aim, I draw on texts from both literary history and popular media: chick lit novels themselves, journalism, online discussion forums, author Web sites and interviews, industry advertisements, and women's lifestyle periodicals.

Though the genre first arose more than ten years ago, the chick lit phenomenon has begun to receive academic attention in the past five years, with Imelda Whelehan, the team of Suzanne Ferriss and Mallory Young, and Caroline J. Smith its pioneering and best-known scholars.[4] Analyses are not copious perhaps because of the fiction's uneasy relationship to feminism: its fetishization of commodity culture and the ambiguity of its protagonists' identities as independent subjects and objects of hetero-sexual exchange. When I first began this study, in the summer of 2003, chick lit was still hoped to be, in the words of journalist Anna Weinberg, "the bright light of postfeminist writing" (47). In the next two years it would do a 180-degree turnaround from its origins. Originally a literary movement in American avant-garde fiction during the mid-1990s, it trans-muted into an unabashedly bourgeois, commercial medium, with its for-mula of urban consumerist fantasy perhaps most accurately perceived as postmodernism's fin de siècle.

At the present time, more than a decade since its migration from ex-perimental fiction to the commercial mainstream, chick lit is thoroughly established as lighthearted fiction for women, with strong ties to romantic comedy, the confessional, and, to a lesser degree, social satire. Its episodic structure and contemporary setting will continue to supply source texts for television and film. For instance, Jennifer Weiner's *In Her Shoes* (2002) and Lauren Weisberger's *The Devil Wears Prada* (2003) were adapted as suc-cessful major motion pictures with A-list casts. Melissa Senate's *See Jane Date* (2001), Cara Lockwood's *I Do (But I Don't)* (2003), Gigi Levangie Grazer's *Maneater* (2003), and Adele Lang's *Confessions of a Sociopathic Social Climber* (1998) aired as cable TV productions. Based on Cecily von Ziegesar's best-selling young-adult series, *Gossip Girl* (2002–2007) pre-miered in the United States on the CW Television Network in September 2007 and continues to command a large fan base.[5] A big-screen adaptation of Emma McLaughlin and Nicola Kraus's *The Nanny Diaries* (2002) starred Alicia Keyes and Scarlett Johansson, though it received lackluster reviews. The film adaptation of Sophie Kinsella's *Confessions of a Shopaholic* (2000), starring Isla Fisher, was released in 2009. Finally, a film version of two stories from Bank's *The Girls' Guide to Hunting and Fishing* (1999) was adapted as *Suburban Girl* (2007) starring Sarah Michelle Gellar as a book editor who falls for an older man, played by Alec Baldwin. Francis Ford Coppola and American Zoetrope are developing a film that is adapted from the last short story in the collection.

This study does not attempt to cover the "chick flick" genre, though Ferriss and Young's edited casebook *Chick Flicks: Contemporary Women at the Movies* (2007) presents an excellent overview, with Negra's *What a Girl Wants?* an exemplary supplement. I provide instead a case study of this strand of women's popular fiction from 1996 to 2006. The beginning date, 1996, marks the publication of the newspaper columns Sex and the City and Bridget Jones's Diary in book form, the two texts most responsible for igniting the chick lit genre. Its end date, 2006, derives from the publication of the dueling anthologies *This Is Not Chick: Original Stories by America's Best Women Writers*, edited by Elizabeth Merrick, and *This Is Chick-Lit*, edited by Lauren Baratz-Logsted, as these volumes recognize, with diametrical degrees of reluctance, the establishment of chick lit as a mainstream genre with a recognizable set of narrative conventions and a romantic-comedic emphasis. Chick lit by this time developed a set of leading authors (Jennifer Weiner, Carole Matthews, Jane Green, Emily Giffin, Plum Sykes, Sophie Kinsella, Marian Keyes, to name the best known), and in 2007, best-selling titles were excerpted in a chick lit daily calendar published by Andrews McMeel. Evidence of this star system in the genre can be found in Lynn Harris's *Death by Chick Lit* (2007), a send-up of the genre intended for chick lit fans. In this satire readers may derive satisfaction in following the struggling literary-novelist-turned-detective's quest to track down a serial killer of best-selling chick lit novelists, a search that in itself works to validate the genre. The study's end date also marks the year that chick lit began to be directly acknowledged in works of literary fiction as a major presence in publishing, with best sellers recognized outside of its fan base.[6]

I focus on chick lit published in America and the United Kingdom partly because of the level my foreign language reading skills and partly because chick lit is primarily a transatlantic phenomenon, with an energetic cross-exchange among these novels and their media counterparts with regard to audiences, their general formulas, and their imbrications in commodity culture.[7] Yet it should be noted that strands of chick lit, which is not originally written exclusively in English, exist outside these regions, and I encourage future scholars to explore especially the overlaps and divergence of chick lit with its non-Western counterparts. For example, Indonesian *sastra wangi*, or "fragrant literature," is a phenomenon whose visual marketing of its authors mirrors representations of Anglo-American chick lit authors. This fiction boom began around 1998, the year of the downfall of conservative president Suharto. BBC journalist Becky Lipscombe described *sastra wangi* as "a marketing man's fantasy made real," as dreamy black-and-white photographs of the young writers, all of whom are beautiful, adorn walls of the country's bookshops. Nukila Amal, who published her first novel at thirty-two years of age, decided against using her photo on her novel so as to resist the *sastra wangi* tag. Other writers, such as Nova Riyanti Yusuf, concede the publicity has been useful and has promoted interest in reading among the younger generation.

An audience for chick lit has recently developed in India, with the consequences for emerging novelists not yet defined; a *Washington Post* editorial published in November 2007 heralded it as the country's "latest and most irreverent entrant into the world of English-language fiction" (Lakshmi). While acknowledging that its typical protagonist represents but a fraction of India's population and is exclusively urban, V. K. Karthika, publisher and chief editor at HarperCollins India, speaks on this new breed of woman: "She is single, has a career and is willing to have fun, take risks and find a man her way, and not necessarily her family's way. It is a woman we have only read about in books from the Western countries and now, suddenly we are finding her on Indian roads" (qtd. in Lakshmi). Best-selling chick lit novelist Advaita Kala elaborated on the reasons for this heroine's growing popularity: "A generation ago, marriage was the only route to independence from parental control in India. Now women are working, living alone in the cities, hanging out with women friends, drinking, dating and having fun in spite of the enormous social pressure to get married. . . . They inhabit a world where women enjoying a drink in the bar are not social outcasts. They are not tragic figures because they are single" (qtd. in Lakshmi).

Chapter 1 presents an analysis of chick lit's tropes to establish the genre as a displacement of the popular romance and a postfeminist alternative to the Harlequin. Chick lit parodies and modifies the latter through greater realism, a picaresque relation to money, and a vast diminishment of the hero. While chick lit is quintessentially postmodern as a romance of consumerism, it also presents a more realistic portrait of single life and dating, exploring the dissolution of romantic ideals or revealing them to be unmet, sometimes unrealistic, expectations.

I chronicle how chick lit began as a literary movement of the American avant-garde in the 1990s, ironically to burgeon commercially from a crisis in romance publishing. While chick lit's proximity to romance fiction has elicited critical denigration, its high visibility in mass consumer markets has worked to further brand it as decidedly unliterary. Chick lit's denigration stems in part from its gendered reclamation of the novel's commodity roots. For example, titles like *Will Write for Shoes: How to Write a Chick Lit Novel* (2006) connect the production of chick lit with the consumption of accessories, as if footwear, a frequent image in the fiction, fuels and rewards composition. As romance authors draw on cultural conventions and stereotypes stipulating that women can always be characterized by their universal interest in clothes, chick lit's fashion and shopping fetish further genders this by-women, for-women genre and compounds its affiliations with mass culture, however upscale. The genre's impressive sales records and presence in secondary consumer markets disinter long-standing mistrust toward the producer of popular fiction and a novelist's deliberate acquisition of commercial gain. Thus the genre enables us to revisit debates surrounding the origin of the novel and the function of prose romance, which has always involved debate about the moral and financial status of the woman writer as well as the educational and entertainment benefits of romance, especially with regard to women readers.

Chapter 2 examines how chick lit reinterprets Austen's legacy, especially *Pride and Prejudice*, enacts an almost grotesque deflation of Elizabeth Bennet, and reopens the tidy endings of Austen's marriage plots. Focusing primarily on Helen Fielding's *Bridget Jones's Diary* and its sequel, I show how in *Bridget Jones's Diary* the ironic novel of development is fused with—and arguably supplanted by—the conventions of romantic comedy supplied in Austen's storyboard. While the plots of these "late-stage coming-of-age stories," as Jennifer Weiner has described chick lit, often chronicle a character's professional or literary achievement, they present a partial parody of the bildungsroman's emphasis on accomplishment and development ("Chick Lit Author Roundtable").

I go beyond a reading of the novel itself to outline how *Bridget Jones's Diary* operates synergistically with the Austen-philia and Darcymania of the last decade, a market encompassing several major movie adaptations, a staggering number of fictional and self-help offshoots, and Austen-inspired board games, paper goods, jewelry, and action figures. Austen's popularity shows no signs of abating, as the novelist is sometimes rhetorically cast as a deity: The Morgan Library presented the exhibit "Women's Wit: Jane Austen's Life and Legacy" (November 2009 through March 2010), which displayed selected Austen letters and manuscripts and included a short film, *Divine Jane: Reflections on Austen* (Dir. Francesco Carrozzini), featuring commentators such as Cornell West. "Jane Austen" in chick lit invokes high culture, the Regency author's name performing the function of a quality brand in chick lit's lexical register. In a blurb for Bank's *The Wonder Spot*, for example, Zadie Smith, whose novel *On Beauty* (2005) won the Orange Prize, analogizes, "What Jane Austen did for marriage, Melissa Bank does for serial monogamy." Yet *Bridget Jones's Diary* and chick lit's role in the commercialization of Austen not only trades in Austen's "author function," but has also strikingly revised and expanded her niche. Though Austen never married, she serves in these newer versions as a travel guide and dating expert, her celibacy complementing that of the paradigmatic chick lit heroine.

Using *Bridget Jones's Diary* as a springboard, I introduce chick lit's parodic, if not simply uniformed, representation of older feminists, a topic taken up again in chapter 5. Feminism is ultimately depicted by chick lit authors as an outdated style and misread as a bilious monolith, its strident tendencies embarrassing and not fully compatible with chick lit's ties to the values of romance fiction and its embrace of commodities, especially beauty and fashion culture. To keep the analysis of Fielding's works primarily in one chapter, I include a reading of her most recent novel, *Olivia Joules and the Overactive Imagination* (2003), a spy thriller inspired by the events of September 11, 2001. The bizarre telos of Fielding's fiction reveals the limitations and domesticity of the original chick lit formula.

Chapter 3 utilizes close readings of Candace Bushnell's *Sex and the City* and its numerous screen adaptations, as well as contemporary novels of manners like Plum Sykes's *Bergdorf Blondes* and Tama Janowitz's *A Certain Age* to focus on chick lit's representations of consumerism and its connections with new-millennial sexual politics, specifically the intersections of heterosexuality and economic value. This chapter considers Bushnell's novel *Trading Up*, a modern take on Wharton's *The Custom of the Country*, and develops the concept of late heterosexuality introduced here through readings of these texts, which satirically chronicle Manhattan's elite, arrivistes, and aspirants. Together they and chick lit meditate self-reflexively on how the tradition of romantic comedy has always linked the successful negotiation of marriage with economic concerns. Chick lit raises the question to what extent the female bildungsroman (with a middle-class, heterosexual protagonist) can dissociate itself from the marriage plot and the marriage plot from the money novel.

Chapter 4 expands the literary genealogies of Austen and Wharton in chapters 1–3 by exploring continuity between chick lit and single female urban fiction classics such Rona Jaffe's *The Best of Everything* (1958), as well as lesser-known texts. Chick lit derives its humor as much from Gail Parent's mental illness comedy *Sheila Levine Is Dead and Living in New York* (1972) as it does from the irony of Austen. For example, chick lit appropriates elements of black comedy present in some women-authored works of twentieth-century mental illness fiction with career-girl protagonists, such as Margaret Atwood's *The Edible Woman* (1970). Critiques of heterosexual institutions in the mental illness novel resurface in chick lit yet are generally sublimated by a romantic ending. This chapter's genealogy is complicit with the media trend of labeling earlier canonical literature as "proto–chick lit" but aims to illuminate issues of literary value that emerge from a thorough examination of chick lit's origins.

The last chapter ponders the genre's negotiation with feminism, one described by some journalists as "antifeminist" but more typically as "postfeminist." I do not wish to claim the term *postfeminist* for myself but instead will explore how chick lit can enrich our understanding of a postfeminist ethos. After presenting a historical chronology of postfeminism, I examine the genre as an implicit commentary on feminism's gains and deficiencies. Our most culturally visible postfeminist fiction, chick lit offers a utopian amalgamation of different strands of feminism fused, problematically, to certain postmodern values. Commercial postfeminism portrays feminism as a bad or embarrassing mother. It positions itself in relation to earlier feminism through inexact oppositions: private pleasure/grassroots politics; humor/dour seriousness; a stylish, polished appearance/dowdiness; desire for marriage and security/mistrust of the male gender.

I then turn to analyze media commentary and author publicity highlighting the chick lit author's appearance. That "the gorge factor" (how sexy the writer is) competes with or upstages any substantial literary considerations seems to be part of a wider marketing impetus in contemporary publishing. The climate of compulsory glamour in publishing is not confined to marketing strategies for the chick lit niche and arguably works in tandem with postfeminism and its relation to beauty culture.

The epilogue examines the state of chick lit as a market beyond the end date of my sample. Interviews with authors and agents reveal that the line between chick lit, women's fiction, and romance is further blurring, with crossover genres—in particular, paranormal fiction—frequently making the best-seller lists. At the same time, "chick lit" as a label is unpopular with publishers because of a market saturation that produced a large number of inferiorly written novels. First-time authors are exhorted to steer clear of pitching a novel as chick lit as well as using its characteristic first-person voice. Nevertheless, chick lit has not lost its vigorous interchange with media and consumer forms. It is now generally perceived as a fiction of bourgeois escapism that will continue to supply source texts for television and film.

At the same time, the global financial crisis has not rendered chick lit redundant as a form of social commentary. While still retaining its hopeful or happy endings, its latest iteration has been dubbed "recession lit," a subgenre featuring privileged protagonists who are forced to belt tighten. The year 2009 brought more than a half dozen titles with plots informed by the housing market collapse, the Bernie Madoff scandal, and widespread layoffs. For example, the protagonist of *The Penny Pinchers Club*, by Sarah Strohmeyer, learns more frugal ways to prepare for divorce, while the main character of *Confessions of a Reluctant Recessionista*, by Amy Silver, becomes thriftier after being made redundant. Consumerism is thus still central to chick lit, but novels have begun to foreground the negative effects of spending. For the texts in my time frame, however, the chick lit universe, with its rare references to an underclass, environmental hazards, or international politics (outside of Parisian fashion), is closer to a utopia than a historically realistic city. Still, it is not accurate to claim chick lit is the exact inverse of post-9/11 fiction best-sellers such as Ian McEwan's *Saturday* (2005), Jonathan Safran Foer's *Extremely Loud and Incredibly Close* (2005), or Don DeLillo's *Falling Man* (2007), as underneath the historical backdrop these works often have a strong character study and domestic fiction component.

While an overlooked site of formal innovation, chick lit's modification of "the personal is political" to "it's just personal" is ultimately a sellout to feminism (or, as Whelehan [2005] has suggested, the germ of the legacy of the consciousness-raising novel). Chick lit's success—its establishment of humorous fiction for women as a full-fledged literary category—is an unnerving reminder of how polemical impulses sit ungracefully in popular fiction and romance. While in chick lit the funny, single woman finds her most developed representation, its shortcomings enable us to call into question the social accuracy of *postfeminism* as a descriptive term and to ask whether this term can still be used responsibly outside the context of white Anglo-American metropolitan feminism.

Ultimately, attempting to introduce a new genre of popular fiction is a type of bloodless violence. Entry into the canon is wrought by a figurative rack, the canon's frame stretched, the newly admitted novel tensed from tests of scrutiny. The scholar writes half-cowering, bracing herself for critical blows. One must work in an aporia, knowing that in the translation from popular to scholarly, part of what makes the former new, or silly, escapes. Popular fiction is subjected to a methodology, packaged in a rigorous argument, a framework adding proverbial scholarly weight. The scholar must develop a split self, detaching herself from her identity as a reader of popular fiction. This is the price all critics must pay, but especially those of popular literature. We have to work with this literature but cannot become too friendly. To devote a book to such fiction is to provoke accusations of succumbing to its contagious quality. Its girly pleasures must prove themselves substantial. A lineage needs to be traced, the pretty orphan's obscure or spurious origins revealed as highborn or respectable enough to pass critical muster—if not an Evelina then a third cousin. That analytical rigor seldom coexists with popular entertainment is no secret; yet for this endeavor such a marriage or at least cohabitation is imperative. The critic of mass fiction commits to her discipline but cannot fully desert what came to endear her to it: its humor, identification, delight, and fun. It is, quite simply, difficult to translate popular literature into academic discourse while retaining the elements that draw its audience. The academic reader is not a popular one. Between the dutiful scholar and devoted reader the tug-of-war commences. We wrestle with these forces; the fight survives as the text.

1 Postmodernism's Last Romance

There seems little doubt that most modern romance formulas are affirmations of the ideal of monogamous marriage and feminine domesticity. No doubt the coming of age of women's liberation will invent significantly new formulas for romance, if it does not lead to the total rejection of the moral fantasy of love triumphant.

—John Cawelti, *Adventure, Mystery, and Romance*

IN SARAH BIRD'S NOVEL *The Boyfriend School* (1989), the heroine, a photojournalist named Gretchen Griner, is assigned to cover a thinly veiled version of the Romance Writers of America's National Conference. The protagonist's conception of the popular romance and its authors is challenged by the organization's conclave of resourceful women. Dialogue exchanges between Gretchen and conference participants serve to revisit historical attitudes toward the romance and its readers, specifically, the idea of the impressionable female unable to distinguish fact from fantasy. When a seasoned author encourages Gretchen to try her hand at a romance novel, she begins to consider it, primarily in light of her growing debts and late rent. Bird's metafiction is significant not only for predating chick lit tropes—Gretchen's noncommittal boyfriend is her editorial supervisor—but also for its articulation of the constraining formula of popular romance. In Gretchen's drafting of her novel, she imagines a "New Wave of readers" who will find refreshing the fact that she dispenses with romance jargon and refuses to postpone the final reward of sexual union. She replaces the usual euphemisms of the romance novel with words like *boner* and substitutes deferred kisses with sex up front (135). She creates a character with the same occupation as herself, lending autobiographical parallels to the manuscript, but confronts opposition from her editor, who points out that the completed novel is devoid of romance. While able to devise a male and female protagonist, she encounters difficulty setting them in scenes of physical rapture, even having them interact amorously at all; the pursuit of love rings hollow and obligatory, the hero and heroine's exchanges listless. The revised manuscript capitulates to romantic conventions, as does Bird's novel itself. For all *The Boyfriend School*'s self-reflexive critique of the romance genre, Gretchen ends up uniting with the brother of her writing mentor after making her way through the usual maze the romance novelist must construct for her pair of intended lovers.

This chapter will explore how chick lit answers Gretchen Griner's yearning for a new type of novel, in its updating of the popular romance and its coupling of the romance formulation with adventure fiction. I begin with some definitional work and historical background with the purpose of differentiating chick lit from its close cousin, the popular romance, often referred to as the Harlequin romance. I intend this chapter as a thorough overview of the chick lit formula, not a comprehensive bibliographic catalog: the sheer number of chick lit titles and its growing subsets impede full coverage.

My explication of the chick lit formula aims to show how this genre dramatically revises the Harlequin romance and, in its modifications, invites historical parallels with early novels' relation to the romance. The rise of the novel in the eighteenth century displaced the romance by adapting that structure, as Northrop Frye in *Secular Scripture* (1976) has demonstrated, to a demand for greater conformity to ordinary experience (39). As a result, the relation of the novel to romance is parodic, the novel, then, a realistic parody of the romance. Drawing on Janice Radway's and Tania Modelski's analyses of the Harlequin formula to present a literary historical framework for this development in popular fiction, I will show that chick lit is a postfeminist alternative to the Harlequin deploying a distinct set of generic tropes. Chick lit is a partial parody of Harlequin romance modifying the latter through greater realism and a different representation of the hero. I then conclude by identifying what cultural values are at stake in chick lit's appropriations of and departures from literary traditions.

Harlequin Romance and the Emergence of Chick Lit

To explain how chick lit emerged as a genre, I backtrack to present a summary of the characteristics of its cousin, the Harlequin romance, from which chick lit developed as a marketing venture. The Harlequin romance possesses one defining constant, an inevitable happy ending, referred to by industry professionals as the "HEA" (happily ever after), which usually takes the form of matrimony or eternal love. According to Romance Writers of America's (RWA's) official definition, the popular romance's central focus is the love story, and the end of the book is emotionally satisfying because its climax resolves the love story.[1] Its main plot must involve a man and woman falling in love, and its conflict must center on the pair's struggling to make the relationship work. It is not a heroine-centered genre, as the male and female protagonist must occupy equal importance in the story. The popular romance is our living descendant of the tradition of *amour courtois,* courtly love, in that it considers romantic love an ennobling, transcendent force. It posits a universe with a clear moral order in which worthy individuals are rewarded. The popular romance validates good character with the promise of love and the implication of lasting happiness.

The proper noun *Harlequin* is roughly synonymous with popular romance, though a text published by Harlequin is not necessarily a romance novel. Harlequin was founded in 1949 by publishing executive Richard Bonnycastle and started out publishing a wide range of books from westerns to romances to cookbooks. In 1957, Harlequin began acquiring the rights to and publishing romance novels from the British publisher Mills & Boon, and by 1964, the company was exclusively publishing romance fiction. In 1971, it purchased Mills & Boon, forming Harlequin Mills &

Boon Limited in the United Kingdom. Today the Toronto-based company, now Harlequin Enterprises Limited, publishes mainstream literary fiction, thrillers, and inspirational fiction along with romance. Popular romance is sometimes still referred to as "Mills and Boon romance" as a vestige of its previous leading publisher.

The popular romance market exploded in the early 1970s with the introduction of Harlequin's Sensual Historical series in 1972 (*The Flame and the Flower* by Kathleen Woodiwiss) and the Sweet/Savage Historical series in 1974 (*Sweet Savage Love* by Rosemary Rogers).[2] Yet throughout most of the twentieth century, romance fiction has been highly visible in mass culture. The Egyptian desert romance *The Sheik* (1919) by E. M. (Edith Maude) Hull was an instant best-seller, and its movie adaptation starring Rudolph Valentino a media sensation. The Gothic romance *Mistress of Mellyn* (1960) was a breakout title for Victoria Holt (Eleanor Alice Burford), whose career spanned five decades and earned her the title "Queen of Romantic Suspense." Other romance writers have enjoyed careers with extraordinary production rates, longevity, and sales, their names staple brands in the literary marketplace. Janet Dailey (1944–) has had 325 million copies of her novels in print, Nora Roberts (1950–) over 400 million, and Danielle Steel (1947–) over 580 million, with all of her more than 75 novels best-sellers. Barbara Cartland (1901–2000), the world's most prolific romance writer, wrote 723 books over more than seven decades. This rapid production, and her sales of more than 1 billion copies, led *Vogue* to crown her with the epithet "the True Queen of Romance." The appeal of the romance has continued into this century. According to RWA, romance generated $1.375 billion in sales in 2008, with over 7,300 novels released; of those who read books that year, one in five read a romance novel, with 74.8 million Americans reading at least one romance novel in the past year ("Statistics"). The Harlequin remains the best-selling subset of category fiction as well as the top-performing genre of paperback fiction.

While one would probably classify the Harlequin as low mimetic fiction in terms of Frye's theory of the modes, the Harlequin, especially its quest plot, has its roots in the mode of romance. Romance initially appeared, observes Frye, as a late development of classical mythology (*Anatomy* 306). The term *romance* derives from the French and was first used exclusively to refer to medieval romances written in French and composed in verse. These narratives were concerned with knightly adventure, chivalric ideals, and arduous quests often set at the court of King Arthur. Later the term was used to refer to any medieval romance, whether in verse or prose, and regardless of country of origin.

Romance portrays a quest for a unique, nonsubstitutable object, the Holy Grail as its archetype. It can end with the protagonist's death or despair, though it closes more frequently with the attainment of or reunion with the beloved. Its primary story often centers on a quest whose main object is the restoration of health and vitality to a king whose infirmity negatively affects his kingdom, either depriving it of crops or exposing it to the depredation of war. In her classic study *From Ritual to Romance* (1920), Jessie Weston demonstrates how the hero's quest works to restore the land laid waste and, simultaneously, the virility of the king and the health of his dominion. The romance's hero is, in this regard, superior in degree to other men and his environment and moves in a world in which the ordinary laws of nature are suspended (Frye, *Anatomy* 33). Romance as a genre presents a narrative that emphasizes action or plot over character development and often lacks clear causal impetus, instead depending on deus ex machina resolutions. The hero's actions are marvelous, and, fittingly, the mode makes common use of fantastic, normally invisible personalities: the presence of angels, demons, fairies, ghosts, talking animals, and elemental spirits reflects the romance's intermediary status between myth and mimetic fiction. The Harlequin retains the quest plot of romance but features a female protagonist whose story focuses on the process of union with a male counterpart.

Chick lit often replicates the quest narrative of the Harlequin in the heroine's union with Mr. Right, but the traditional HEA is not requisite. Frequently Mr. Right turns out to be Mr. Wrong or Mr. Maybe. Sometimes a novel chronicles a succession of Mr. Not-Rights. In this depiction of "serial dating," chick lit strays from what Harlequin readers have articulated as the cardinal "one woman–one man" tenet: the stipulation that a romance focus only on one male complement for the heroine (Radway 171). Though the chick lit genre originates, like the Harlequin, from North America and the United Kingdom, the quest for self-definition and the balancing of work with social activity is given equal or greater attention than the Harlequin's relationship conflict. For example, editorial guidelines for Harlequin's NEXT imprint advise that while stories need to end in a happy manner, a romantic resolution is not compulsory: romance should comprise "a piece of the pie, rather than the whole one" ("Learn to Write").

Despite blurbs claiming to address "universal female dilemmas" and the struggles of an "everywoman," a characteristic chick lit novel features a first-person narrative of a twenty- or thirtysomething, white, middle- or upper-middle-class, never-married, childless, Anglo or American, urban, college-educated, heterosexual career woman engaged in a seriocomic romantic quest or dating spree.[3] While the classic heroine of Harlequin romance is an ideal beauty, often no older than twenty-five, the chick lit heroine, typically twenty-seven to thirty-eight, is often highly conscious or critical of her own physical appearance, with obsessive concern about caloric intake. In contrast to the Harlequin heroine, who often possesses acute intelligence and a fiery, or at least feisty, disposition, a chick lit heroine can be described as "quirky" or "creative" at best, with even the intelligent, type-A protagonists more ambivalent or confused, however gregariously, than "fiery" (Cooke 18). Workplace obstacles, which the heroine confronts and negotiates, run concomitantly with dating circuit adventures. This multitasking complements a self-improvement regimen as the protagonist strives to eliminate clutter, quit smoking, or read the classics. The action-packed plots and the vitality of the protagonist challenge single-at-thirty stereotypes to sometimes contain them, as the denouement frequently involves the protagonist's attainment of a "serious boyfriend," proposal, or matrimony. While many narratives are truncated by marriage plot conventions, others depict a comfortable but static suburban telos as a potential crisis, with heroines vacillating between the more secure status of marriage and the open-ended possibilities of the single state.

The fiction's telos frequently parallels the heroine's courtship progress with promotions, as she moves up the editorial ladder, acquires her own office or column, or authors a book, lending some chick lit the quality of a female *Künstlerroman*. While the dissolution of a relationship may coincide with the termination or resignation of employment, at other times progress as a journalist—being designated with a regular editorial spot, for example—affirms that an unattached character has achieved an admirable level of self-sufficiency and will find Mr. Right if and when she makes it a priority. The most invigorating texts, however, leave the protagonist presented with the opportunity to marry while she rushes off to more glamorous matters or relishes inviolate solitude. The desire to be beautiful, rich, and adored receives ultimate validation when the heroine enters the realm of narrative, her life story circulated in the gossip papers or her image photographed by paparazzi as an exciting artist, editor, or style icon. Regardless of the specific outcome, the heroine's aspirations for social mobility dovetail with the picaresque, as do her status as an orphan, the absence of one parent, and often entry-level occupation. In its formal tropes such as first-person autobiographical voice, episodic structure, urban setting, and approximate realism, chick lit retains elements of this literary tradition, with some protagonists, as I will examine later in greater depth, bearing traits of the *pícara*.[4]

One of chick lit's most salient characteristics is its city setting. Chick lit occasionally is called "metro lit." The city does not frequently appear on Harlequin romance covers, while it is popular in chick lit's iconography. Chick lit's city setting differs from early romance in that it does not present a pastoral or Arcadian world. A sylvan landscape often characterizes romance, one, according to Frye, full of glades, shaded valleys, babbling brooks, the moon, and other images closely connected with the female and maternal aspects of sexual imagery (*Anatomy* 200). Chick lit transports elements of the romance into a specific urban setting, as opposed to Harlequins, which, as Ann Barr Snitow has noted, avoid references to local detail beyond the merely scenic (148). In this sense, the chick lit genre offers what Michael McKeon has termed "emplacement," as the city is a bona fide character (14). The city's capacity for self-invention and atmosphere of possibility complement its protagonist's desire for what Lee Edwards has termed "an epic life" as well as its heroine's "great, half-formed aspirations" (624). The city's frenetic activity parallels chick lit's fast-moving plots that contain a minimal amount of stopped-action scenes. Such scenes, as Wendy Steiner in *Pictures of Romance* (1988) notes, include "the suspension of the heroine either in prison or in more literal states of immobility as in *Snow White;* the topos of love at first sight as a moment apart from time in which the two viewers are united by pure vision; or the moment of emotional or sexual transport treated as time outside time," and they are constantly used by the romance in representations of love (3). Chick lit does not employ the romance's frozen moments that, paradoxically, so often initiate the blossoming of love, as Steiner argues, partly because of the city's acutely time-conscious world.

The metropolis functions prominently in chick lit because many pro-tagonists work in journalism or the publishing sector, where they report on urban life. Because the protagonist's day-to-day work activity occu-pies a substantial portion of the chick lit plot, the genre can be viewed as an heir to Harlequin's "career romance" titles. In the mid-seventies the typical Harlequin heroine was either just emerging from home or was a secretary or nurse who quit her job at marriage, yet by the late seven-ties, many Harlequin heroines had unusual and interesting, if not bizarre, careers (Rabine 167). Insofar as many chick lit heroines have crushes on or full-fledged affairs with their bosses or senior colleagues, the genre extends Harlequin's "Temptations" series, where the boss figure remains the pro-totype for the career romance hero (Rabine 168, 170). When the Harlequin career romance's plot begins to thicken, however, the heroine's job that initially imbued her with glamour becomes temporary. Women's work in popular romance operates merely "cosmetically," as Ann Rosalind Jones notes, since the formula's demand for the heroine's total commitment to a man undermines the career romance from portraying the protagonist's job responsibilities with verisimilitude (207). The overwhelming popularity of chick lit, as Lisa Guerrero has theorized, can be traced to the social real-ity of its readership with regard to work—in her words, "Young women, who, after reaping the benefits of the opportunities secured for them by the fights waged during the preceding decades, found themselves in the virtu-ally uncharted territory of being professionally powerful but relationally adrift" (89). In its greater integration of the professional sphere into the romance plot, chick lit offers less romance than its predecessor but greater realism, and in its attempts at synthesis of work and love it shows the chal-lenges of straddling both realms.

While not all chick lit novels contain the compulsory elements of a Har-lequin, such as a hero and his eventual union with a heroine, romance pub-lishers have not shied away from capitalizing on this evolution in roman-tic comedy. The chick lit genre emerged in part from a crisis in romance fiction publishing itself. The popularity of *Sex and the City* and *Bridget Jones's Diary* opened an opportunity for romance publishers to prepare for the future. Specifically, romance authors were getting older, and their publishers did not have a new cohort in the wings. In the case of Harle-quin's Red Dress Ink (RDI) series, which published chick lit titles from November 2001 to December 2008 and was highly influential in launching the careers of numerous leading chick lit novelists, the imprint arose from editors' confronting a dearth of younger romance fiction writers: "There was this realization that we weren't finding an incredible new crop of twenty-something romance writers," confided Isabel Swift, vice president of editorial for Harlequin Enterprises (qtd. in Marsh). The relatively young women writing chick lit brought fresh talent not to popular romance per se but to a promising and lucrative variant. Harlequin saw in chick lit a strategy to expand its demographic along age and regional lines. The typical romance reader is married, from the South (29 percent) or Midwest (27 percent), on average between thirty-five and forty-four years of age, with 60 percent of readers living in towns with populations under 50,000 (RWA, "Statistics"; Marsh). The introduction of chick lit through news releases and special-offer listserv announcements to the existing romance audience has been a marketing strategy of Harlequin. While most promotions and sweepstakes advertise the more traditional romance imprints, a chick lit title is sometimes included as an effort to draw greater numbers of college-age and young professional women, specifically those under thirty-five.

Harlequin is not alone in this initiative. To draw a younger, hipper audience, Dorchester Publishing, the fourth-largest publisher of romance novels, launched its "2176" action-adventure romance series in April 2004. The RWA industry publication *Romance Writers Report* has begun to include chick lit titles in its advertising pages. The inclusion of chick lit in romance publishers' title lists is a strategy to cultivate high sales and an indicator of chick lit's status as a subgenre within romance fiction. In 2004, chick lit was recognized in two of the RWA award categories, the Golden Heart and the RITA Awards' Mainstream with Romantic Elements class.[5] That year witnessed the founding of an official RWA chapter devoted to chick lit, the online community Chick Lit Writers of the World. Chick lit's strong ties to romantic comedy have created unprecedented opportunity for publishers to expand their customer base and to develop new categories within romance fiction.

Chick Lit's Recasting of the Hero

Having established a working definition of chick lit and its historical link to the Harlequin, I will now explicate in greater detail chick lit's appropriations and departures from the Harlequin to offer a lucid and thorough picture of the general chick lit formula. Chick lit's most significant deviation from the Harlequin lies in its representation of men. Men serve various functions, and while men are sometimes love objects, the chick lit heroine's relation to men is often closer to that of the picaresque than that of romance. Though an offshoot of popular romance, chick lit transforms it significantly, virtually jettisoning the figure of the heterosexual hero, with Manolo Blahniks upstaging men. Titles like *Shopaholic Takes Manhattan* (2002) by Sophie Kinsella and *She Who Shops* (2005) by Joanne Skerrett give commodities and their social significance such a central position that they come to displace the hero. The hero is relegated to a cipher as the protagonist's suitor or fiancé figures analogously to men in bridal magazines. The hero is a shadow presence or background figure, and a gay male best friend instead functions prominently as the protagonist's confidante. More often than not we know more about the Plaza Hotel, the wedding reception venue par excellence, than we do about the heroine's groom. Men are not really valued as individuals as much as a means to a lifestyle, wedding, or in some cases beauty boost. Plum Sykes's gossip novel *Bergdorf Blondes* confides to the reader the fact that the single Park Avenue Princesses seek betrothal not to share a life with one particular man but to reap the dermatological benefits of being engaged, rumored to be superior to any chemical peel. Sometimes the hero is upstaged by someone from outside his species: in Elizabeth Young's *A Girl's Best Friend*, Henry, the protagonist's wolfhound mix, occupies the alpha male slot. The concluding pages describe an engagement, but Nick, the love interest, conveniently happens to be a vet.[6]

There is almost nothing compelling about male sexual prowess, either for the single or especially for the married woman. For example, the beau of Bank's "My Old Man" is impotent. The married protagonist of Kathleen Tessaro's *Elegance* evaluates her desire for her thoughtful but libido-challenged spouse: "The truth is I don't want him to notice me, to cuddle me, to touch me, or to say how pretty I am. I just want him to leave me alone. After all that, I don't want to fuck him either" (90). Tessaro's international best-seller presents something unheard of in a Harlequin, as a closeted gay male is the heroine's husband. After their long-nonexistent sex life, the divorce that finally follows allows the protagonist to move in with her affluent boyfriend. The protagonist of Jennifer Weiner's chick lit murder mystery *Goodnight Nobody* (2005) experiences a similar degree of sexual satisfaction from her husband: she discloses that a few years into her marriage her orgasms became mostly of "the DIY variety" and now she "probably had more fun in the shower" with a massage attachment (117).

The cardboard groom becomes a corpse in some chick lit. The protagonist of Deanna Carlyle's short story "Dead Men Don't Eat Quiche" (2006) refers to her ex-boyfriend who was murdered by poison as "late, not-so-great," as she "was over [him] even before he died" (103). In Bushnell's *Four Blondes* (2000) a character confesses:

> I wanted to be a painter. But I had the big white fantasy—that dream you have about your wedding day. And then it comes true. And then, almost immediately afterward, you have the black fantasy. . . . You have this vision of yourself, all in black. Still young, wearing a big black hat, and a chic black dress. And you're walking behind your husband's casket. . . . You still have your children and you're still young, but you're . . . free. (243–44)

Even texts that end with marital happiness present a predominantly depressing take on marriage. The newlywed protagonist of Kavita Daswani's *The Village Bride of Beverly Hills* (2004) seeks marriage counseling, her husband a sloppy, wheezing mama's boy who calls his parents twice a day on their honeymoon. Because the husband shows more allegiance to his live-in parents, who treat his wife as a maid-of-all-work, the protagonist returns to her home in Delhi, planning to divorce, which will render her socially a virtual untouchable. In a somewhat unrealistic turnaround, the husband undergoes considerable character growth (and presents her with an impressive new engagement ring) to justify their reconciliation.

Both chick lit's narration and paratexts arguably lend one-dimensionality to male characters, besides the fact that many are debut works. Male speech is often indirect because of the genre's typically first-person female narration. First-person perspective, a narrative method normally absent from the Harlequin, is popular in chick lit, and as a result, many novels border on internal monologues.[7] The frequency of the pronoun *I* emphasizes the heroine's development or produces, as critics have claimed, a juvenile solipsism. While the Harlequin employs a "clinch" cover depicting a hero and heroine welded in a half-naked embrace, only the heroine makes chick lit's cover iconography. In the few instances when men do appear on covers, they are fragmented or featured in a downstage position.

Given this unflattering representation of men, it is no surprise that chick

lit novels treat marital fidelity with ambivalence. For example, the protagonist of Alison Pearson's *I Don't Know How She Does It* (2002), an Oprah
book pick, has an e-mail flirtation with a coworker in an overseas office.
The two share a kiss on the mouth and bad food and great songs in the
Sinatra Inn, but she never goes to bed with him, leaving her with "a regret
the size of a continent" (349). The married protagonist of Marian Keyes's
Sushi for Beginners (2001) is not as abstemious as Pearson's heroine and has
an affair with a stand-up comic. After their third clandestine "Harder!" and
"God!" session, her paramour asks if he can shower at her place; the pampered mother of two answers with a curt "Be quick about it" (414). The
protagonist of Sue Margolis's *Neurotica* (1998) is commissioned to write a
fictional article on three women's experiences with swinging agencies and
uses the piece to come clean about her own marital infidelity. Adultery in
chick lit, though a deviation from the Harlequin, is rarely unapologetic.
The protagonist's own conscience or economic hierarchies contain sexual
transgressions, a pattern that arguably stems from the genre's romance
vestiges.

Chick lit may share some of the conservative tendencies of the Harlequin romance on the point of adultery, yet it differs from the earlier genre
in its attitude toward premarital female sexuality. Romance traditionally
has as its heroine a virgin or a virtuous married woman, with the virgin
reaching her initial sexual contact on the last page as a bride. In chivalric
romance, as Frye observes, the action of the story sublimates erotic feeling (*Secular* 183). Popular romance still has the trembling virgin as a stock
character, though by the 1980s Harlequins began to introduce sexually
experienced heroines. In chick lit, heterosexual female desire and consummation drive plot. Writer's guidelines for the Christian subset, however,
stipulate no premarital sex and a minimum of sensuality.[8] Though there is
at present not a large number of chick lit novels in English by South Asian
writers, novels such as Daswani's *For Matrimonial Purposes* (2003) present
virgin protagonists encountering the new appearance of condom advertisements in popular media.

Chick lit is significant not only for its inclusion of graphic sexuality in its
romance plot but also for its frankness on the degree of erotic gratification
its heroines experience. According to Margaret Doody in *The True History
of the Novel* (1996), forms of the god Eros in the novel's history have been a
key trope, where Eros has been represented in nature as a garden setting or

in interiors as a Cupid icon carved in a fruitwood mirror. In chick lit, there are minimal instances of genuine eroticism between men and women; men themselves are infrequently depicted as objects of desire. This representation of men differs dramatically from the Harlequin, whose hero's masculinity, as Ann Douglas notes, operates to provide the reading experience of "porn softened to fit the needs of female emotionality" (27). In chick lit, Eros is manifest instead in the protagonist's longing for luxury goods and professional or literary achievement. Beautiful or extremely fashionable objects, not a physical male, serve to create desire and cultivate worship. Chick lit retains the romance's pattern of desire originating through sight, but the desire normally bestowed on the romance's beloved is now attached to products that create or enhance female beauty.

A mixture of satisfaction and dissolving romantic expectations therefore characterizes the postcoital musings recorded in chick lit. For example, a character in *Sushi for Beginners* judges an initial sexual encounter and levelheadedly weighs its pros and cons:

> The sheets were fresh, the candles a surprising touch, he was thoughtful and attentive and he never once remarked on her absence of waist, but she had to admit that no, she wasn't entirely transported. However, he was very appreciative, and she enjoyed that. It certainly wasn't the worst sexual experience she'd ever had. And the best sex had always been slightly unreal, usually taking place after making up with Phelim, when the joy of being reunited added an extra piquancy to an already compatible experience.
>
> She was a big girl now and expecting the earth to move was unrealistic. Anyway, the first time she had sex with Phelim it hadn't set the world on fire either. (394)

In chick lit sexual encounters are not entirely unromantic, but they are not rapturous either; male characters seldom possess the phallic intensity of the Harlequin hero.

Even when the sex itself is satisfying, the backdrop lacks the Harlequin's ambience. Although the protagonist of Lisa Jewell's best-selling *Thirty-Nothing* (2000) experiences *"mind-blowing"* relations with an old flame, descriptions of physical pleasure are upstaged by setting and material detail: a garage reeking of cat urine, the too pale male attired in bright lemon underpants (218, original emphasis). With the light of day the heroine asks herself, "What the hell was she doing down here?" and becomes conscious that her partner's long and shapely legs appear womanly, his lack of muscularity underscored by his hands' smoothness and absence of hair. More "sex scenes" than "love scenes," these episodes in chick lit offer a frank appraisal of the sexual revolution's aftereffect: the relaxation of premarital sexual constraints, while physically gratifying, guarantees neither fireworks nor intimacy. The high number of sexual partners the chick lit protagonist experiences parallels the romance's pattern of the questing hero's confronting false or imposter versions of his eventual beloved. The quest plot of partner search enables chick lit to fall under the popular romance classification without matching the eroticism that is stock fare in the Harlequin.

When they are not sketchily drawn, male characters are sometimes depicted as physically violent. Violence is not a trope in chick lit but is notable as one of the few subjects the genre does not treat humorously. The protagonist of Karen Quinones Miller's *Using What You Got* (2003) is badly beaten and handcuffed to a radiator by her boyfriend, who is exposed as active in the drug trade, while the leading lady of Carlyle's "Dead Men Don't Eat Quiche" is slammed against a stall as a male sexual predator clandestinely enters a public bathroom and tears off her underwear in a misogynist dare. A character in Valdes-Rodriguez's *The Dirty Girls Social Club* (2003) incurs a beating by her husband that causes a miscarriage and hospitalization. The protagonist of Michelle Curry Wright's *Miranda Blue Calling* (2004) leaves Aspen partly to escape memories of an ex-boyfriend's beating. Despite two black eyes, a broken nose, and reoccurring headaches that persist years later, she remains ignorant of outreach organizations: "She thought about calling one of those hotline numbers pasted in the stalls of public bathrooms but was afraid they would tell her what she already knew; that she had brought it all upon herself" (34). A novel more enlightened in its stance toward violence against women, Kate Harrison's *The Starter Marriage* (2005), features a secondary character who has been repeatedly beaten by her ex-husband and finds shelter with another member of a "Divorce Survival Class" group therapy circle. Her ex barges into a session wielding a knife, but thanks to the smart thinking of the group, he is overpowered, arrested, and sentenced.

Thus, physically violent men could be seen as chick lit's version of the villain figure of the romance, a stock type who serves as a moral foil to the hero. In versions of the romance such as Shakespeare's *Cymbeline* and the Harlequin, for example, the villain's attempted assaults on the heroine form one of two poles of her career in the story; violence, sexual force, and other types of character defamation effect the heroine's ritual death, the nadir of her fortunes. In the romance's cyclical pattern, the heroine then passes upward from the descent of ritual death into an eventual triumph that includes marriage and the recovery of her identity (Frye, *Secular* 80). Harlequins, especially before second-wave feminism, sometimes featured a male protagonist as an abductor or rapist who moves into the hero position by becoming more subdued and attentive to the needs of the heroine: through the falling action, he regards his earlier violent behavior an error of excessive phallic energy and commits deeply to pleasing the heroine. While violence in the Harlequin is not directly condemned, it is shown ultimately to be an indicator of the hero's need for greater character development, and the Harlequin formula is devised to ensure his emotional growth. Chick lit, as a beneficiary of feminism in this respect, falls clear on its judgment of violence against women: perpetrators are legally punished and communication with them severed by the female protagonist. While some protagonists may have difficulty perceiving that their abuse is inexcusable, the chick lit genre dissociates the forceful male from the hero.

The final difference between the Harlequin romance and chick lit concerns the status of money in the marriage contract. This difference is a central subject of my next two chapters, but I wish to introduce it here within the catalog of chick lit's tropes. Chick lit concerns itself with money and wealth in upper-middle-class society, whereas the Harlequin does not exclude the blue-collar male from the hero position. Most manifestations of the romance oppose love with deliberate monetary gain, as the gold digger or social climber functions as a foil to the less-worldly heroine. Chick lit, however, does not condemn the ambitious husband hunter, typically united with a man she does love but also one who is, conveniently, financially fit. Popular romance novels must be careful, as Tania Modleski notes, to show that the heroine never machinates for a man and his estate (*Loving* 48). Many chick lit novels such as Gigi Levangie Grazer's *Maneater* (2003), invert, or at least complicate, this trope. Deliberate social climbing on the part of the woman is diffused through humor or presented in semifarcical husband-hunting tales of cunning and endeavor. Precedents for this kind of heroine can of course be found in picaresque works such as Daniel

Defoe's *Moll Flanders* (1722) and Haywood's *The City Jilt* (1726) as well as her *Anti-Pamela; or Feigned Innocence Detected* (1742).

It can be suggested that the chick lit heroine, with her sometimes upfront gold digging and sexual carousing, is a kind of prostitute *pícara* made safe and acceptable in an unapologetically materialistic age. For example, in the initial sentence of Bushnell's "Nice N'Easy" (2000), the third-person limited narrator objectively informs us that thirty-two-year-old Manhattanite Janey Wilcox has spent the last ten summers in the Hamptons without renting a house or paying for anything except an occasional Jitney ticket. In the early nineties Janey's modeling success earned her a part in an action flick. Janey never acted again, but with her semicelebrity "thinking man's sex symbol" status established, she has figured out that as long as she maintains her high-finish exterior she can "get . . . things and keep on getting them" (3). That Janey has no money is irrelevant, the narrator claims in the first entry of *Four Blondes'* short story quartet, as long as she has rich friends and can get rich men; the secret for attaining the latter is simply to abandon any illusions about marrying them: "There was no rich man in New York who would turn down a regular blow job and entertaining company with no strings attached. Not that you'd want to marry any of these guys anyway" (3). Janey forgoes the long-term investment of a committed relationship for the quick return of a prime area Hamptons rental and, usually, as a fringe benefit, the man's car. Janey sells herself seasonally as what economists Samuel Cameron and Alan Collins have termed a "recreational consumption good" and realtorlike, appraises men, a mere means to the fetishized housing, based on their ability to offer "location, location" (126). When a friend asks her whether she worries if men will figure out they're being used for their houses, she replies, "I'm a feminist. . . . It's about the redistribution of wealth" (10). In its closing episode, Janey, who secures an $8 million windfall contract with Victoria's Secret, pulls her Porsche Boxster convertible, a contract bonus, into the driveway of a Daniel's Lane five-bedroom rental with sauna, Jacuzzi, and pool.

We can only wonder if Bushnell is offering a case study or self-help template in which the self-conscious use of the female body as a type of currency is offered as a materialist ethos. Though Janey is not the most typical chick lit heroine because of her remarkable physical beauty, "Nice N'Easy" offers an entry point into a broader narrative pattern. In chick lit, marriage or the assurance of a serious relationship concludes the novel technically within the frame of romance while intenerating the picaresque drive of acquisition.

Together these tropes indicate that chick lit has worked to lend the popular romance greater and more contemporary psychological realism. As a chick lit novel does not necessarily culminate in marriage or long-term union, it presents a more realistic portrait of single life and dating, exploring, in varying degrees, the dissolution of romantic ideals, or showing those ideals as unmet, sometimes unrealistic, expectations. It appears, approximately three centuries later, that the novel has come full circle, or, in its partial parody and reformulation of romance conventions, has renewed this cycle.

Chick Lit and the Historical Denigration of Women's Popular Fiction

The moniker *chick lit* does not connote serious, difficult reading. In fact, the question "Isn't that a gum?" is one typically asked of chick lit authors. Trivializing both author and narrative in gendered terms, the label *chick lit* inevitably casts the genre in the figure of a bubbly but dumb blonde. Corollary labels such as "year-long beach reading" and "the treadmill book club" associate the genre with escapism and minimal intellectual effort (Allison; Napalkova). Titles operate as a further roadblock: *See Jane Date* implies a grade-school mentality, while *Run Catch Kiss* suggests a primitive take on love and sexuality. The genre's characteristic kitschy covers imbue chick lit paperbacks with a quick-fix consumable status and have earned it the derisory classification of "snack-food literature" (Barrientos). Bad press of this sort may render my study also vulnerable to the charge of triviality. But we should bear in mind that this kind of charge regarding the triviality of romance fiction is not unheard of historically, as it has for many years carried a certain kind of antifeminist burden. For example, a *New Yorker* cartoon from 2004 (figure 2) echoes these familiar charges and value judgments. One cannot help but notice how the cartoon, depicting a living-room battle of the books, portrays the male's reading material as larger, more robustly bound than his wife's.[9]

The critical reception of chick lit can be seen as another cycle of gendered antinovel discourse directed at the composer of romance and ama-

"Go bother your mother. She's only reading chick lit."

FIGURE 2. Cartoon representing chick lit as gendered anti-novel discourse, from the *New Yorker*, 28 June 2004: 8. (Image supplied by The Cartoon Bank / Condé Nast Publications.)

tory fiction, a discourse that has punctuated the novel's three-hundred-year history. Chick lit, though a new marketing niche, has provoked historical tensions between popular and literary culture. The chick lit genre's unabashed femininity seems to embrace the gender coding historically attributed to the novel reader, or more specifically, the reader of second-tier (i.e., romance or sentimental) fiction. The oil painting *The Novel*, sometimes also referred to as *Lounging Lady in Pink*, by Fabio Cipolla (1854–?) embodies this trope, as its lady reader's blushing cheeks match her attire (figure 3). While chick lit may be a trend, it invites us to revisit major debates around the novel and literary (and monetary) value.

Romance fiction—of which chick lit is the latest manifestation—has always invoked debate about the woman writer's moral and financial status as well as the educational and moral benefits of her writings, especially with

FIGURE 3. *The Novel* (date unknown) by Fabio Cipolla (1854–?).

regard to women readers. Though the French *roman* and the Italian *novelle* do not distinguish the novel from the romance, the history of the novel in English is a history of secession and appropriation from this form.[10] Indeed, many early novels, to differentiate themselves from romance and to stake their claim to veracity, presented themselves as histories to benefit from that genre's masculine and authoritative valence. According to Annette Townend, judgment of the romance as "unserious" literature, appears as early as the end of the sixteenth century as a consequence of the romance's shift from a male to a female protagonist and the transition to a single-sex readership (19). The "feminine" temper of the romance, argues Gillian Beer, can be traced to the increased role of women, a role that in her view is the chief distinction between Arthurian romance and earlier related Carolingian literature (25).

In the eighteenth century, criticisms of romance fiction—its quality and baneful effects—became a staple in conduct book literature. Romance novels were deemed "dangerous fictions" and "instruments of debauchery" by Oliver Goldsmith in 1761, for their potential to inspire licentiousness and villainy in youth of either sex (232). Though they commonly closed with a marriage, the consent of parents, and a ceremony prescribed by law, the plot of romantic novels is rife with passages that in their "overthrow of laudable customs" expose virtue to the most dangerous attacks (232). Critics incessantly cautioned against the habit of reading romance fiction because of the stories' capacity to lead female readers into affectation and false character. For example, John Trumbull in his *The Progress of Dullness* (1773) mock-grieved romance's bluster, as it fills ladies' heads "brimfull of purling rills" and "swells the mind with haughty fancies," "am'rous follies," and "whims" (19). Trumbull articulates what is now a critical commonplace in gender and literary history—passionate acts and emotions found in romance fiction inspire delusions and compromise inherently vulnerable female judgment:

> For while she reads romance, the Fair one
> Fails not to think herself the Heroine;
> For ev'ry glance, or smile, or grace,
> She finds resemblance in her face,
> Thinks while the fancied beauties strike,
> Two peas were never more alike,
> Expects the world to fall before her,
> And ev'ry fop she meets adore her. (19–20)

Sometimes titled *The Progress of Coquetry*, Trumbull's couplets indicate the historically negative value charged to romance reading as well as its ascribed convergence with flights of fancy in women.

While in the earlier decades of the eighteenth century a critical discourse rose against amatory fiction, another surfaced two and a half centuries later against the contemporary romance novel. The romance novel came under attack as mass-produced and silly, its characterization by women as retrograde and deleterious emanating from the advent of second-wave feminism. For example, in the best-selling feminist classic *The Female Eunuch* (1970), Germaine Greer penned one of the first critiques of Harlequin romances of the mid-twentieth century. For Greer, the novels merit one-word classifications, specifically, "trash" and "mush" (185). By presenting an "utterly ineffectual heroine" the novels thwart female liberation aimed at counteracting the fiction's capacity to breed "sterile self-deception" (185). The female reader is masochistic, "cherishing [her] chains of bondage," a slave to the romantic myth (176). Echoing criticisms of early romance fiction, Susan Ager of the *Detroit Free Press* judged the popular romance as not merely "bad" for women but emphatically "evil," condemning it as "more crippling than high heels" and "worse than whipped cream"—which is, of course, edible froth (qtd. in Grescoe 217). Ann Douglas in the essay "Soft-Porn Culture" (1980) similarly assesses Harlequins as unfailingly portraying a "duel of sexual stupidity" between "emotional illiterates" in a "totally anti-feminist world" (26). Even the more dispassionate studies of Harlequin's empire cannot entirely escape casting the romance as fundamentally commercial, hence inferior as literature. For instance, *Merchants of Venus*, Paul Grescoe's book-length examination of the world's largest paperback publisher, implies in its title that Harlequin does not so much create novels as sell them. He claims, further, that romance novels are not inherently literary as much as products of and about a female grotesque. His allusion to Shakespeare in the study's title, while playful, nevertheless distinguishes the modern romance from "authentic" literature by connoting a keen hunger for commerce.

The origin of the term *chick lit* clearly fits within the historical trend of denigrating the prose romance and commercial writing by women. *Chick lit* was first used in English-speaking circles by Princeton University students as a dismissive tag for Elaine Showalter's "Female Literary Tradition" course. The first print reference appears in Don Betterton's *Alma Mater: Unusual Stories and Little-Known Facts from America's College Campuses* (1988) (113).[11] The term *chick lit* was then employed by Cris Mazza and Jeffrey DeShell in their groundbreaking anthology *Chick-Lit: Postfeminist Fiction* (1995), where the term was used in a less casual and deprecating way. Intending to herald new voices in American women's experimental composition, Mazza and DeShell sought to bring more women to the then male-dominated title lists of the publisher Fiction Collective 2 (FC2), an Illinois State University–based publisher of avant-garde fiction. The volume sought to articulate a metalanguage for female experimentation in American fiction that, in the view of the editors, lacked a tradition with accompanying critical support. Assisted by a kicky hyphen, Mazza and DeShell announced a feisty and unapologetically female literary category that distanced itself from a staid second-wave disposition: the *chick* of their *Chick-Lit* supplanted the serious *woman* and gynocentric *womyn* of an earlier, more inviolate, feminist age.

The title attempted to reclaim connotations of *chick*, a noun typically conjuring a physically attractive woman who, in her highly apparent femaleness, is nonthreatening to power hierarchies. Mazza, the winner of the

1984 PEN/Nelson Algren Award and author of more than ten books of avant-garde fiction, outlines this postfeminist temper in the preface:

> It's writing that says that women are independent and confident, but not lacking in their share of human weakness & not necessarily self-empowered; that they are dealing with who they've made themselves into rather than blaming the rest of the world; that women can use and abuse another human being as well as anyone; that women can be conflicted about what they want and therefore get nothing; that women can love until they hurt someone, turn their own hurt into love, refuse to love, or even ignore the notion of love completely as they confront the other 90% of their life. Postfeminist writing says we don't have to be superhuman anymore. Just human. (n.p.)

Embracing a paradigm of and/and/and rather than either/or, Mazza and DeShell's *Chick-Lit* aligned itself with a postmodern value system. Their sequel *Chick-Lit 2: (No Chick Vics)* (1996) attempted to problematize the category of female victim employed in the early literary criticism of Sandra Gilbert and Susan Gubar as well as in the antiporn polemics of Andrea Dworkin and Catherine McKinnon. In their sequel, the editors instead opted for an exploration of women characters not only as victims in relation to men but also, more subtly, as victimizers and victims of their own priorities (Zolbrod 47). The editors were not contending that feminist causes are unnecessary or that women are never victims; instead, the volumes' manifestos insisted that women exceed the status of victim in their individual personalities. Thus the term *chick lit* was transformed through Mazza and DeShell's anthology from a joke about women's writing to a more serious intervention in contemporary women's fiction.

Chick lit's reclamation as a term, however, would be short lived. Mazza and DeShell's term, for the most part unknown to the literary mainstream, was subsequently appropriated as an idiom by journalist James Wolcott in a May 1996 *New Yorker* editorial entitled "Hear Me Purr: Maureen Dowd and the Rise of Postfeminist Chick Lit." With Maureen Dowd, the op-ed columnist of the *New York Times*, as his target of derision, Wolcott appraised 1990s women's journalism as "popularity-contest coquetry" and maintained that this "sheer *girlishness*" was an "odd aftereffect" of feminism (57, original emphasis). The successes of the women's liberation movement, he argues, ultimately squashed women's "journalistic swagger," leaving in its wake "flirtational" writing, propelled by a "Tell me I'm cute—or else" mentality (57). In Wolcott's view, Maureen Dowd and other "chick writers" have been so marketable because they are non-threatening: some are "gifted and amusing" but all are approval-seeking "chicks" (58). The FC2 anthology, its title providing the chief thematic for Wolcott's argument, is referenced in one sentence toward the article's end, where it is misidentified as popular fiction, its characters summarily judged by Wolcott as "fairly divided between getting laid and not getting laid" (58). Wolcott stripped *Chick-Lit* of its hyphen, the term entering the New York publishing conversation as a stylish sneer. Through Wolcott's editorial, the assertive *ch* of the FC2 anthologies lost its muscle, devolving into cutesy assonance.[12] The term *chick lit* itself became wobbly, as it has vacillated in print between *chick lit*, *chick-lit*, and *chicklit*.

Chick Lit's Ties with Consumer and Fashion Culture

While chick lit's proximity to romance fiction has elicited critical denigration, its iconic status in consumer markets has worked to further brand it as decidedly unliterary. Chick lit's strong visual presence in secondary commercial markets is a target for critical sneers that duplicate condescension surrounding early romance fiction. Journalist Anna Weinberg's satirical recipe "Make Your Own Chick-Lit Novel!" (figure 4) acknowledges chick lit's distinct visual identity, while NPR *Fresh Air* critic Maureen Corrigan has assessed the genre as a "veritable Pepto-Bismol tidal wave." Chick lit has brought a new visual contribution to the marketplace. This contribution reveals, embarrassingly for some, a strong interplay with advertising and commodity culture. For instance, Lord & Taylor in 2004 introduced two chick lit–inspired designs among its selection of gift card faces. Chick lit covers share a similar aesthetic with the flirty, almost hyperfeminine designs of Lulu Guinness and Nanette Lepore, upscale fashion and fragrance lines that took off concurrently with the genre's growth. Victoria's Secret, which for many years featured pink-and-white pinstripe cosmetic and accessory cases as part of its permanent inventory, brought this signature motif to a new level in 2003: a form-fitting "pyjama" short line, bearing strong resemblance to RDI covers such as Ariella Papa's *Up and Out*, proclaims pink, spelled out literally, the "Pink" line now with coordinating laundry bags, throw pillows, cotton panties, and T-shirts. And to have one's legs appear to their best advantage, women can use Gillette's "Passion Pink Venus" razor, the advertisement for which appeared the same year as the Pink line and depicts swimsuit-clad models cruising in a pink convertible.

This valorization of pink—embodied in Gillette's associations with fun, mobility, music—has failed to cross over to the genre's reception: critics such as Corrigan have labeled its protagonists "powderpuff girls," and this particular figurative language is not completely unwarranted given the genre's interchange with the beauty industry. For instance, "Lucky Chick" body-care products, utilizing an icon of a woman in a pink turban with her arms outstretched like a diva, aim to cultivate "a positive attitude focused on fun and pampering," dovetailing with that of the genre's protagonists. *Lucky* magazine beauty department alum Tia Williams has inspired a lip gloss shade called "Billie," named after the heroine of her novel *The Accidental Diva* ("Hot Gloss").[13] Lancôme's fall 2003 "Urban Eve" collection, drawing its inspiration from "an urban cityscape and the multifaceted woman who inhabits it," not only offers makeup to a new breed of city sirens but also complements protagonists' gravitation toward all things coordinating. The genre has permeated the realm of writing materials itself as both the R. Nichols and Caspari stationery lines feature chick lit–inspired designs.

Chick lit's packaging aims to attract and bring back readers through visuals women gravitate to as consumers. Chick lit covers appear as almost caricatured versions of women's lifestyle periodicals, as if chick lit offers the book-length version of a *Cosmopolitan* fiction feature. This marketing tactic seeks to attract the urban young professional demographic who may be reluctant to purchase a romance paperback with a clinch cover. The cover makeover brought about by chick lit—in height and width the novels are larger than Harlequins—draws on women's penchant for designer commodities and works synergistically with the retail. The covers of chick lit novels, frequently depicting an exposed female knee or lower limb, are often in some shade of the pink color palette. Chick lit then also operates in a feedback loop with fashion trends: the color pink was the new black from 2003 through parts of 2005, years in which the number of chick lit titles grew dramatically. Given these factors, chick lit's commercial success is not entirely surprising: market research consistently finds that American women comprise 80 percent of readership for adult trade fiction, and chick

Make Your Own Chick-Lit Novel!

1. START WITH ONE YOUNG URBAN FEMALE

$\left(\begin{array}{c}\textit{who's a low-level}\\ \textit{employee in:}\end{array}\right)$

2. CHOOSE ONE OF THE FOLLOWING:

a) PUBLISHING	*b*) PUBLIC RELATIONS
c) ADVERTISING	*d*) JOURNALISM

------------------------- *add* -------------------------

3. ANXIETY ABOUT ONE OR ALL THE FOLLOWING:

a) BODY	*b*) SEX LIFE
c) BIOLOGICAL CLOCK	*d*) ANNOYING MOTHER
e) EMOTIONALLY IMMATURE MEN	*f*) DYING ALONE
g) SHOPPING ADDICTION	*h*) INSUFFICIENT COLLECTION OF SHOES
i) NICOTINE ADDICTION	*j*) CRAPPY SALARY
k) EXCESSIVE ALCOHOL CONSUMPTION	
l) FINDING LOVE IN THE CITY OF:	

1. NEW YORK	2. MANHATTAN
3. GOTHAM	4. LONDON

------------------ *Mix it all together* ------------------

4. ZANINESS ENSUES.

Your book should look something like this:

 *or*

FIGURE 4. "Make Your Own Chick-Lit Novel!" A satirical recipe for the chick lit formula from *Book*, July/Aug. 2003: 49.

lit directly targets women through fashion, gendered cover visuals, and heroine-centered plotlines.

While careful attention to the style, color, and detail of women's fashions is among the most fundamental of devices that constitute the popular romance's mimetic effect, chick lit's reception history elicits notable parallels on the point of fashion with censure surrounding early English novels. Regarding Francis Coventry and his satirical novel *The History of Pompey the Little* (1751), novelist Henry Fielding urged the female reader of amatory trifles to "leave this extravagance to their Abigails with their cast cloths" (qtd. in Warner 8). Romance reading is not only pathological but also here associated with women's rabid appetite for new fashions. The right novels will inoculate against this, encouraging women to pass on their old dresses to their maidservants in exchange for more sensible garments. In her study *Ladies of Labor, Girls of Adventure: Working Women, Popular Culture, and Labor Politics at the Turn of the Century* (1999), Nan Enstad documents how leaders in the International Ladies Garment Workers Union and the Women's Trade Union League regularly upbraided members for their untiring interest in fashion as well as their voracious reading of dime novels about working heroines who marry millionaires. The wearing of French heels, delicate and typically three inches high, for both work and leisure, worried leaders who feared they not only distracted women from the more practical concern of labor organizing but also intensified middle-class perceptions of working women as too frivolous to be viewed seriously as employees or political actors (Enstad 3). A century later, the connection between frivolous novels and fashion has resurfaced again with chick lit; critics, judging a book by its cover, have conflated its fashion-conscious exteriors with inferior literature, as a fixation with clothes permeates the genre in content and form.

The genre unequivocally expanded the women's style guide market, with self-help manuals with titles like *City Chic* (2003) now overexposed. Stylish female clothing or high heels more often than not appear on covers. Simon and Schuster Pocket Books' "Downtown Press" imprint logo utilizes a shopping bag, while the imprint titles "Strapless" and "Red Dress Ink" (RDI) reflect their protagonists' typically strong penchant for apparel. Before the imprint was discontinued in 2008, RDI employed the tagline "Fiction with Style." Avon Trade, an imprint of HarperCollins, employs a tote purse as its logo, the imprint slogan—"because every great bag deserves a great book!"—exclaims a marriage between accoutrements and reading, yet in its order privileges the female term, "book" ultimately a complementary accoutrement. The chick lit–inspired self-help volume *The Handbag Book of Girlie Emergencies* (2001), featuring a white stick-figure sketch of a handbag superimposed on the pink-on-hot-pink front cover's center, blurs the categories of book and accessory. A 2004 RDI advertisement for monthly shipments invites readers to "try . . . books on for size" and offers two free gifts for doing so: a copy of Lynda Curnyn's *Engaging Men* and a *Cosmopolitan* Virtual Makeover CD.

Chick lit has been described by Elizabeth Merrick as "the stepsister to the fashion magazine," and, not surprisingly, a substratum of texts presents a satirical treatment of the Manhattan fashion sector (vi). As romance authors draw on cultural conventions and stereotypes stipulating that women can always be characterized by their universal interest in clothes, chick lit's fashion and shopping fetish further genders this by-women, for-women genre and compounds its affiliations with mass culture, however upscale (Radway 193). While chick lit actively produces discourses of feminization, it is equally burdened by the negative values charged to women's participation in mass culture.

Chick lit's denigration stems in part from its gendered reclamation of the novel's commodity roots. Its covers and even its authors seem to court a consumerist ethos and thereby call attention to the novels' commercial origins. For instance, Ford Motor Company made a deal with best-selling chick lit author Carole Matthews to feature one of its cars in her novel *The Sweetest Taboo* (2004). The product placement has the heroine driving a Ford Fiesta: "She's red, raunchy and drives like a dream," reads a snippet from the book ("Literature, Sponsored by . . ."). Further, many chick lit authors maintain Web sites to link readers to book vendors and also manage listservs to announce their new releases, book signings, and special appearances.

Chick lit authors, who create characters who like to shop, have not been shy in admitting to the pleasures of shopping. Back cover author bios, like that of Michelle Cunnah, unabashedly reveal the novelist's affinity for consumption, as we are informed that the author of the award-winning *32AA* (2003) is a frequent visitor to shopping outlets and the proud owner of approximately forty pairs of shoes. Shanna Swendson, a member of Yahoo!'s Chick Lit: Women's Fiction Markets and Tips discussion board and author *Enchanted, Inc.*, encourages her virtual sisters to persevere in writing "these books that others may dismiss as fluff."[14] The best-selling novelist concludes her post with a defense of shopping: "Now's [*sic*] I'm off to Barnes and Noble with my Master Card to spend more money than I should. It's market research right?" ("Relevance of Chick Lit"). Author of the international best-selling Shopaholic series Sophie Kinsella in 2003 participated as one of the "bridal industry superstars" in the annual "Wedding March on Madison" bridal weekend sponsored by *Brides* and *Modern Bride*. Intended to help brides-to-be "learn from the pros and shop like a star," the Manhattan-based extravaganza featured Kinsella presenting "Shopping Advice from a Shopaholic." RDI authors Melissa Senate, Lynda Curnyn, and Wendy Markham participated in a reading on October 1, 2003, as a cross-promotion with Bloomingdale's Manhattan flagship store. Attendees who purchased $100 worth of Y.E.S. clothing received an autographed book of their choice and the opportunity to meet the respective author, who sat in of one of the clothing aisles. A Lord & Taylor June 2004 private sale invitation aimed to grab recipients' attention by appropriating the title of a chick lit novel by Kinsella concurrently on best-seller lists. Appearing in green on the invitation, the question "Can You Keep a Secret?" is germane enough given the context of the private sale, yet this query attempts continuity with Kinsella's Shopaholic novels. Potential shoppers familiar with the series may chuckle at their relation to its protagonist, Becky Bloomwood. The invitation's allusion to the protagonist's extravagant compulsive shopping makes the receiver feel financially conservative in comparison. Once the recipient processes the comparison, the invitation can incite consumer sales, if not heavy spending.

The 1980s witnessed a vast increase in cultural analyses of consumption concomitant to the development of postmodern cosmologies. Chick lit's revelry in consumerism, however, exceeds the reification depicted in novels reflective of postmodernism such as Don DeLillo's *White Noise* (in its supermarket and "most photographed barn in America" scenes, for example) and Tom Wolfe's *Bonfire of the Vanities* (with the media frenzy that accompanies the court case, its frequent mention of brand names, and its portrayal of the fixes and ephemeral quality of news and consumer culture). Paterian in intensity as a Prada sample sale burns with a hard gemlike flame, chick lit is quintessentially postmodern as the romance of consumerism. Chick lit's deep imbrications with commodity culture are reflected in many of its titles: besides Kinsella's Shopaholic series, titles like Cecily von Ziegesar's *All I Want Is Everything* (2003) and the Christmas novella trilogy *Shop 'til Yule Drop* (2004) celebrate consumerism. Blurbs too playfully link reading chick lit to shopping, as reviewers tout the number one *New York Times* best-seller *Shopaholic and Baby* (2007) as being "as fun as a shopping spree at Miu Miu" (*Entertainment Weekly*), while another blurb invites the potential book buyer to "give your credit cards a rest and indulge in a vicarious splurge" (*Glamour*). As protagonists aspire to attain the material trappings of success, either affirmed or, more typically, reevaluated, chick lit reflects the culture of "lifestyle," a term acquiring a distinctly commodified valence in the 1990s.

One can argue that the genre "yuppified" the popular romance novel or perhaps "girled" the not especially gender-specific concept of the young urban professional. Indeed, the term *thirtysomething*, now vernacular to describe the age group of Bridget Jones and cohorts, takes its roots from the TV series of the same name.[15] More broadly, the chick lit genre's materialism reflects how the steep rise in single-woman households has enabled women to engage in greater consumer activity, as women now account for about 90 percent of all apparel transactions and 80 percent of purchases overall in America (Seckler). There is also less guilt attached to luxury spending, with purchases ranging from fine apparel, exotic vacations, and spa weekends to massage therapists and fitness trainers.[16]

As this latest development in Anglo-American fiction revisits the English novel's early decades, chick lit's reception invites a backward glance at debates around the long-standing tensions between media and literary culture. In its triple embrace of shopping, femininity, and mass culture, the chick lit genre greets the novel's closet skeletons in a new marketplace.

A Postmodern Marriage:
Chick Lit and Generic Amalgamation

While chick lit both appropriates and parts company from the genre of romance, it frequently dovetails with the self-help genre. Though the speed at which chick lit can be consumed renders the genre, as Jennifer Weiner puts it, "comfort food between . . . covers," chick lit is a distinctive amalgamation of canonical and noncanonical forms, and this amalgamation parallels the protagonist's search for what romantic and lifestyle values are worthy of emulation.[17] For example, Kathleen Tessaro's *Elegance* (2003) doubles as a self-help book on the subject of its title. London box office sales clerk Louise Canova stumbles upon a forty-year-old encyclopedia of style by French fashion expert Genevieve Antoine Dariaux, and the novel structures its chapters around sections reprinted from Dariaux's 1964 tome. Advice on apparel suitable for a yachting excursion complements the protagonist's attempt to attend the male love interest's boat-christening party. Laura Zigman's *Animal Husbandry* (1998) appropriates anthropological and evolutionary thought as its protagonist, aptly named Jane Goodall, formulates a "New-Cow Theory" to explain why men, sexually satiated, leave women for a different mate. The lighthearted *How to Meet Cute Boys* (2003) by Deanna Kizis includes dating and relationship statistics as well as quizzes and magazine articles from the *Cosmopolitan*-like magazine its protagonist edits. Laura Wolf's debut novel, *Diary of a Mad Bride* (2002), chronicles a year in the life of associate features editor Amy Thomas. Happily single and dating, Amy is bewildered over her friend's obsessive wedding planning syndrome. She tries in vain to convince her best friend that having to use folding chairs for her outdoor service won't make the ceremony look like an AA meeting, yet after the bridesmaid unexpectedly becomes engaged, she finds herself also mutating into a mad bride. Amy begins by making a twenty-item wedding to-do list, which, after she consults some bridal magazines, grows to seventy items. The list, which appears in full in the text, is reprinted several times with lines through its completed or jettisoned tasks. The list becomes a diary that doubles as a keepsake book, featuring a reprint of the invitation, wedding-gift thank you notes, and a series of "while you were out" messages, the last of which is from Amy's assistant, who, exasperated by a delegated wedding-related work overload, conveys her resignation. Chick lit's accessibility, humor, playfulness, and barrage of brand names at times overshadow innovative generic fusions and reflexivity.

Chick lit's synthesis of disparate textual sources reflects contemporary woman's search for new models and new ways of loving. For example, the front cover of *The Princess-in-Training Manual* (2003) by Princess Jacqueline de Soignée depicts a tiara-clad aspiring aristocrat who coyly commands us to flip her over. The back cover then reveals two books in one, as it presents a sultry brunette with a martini in one hand and in the other the title itself, Erica Orloff's seriocomic manual *Divas Don't Fake It*.

The authenticity of the authors' identity is deliberately tenuous: *Soignée* is French for an impeccably polished woman, and *Orloff* is both a fur brand and a spurious aristocratic name, specifically "Eagle" in Russian. These two titles, presumably written by one author, are thinly separated by three pages of blurbs and thumbnail front cover reproductions of forthcoming RDI imprint releases. These self-help guides straddle the borders of fiction and nonfiction and represent some of the difficulties in classifying chick lit generically. As Yahoo! Chick Lit Discussion Group member Stephanie Elliot maintains, "I don't think chick lit can be classified as romance, and I don't think it can be classified as literary—I think it's a genre all on its own." The specious manuals approach farce in their tone and caricatured illustrations, yet they are not entirely spoofs. They simultaneously make fun of but embrace chick lit's excesses. An over-the-top tone works to mitigate the manual's strategies for co-opting power, albeit power too dependent on material finery and sybaritic consumerism.

Diva purports to offer a primer for primas. Its ten-chapter structure issues secular commandments decreed by the book's mouthpiece, the fictional Xandra Kingston, a self-proclaimed diva from a long line of passionate Russians. Some tenets of this faux autobiography are subjective ("A Diva Is Spontaneous"), others fortifying ("A Diva Knows How to Reinvent Herself"). Others, like the chapter title "Silicone Sluts and Implant Invasions: Divas Aren't Afraid of the Word *Fuck*," connote a disastrous cultural studies endeavor. More sensible commandments like "A diva doesn't demand the best from others, she demands it of herself" appear between dialogue-heavy episodes featuring Xandra's interactions with friends, boyfriends, and retailers (66). Her consciousness raised to megalomaniac proportions, the diva may well be the most exciting woman in the room, but she is also rude and destructive, as Kingston advocates cutting lines and china-smashing tantrums. *Diva*, like the chick lit genre in general, challenges the lines between narcissism and self-expression, humor and veiled seriousness.

The Princess-in-Training Manual's preface offers a Paris Hilton–type confession as Soignée recounts that the manual's vision came "after a few saketinis too many at Nobu" (9). Like some *Sex and the City* viewers, readers may derive satisfaction in their familiarity with the gourmet Japanese fusion restaurant and celebrity hot spot. Chick lit, functioning in part like a Zagat guide, often describes the décor and fare of London and New York's premiere restaurants, and the reader may put them on her to-visit wish list or feel pride and nostalgia if she has already dined there. Those open-minded enough to keep reading encounter chapters on topics such as "On (Inner and Outer) Beauty" followed by headings marrying princessdom with self-help clichés such as "A true princess knows that she is beautiful from the inside out" (57). The chapter body then features episodes of pampering in the Elizabeth Arden Red Door Spa, offering vicarious indulgence or irritating envy. Scenes of what we may call power femininity are interspersed with boldface headings emphatically advocating a code of self-reliance: "*Rely on yourself. No matter what*. This is what a true princess does" (87, original emphasis). The tutorial devotes scant discussion to Prince Charming, relegating commentary to a few paragraphs in the final chapter. Part nonsense, part good advice, part crash course for social aspirants, the manual tells us that the Inner Princess requires no prince for completion. *Happily-ever-after* is defined as a faith that love exists, is on its way, and is attainable only with a foundation of self-respect and personal care.

To equip readers for turning their lives into a man-optional fairy tale, the guide concludes with an eight-page glossary. Entries ostensibly continue the book's attempts to marry frivolity and utility to the extent that nothing is frivolous if it can be channeled toward self-fashioning and the cultivation of pleasure:

J'aime Paris: French, meaning "I love Paris."

occhiali: Italian, meaning sunglasses.

pavane: a stately European court dance popular during the sixteenth century.

Predictably, designer and chic more often than not trump mid-tier or even American brands. The foreign-language entries denote accessories and upscale baubles functioning as a romance-language edition *Vogue* Guide for Dummies. They ostensibly challenge tropes of earlier conduct books, namely, their tradition of chastising middle-class women for aspiring to the practices of their aristocratic counterparts, whether in the form of fashionable dress or the desire for polite society. Additionally, the manual, like Jennifer Sander's *Wear More Cashmere: 151 Luxurious Ways to Pamper Your Inner Princess* (2003) and Francesca Castagnoli's *Princess: You Know Who*

You Are (2003), offers an adult counterpart to the phenomenon in young-adult and children markets. The primer works in tandem with the best-selling Princess Diaries series by Meg Cabot and the pink princess aesthetic in girl's bedroom linens and décor.

While chick lit novels often contain an education manual or lifestyle primer, they sometimes mock or, serving as meta-self-help books, offer a corrective to popular self-help tomes. Protagonists critique best-sellers such as *The Rules: Time-Tested Secrets for Capturing the Heart of Mr. Right* (1995) by Ellen Fein and Sherrie Schneider.[18] Others can be read in part as a counter- or unofficial version of Fein and Schneider's *Rules for Online Dating* (2002), as protagonists utilize Internet introduction services. Sometimes chick lit authors use a foreign protagonist to report on a city's peculiar customs or new trends. For instance, on a trip to New York the Shopaholic series protagonist is taken aback at an Upper East Side spa's offering of a Brazilian bikini wax as well as its variants and embellishments. Neophytes are educated in the nuances of contemporary style. Andrea Sachs of *The Devil Wears Prada*, for example, learns that "M.J.s" is fashion industry shorthand for Marc Jacobs. At times a fashionista's knowledge will be refined, as when one learns the couture label Badgley Mischka is not one person but the collaboration of Mark Badgley and James Mischka. Readers of Sykes's *Bergdorf Blondes* are educated in lingo used by Manhattan's young female elite when, in a gesture comparable to Soignée's inclusion of a glossary, Sykes provides a list of shorthand expressions in between chapters 2 and 3 to translate the book's frequently used terms. For instance, "Chip's" refers to the restaurant and social scene Harry Cipriani at Fifth and Fifty-ninth Streets, "A.T.M." means a rich boyfriend, and an "M.I.T." is a Mogul in Training (more desirable than an A.T.M. but not as much so as the scenario of a woman rising to the rank of M.T.M.—that is, "Married to Mogul"). In sum, the chick lit narrator frequently serves as an ethnographic guide and point of comparison with the reader's knowledge of courtship and material culture.

While chick lit has established itself as a lucrative market niche, the formula cannot be pegged into a simple generic classification. It possesses greater realism than the Harlequin in its treatment of modern relationship dynamics but cannot be deemed realist literature. It blends the realist tendencies of the bildungsroman with the fantasy elements of romance. What compromises chick lit's realism despite its mimetic detail is its engagement with the "success story." Its trope of professional ascendancy leaves the impression that every media employee will become a columnist, a best-selling author, or TV personality—and while she is still under thirty-five.[19] Chick lit presents a genuinely innovative mixture of forms, both literary and nonliterary, while reminding us that more genres do not necessarily a better novel make. While marketed as different from the Harlequin novel, chick lit novels are ultimately romances of the self. Their amalgamation of generic forms must be seen as an attempt not only to find a way to articulate a new-millennial novel of female development but also to synthesize romantic comedy with consumerism.

2 *Bridget Jones's Diary* and the Production of a Popular Austen

They both knew that while they were not
impoverished ladies of an earlier era for whom
marriage "must be their pleasantest preservation
from want," it was equally true that married life
formed the core of their expectations and desires.
Whatever they claimed to believe to the contrary,
neither of them was likely to be happy without it.

—Rachel Pastan, *This Side of Married*

LIKE *Sex and the City*, the phenomenon of *Bridget Jones's Diary* has its origins in an eponymous newspaper column successfully adapted to book and to screen. Helen Fielding's weekly column first appeared in the *Independent* (London) on February 28, 1995, and was later moved to the *Telegraph* in 1997. In August 2005, Fielding resumed writing the diary column for the *Independent*, with the final column appearing a month before the birth of her second child. Although an exaggerated portrayal of the author's own experiences as a single urban woman, the column featured a byline photograph of Susannah Lewis, a secretary at the *Independent*, holding a cigarette and wine glass. The column's faux iconography fostered the notion of an actual Bridget and garnered fan mail and marriage proposals. The book format of *Bridget Jones's Diary*, published in the United Kingdom in 1996 and the United States in 1998, won Book of the Year at the British Book Awards in 1998. Translated into more than thirty languages, *Bridget Jones's Diary* has sold more than 2 million copies. Fielding's work is the most canonical of chick lit titles as well as the most acknowledged by professors who feature the text on contemporary British novel and Austen-related syllabi. It has begun to attain significance in the wider literary canon, evidenced in its excerpted inclusion in *Literature as Meaning: A Thematic Anthology of Literature* (2005), edited by Wendy Steiner and published by Pearson Longman's Penguin Academics series imprint. Additionally, it is the only chick lit novel to which a book-length reader's companion is devoted: Imelda Whelehan's *"Bridget Jones's Diary":* *A Reader's Guide* (2002) imparts a thorough introduction for generalist audiences. Bridget—a journalist, like her creator—has come to represent the paradigmatic chick lit protagonist, with *Bridget Jones's Diary* a source text for chick lit tropes.

Readers worldwide recognized themselves in the titular character's self-improvement drives, declaring Bridget Jones an everywoman. Bridget's average body weight, middle-class background, professional rank, and certainly her surname, qualify her as a modern everywoman and a departure from the beautiful heroine of historical romances. The protagonist's down-to-earth quality is produced by a quirky comic vernacular that brought the terms *singleton, emotional fuckwittage,* and *smug married* into English colloquial usage. Salman Rushdie deemed the novel "a brilliant comic creation," rightly highlighting its parody of the bildungsroman's emphasis on development. At the end of the calendar year, Bridget Jones calculates her daily weight and caloric tallies to discover that while she has lost seventy-two pounds she has gained seventy-four. As Austen's *Northanger Abbey* is a parody of Gothic romance, chick lit enacts a realistic parody of the popular romantic formula and reconsiders traditional bildungsroman patterns. Bridget's "development" is measured foremost by self-acceptance and ability to find humor in her all-too-specific personal improvement goals.

A mistress of self-deprecating humor, Bridget stars as the heroine of a modern-day *Pride and Prejudice*, and the novel's self-reflexive affiliations with this classic novel of manners serve to anchor the chick lit genre in respectable origins. Fielding names *Pride and Prejudice* as her "favorite book of all time" and unabashedly admits that from it she "pinched the plot for . . . *Bridget Jones's Diary*" and "came as near as [she] could to stealing its hero, Mr. Darcy, by turning him into Bridget's Mark Darcy" ("Helen Fielding's Bookshelf"). Fielding is hardly alone in her high opinion of Austen's story: in her study *A Natural History of the Romance Novel* (2003), Pamela Regis titles a chapter devoted to the text "The Best Romance Novel Ever Written: *Pride and Prejudice*, 1813" to introduce its paramount status among romance writers and readers. The self-conscious use of a universally beloved novel deflects from the pathetic earthiness and chronic insecurity of Bridget, qualities hardly prominent in her predecessor, Elizabeth Bennet. *Bridget Jones's Diary* is essentially a romance, and its sequel, a frustrated marriage plot, relies on a flimsy exotic travel narrative to distract the reader from the emptiness of Bridget's life and the depressing consequences of romantic failure. To its credit, the sequel indirectly problematizes the neat endings of Austen's marriage plots and underscores the fantasy dimensions of *Pride and Prejudice*'s Elizabeth-Darcy and Jane-Bingley pairings, specifically, the heroines' vastly different economic position from their husbands'.

Though foremost a comic work (Fielding's longtime boyfriend is Kevin Curran, a writer for *The Simpsons*), *Bridget Jones's Diary* also offers a template to examine chick lit's engagement with feminism. The romance of Austen's *Pride and Prejudice* works as a screen over *Bridget Jones's Diary*'s conservative, or at least status quo, messages and its vexed relationship to the women's movement. *Bridget Jones's Diary*'s stance on feminism, though ironic, seems to have been interpreted literally by chick lit novelists who, inspired by this best-seller, draw upon the stereotype of feminists as angry and unremittingly serious. In consequence, aspects of radical feminism are appropriated to make negative blanket statements about the larger feminist project. A poor or outdated fashion sense layers these unflattering characteristics. Lightheartedness, saucy humor, and upscale or trendy style, the latter a focus of chapter 3, are presented as an alternative paradigm (or antidote) to feminism. The reader is more likely to notice how Fielding pulls off plot parallels with Austen's novel or simply to enjoy the book as humorous fiction than to perceive Bridget's being an almost grotesque deflation not only of Elizabeth Bennet but of the liberal feminist tenets of autonomy and choice.

Bridget Jones's Diary additionally serves as a historical marker and index into in the Austen-philia and Darcymania of the last decade, a cottage industry encompassing a staggering number of fictional offshoots to Austen-inspired stationery and board games. In March 2007, for instance, a BBC online survey of more than two thousand book lovers to mark World Book Day, *Pride and Prejudice* was voted England's favorite book, outranking Tolkien's Lord of the Rings trilogy in a reversal of BBC's "The Big Read" poll conducted in 2003 (*"Pride and Prejudice* Is Top Read").[1] Piggybacking off the popularity of the landmark BBC production of *Pride and Prejudice*, Fielding's novel co-opts Austen's status as a traditional author while serving as a catalyst in the attribution of new credentials to Austen, such as travel guide and dating coach. These consumer and media forms reify Austen but also lend an optic into the playfulness of postfeminism and its joining of romance with self-help, commodity fetishism with nostalgia for courtship and civility.

Bridget Jones's Diary as Ironic Bildungsroman

Bridget Jones's Diary consists of twelve chapters spanning one calendar year and commences with its protagonist's New Year's resolutions. Each chapter features dated diary entries, sometimes with minute-by-minute detail of Bridget's hours. This meticulous temporality lends an immediacy and plot-driven component to the diary form. It also adds a narrative drive to its traditionally meditative emphasis. The diary structure was inspired by Fielding's looking back over the calorie-obsessed diaries she produced during her college years (Whelehan 12). Bridget devotes the first two pages to converse "I WILL NOT" and "I WILL" lists, with entries like the following:

I WILL NOT

Behave sluttishly around the house, but instead imagine others are watching.

Have crushes on men, but instead form relationships based on mature assessment of character.

Sulk about having no boyfriend, but develop inner poise and authority and sense of self as woman of substance, complete *without* boyfriend, as best way to obtain boyfriend.

I WILL

Reduce circumference of thighs by 3 inches (i.e. 1½ inches each), using anticellulite diet.

Go to gym three times a week not merely to buy sandwich.

Learn to program video. (2, 3)

The resolutions and subsequent entries focus on the mundane and riff on the protagonist's desire for self-improvement. From its initial pages, the text parodies the unilinear progress characteristic of the heroes and heroines of the traditional bildungsroman (also called "novel of formation" or "novel of education") (Franken 732). Bridget's great expectations and comic shortcomings offer readers a caricatured portrait of their own visions and deficiencies. In her goal to "read books and listen to classical music," she aspires to the trappings of sophistication and accomplishment (3). This motive, compounded with her wish to present a "poised and cool ice-queen" persona, links her to *Pride and Prejudice*'s Caroline Bingley; though urbane, this haughty character pursues advancement in the fine arts but perfunctorily, with her real goal to marry advantageously (2). In the end, Bridget's year-end summary reveals but one kept resolution, 114 hangover-free days, and the receipt of 33 Christmas cards. The novel's final line—"An *excellent* year's progress"—is reflective not only of its ironic attributes but of Fielding's ability to imbue Bridget with a distinct comic voice (271). While the Harlequin may contain scenes of playful banter, chick lit deliberately aims for a humorous effect: Bridget Jones's popularity stems in part from her ability to laugh at her self-improvement quests. The mock bildungsroman balances its protagonist's neurotic accounting tendencies with self-deprecating humor and jocularity.

In its structure and characterization, Fielding's novel essentially supplied a storyboard for aspiring chick lit novelists. The numerous chick lit authors who use months of the year as chapter frames demonstrate the influence of the larger structure of Fielding's international best-seller. Bridget's "urban family" of single friends also became a stock feature of the genre. The friendship circle stands in for family, as immediate relatives are often dead or absent. However, some chick lit titles by authors of color, such as Kavita Daswani's *The Village Bride of Beverly Hills* (2004) and Kim Wong Keltner's *The Dim Sum of All Things* (2003), put more, sometimes central, emphasis on the protagonist's relationship to her family, both immediate and in-laws, and the negotiation between the expectations of her elders and extended family and the life she wishes for herself as an immigrant or first-generation American. While these novels offer significant departures from chick lit's vague or nonexistent representation of the family, as Butler and Desai (2008) have thoughtfully contended in an article on South Asian American chick lit novels, they are, at this time, relatively few in number.[2] In the genre as a whole, the urban family acts of a type of Greek chorus that, according to Christien Franken, offers commentary, issues warnings when necessary, and, when a heart is broken, rallies around the character to prevent the worst damage (735). The trope of the urban family also appears in the popular sitcoms *Friends* (1994–2004), *Allie McBeal* (1997–2002), and *Coupling* (2000–2004), featuring representations of urban singles culture and apartment living.

Bridget's ineptitude in the kitchen is a frequent motif of the genre, as most protagonists flirt with the idea of cooking gourmet but rarely venture further than purchasing a recipe book. For example, the central character of *The Boyfriend School* lives off a diet of Cup-o-Soup. The protagonist of Naomi Neale's *I Went to Vassar for This?* (2006) uses her state-of-the-art dishwasher at most twice a month to rinse wine glasses and coffee cups. The narrator of Bushnell's "Highlights (For Adults)" remarks, "None of the women in this group are good cooks," while *Sex and the City*'s Carrie Bradshaw confesses she uses her oven for storage (*Four Blondes* 83). *Bridget Jones's Diary* would foreshadow how chick lit detaches domestic management from class and respectability, with heroines investing greater time and income in their physical exterior.

The protagonist's earnest attention to female day-to-day ritual, her pattern of goodwill met with bumbling gaucheness, has inspired literary emulation by young women writers. Passages like the following have inaugurated a new kind of feminine mundane:

8:45 a.m. Start on black opaque tights. Pair one seems to have shrunk—crotch is three inches above knees. Get second pair on and find hole on back of leg. Throw away. Suddenly remember had Lycra miniskirt on when returned home with Daniel last time. Go to living room. Triumphantly locate skirt between cushions on sofa.

8:55 a.m. Return to tights. Pair three has hole only in toe. Put on. Hole transforms into run which will protrude tellingly from shoe. Go to ironing basket. Locate last pair of black opaque tights twisted into ropelike object speckled with bits of tissue. Untangle and purge of tissue.

9:05 a.m. Have got tights on now. Add skirt. Begin ironing shirt.

9:10 a.m. Suddenly hair is drying in weird shape. Search for hairbrush. Locate in handbag. Blow-dry hair. Will not go right. Spray with plant spray and blow some more. (80)

In this emphasis on the quotidian, the popularity of *Bridget Jones's Diary*—and by extension, the chick lit genre—stems from its more realistic and partly parodic version of 1980s women's popular fiction, exemplified by the novels of Judith Krantz (*I'll Take Manhattan* [1986]), Jackie Collins (*The Bitch* [1979]), Shirley Conran (*Lace* [1982]), Judith Gould (*Sins* [1983]), and Barbara Taylor Bradford (*To Be the Best* [1988]). The glamour novels of these authors—also referred to generically as the "bonkbuster," "the sex and shopping novel," and even the "S[hopping] and F[ucking] novel"—foreground a self-confident protagonist's meteoric career rise from humble or middling origins.[3] While the protagonist fights for personal independence through the fierce negotiation and acquisition of capital, she is not a mentor to women and feels no debt to feminism (Philips 16). The protagonist's entrepreneurial savvy and compelling looks are met by man-eater cunning and bedroom athletics.

Chick lit writers claim this fiction lacked authenticity as a depiction of their experience as working women. Sarah Mlynowski, the author of *Milkrun* (2001) and a former Harlequin employee, comments as follows on this gap between expectations and actual circumstances: "I found the ironic juxtaposition between the books I marketed and my single-in-the-big-city life the perfect experience to explore in fiction."[4] While chick lit characters share their predecessors' revelry in the consumption of fashion and luxury commodities, they are not as self-driven or solitary, preferring instead camaraderie in which to vent or party (Philips 17). In other words, chick lit authors created a more identifiable heroine, one frequently struggling with consumer debt, while retaining the sex and shopping novel's urban occupational settings such as magazine publishing, public relations, or design.

Bridget's capacity for eliciting readers' identification and her alacrity for life's experiences hark back to the same qualities in the heroine of the novel's source text, Austen's *Pride and Prejudice.* In a presentation given at a meeting of the Dallas Area Romance Authors in May 2005, Shanna Swendson has argued that Austen, who "puts the 'chick' in chick lit," offers an ideal model for the key ingredient contemporary publishers are looking for in manuscripts: a protagonist who is "someone you would want to be but that you could actually imagine being" ("Jane Austen"). Though an only child, Bridget figures as the novel's Elizabeth Bennet, while Mark Darcy, a divorced London barrister, shares the surname of *Pride and Prejudice*'s hero. Bridget's mother, the Mrs. Bennet equivalent, tries to pair the two at a family friend's New Year's Day turkey curry buffet. Defensive about her never-married status, Bridget is put off by the modern Darcy's pomposity. She observes, with full awareness of the intertextual ironies, how he stands with his back to the room, scrutinizing the contents of bookshelves: "It struck me as pretty ridiculous to be called Mr. Darcy and to stand on your own looking snooty at a party" (12). The novel deploys a succession of plot parallels that develop its intertextual link with Austen. Bridget's shock upon seeing the stateliness of Darcy's home mirrors Elizabeth's shock on first sight of Pemberley. One of my students has pointed out that as Austen's Wickham sees no reason why he and Elizabeth shouldn't be good friends still, Daniel Cleaver, Bridget's boss and onetime boyfriend, sees no reason why he can't sleep with Bridget whenever he wants. Cleaver's flirtatiousness renders him closest in personality to Wickham, though he sleeps with Mark Darcy's wife instead of attempting to run off with Fitzwilliam Darcy's sister, Georgiana.

The Wickham/Lydia elopement has its closest approximation in a subplot involving Bridget's mother (Pamela) and her criminal paramour, Julio, in which Pamela's flightiness and lack of character judgment render her a hybrid of Lydia and Mrs. Bennet. This subplot's obvious clues to Julio's less-than-legitimate business dealings, compounded with Bridget's clumsiness and laughable progress, render *Bridget Jones's Diary* both a metafiction and a screwball comedy. Julio's fraudulent schemes are uncovered and her mother's situation rectified with Darcy's help, and both Darcys finally recognize the authentic spirit of their beloved. Mark highlights Bridget's contrast to the typically ostentatious women of their set when he asks her out by saying, "Bridget, all the other girls I know are so lacquered over" (207). All in all, the Austen intertext in *Bridget Jones's Diary* evokes fond affect in the reader as it imparts a romantic undertow to what is at heart a comic work.

Fielding further underscores the intertextuality by setting the novel in 1995 and referencing the BBC adaptation of *Pride and Prejudice*. Bridget muses on her investment in a media event of veritable national addiction: "The basis . . . I know, is my simple human need for Darcy to get off with Elizabeth. . . . They are my chosen representatives in the field of shagging, or, rather, courtship. I do not, however, wish to see any actual goals. I would hate to see Darcy and Elizabeth in bed, smoking a cigarette afterwards. That would be unnatural and wrong and I would quickly lose interest" (215). Bridget merges with Elizabeth Bennet as the penultimate diary entry confesses Mark and Bridget's erotic union. The Bridget-Darcy coupling is paradigmatic of the fusion of realism and wish fulfillment in chick lit.[5] On top of his busy schedule, Mark, it is implied, devotes significant time exonerating Pamela from the threat of prosecution, a highly unlikely investment if he were only interested in Bridget for a hookup. Yet a careful reading reveals that he sleeps with her on their first real date, which isn't even a dinner. After a gourmet Christmas brunch, he reveals that he booked in advance a lavish hotel suite, and despite the romance and champagne of the afternoon's setting, Bridget's admission that right before the consummation he "told me all this stuff about how he loved me: the sort of stuff, to be honest, Daniel was always coming out with" problematizes an easy connection with Austen's Darcy (266–67).

Despite the novel's deliberate intertextuality with Austen, Bridget is very much her own character. In word and deed, the protagonist is more of a humorous creation than a heroine of emulation. Slang and colloquialism are her verbal mainstays, while Elizabeth Bennet's speech acts with Darcy are those of a self-assured rhetorician. Although verbal communication, whether direct speech or letters, is the principal force in both sets of characters' union, Fielding opts for much shorter sentences, with Bridget's diary entries predominantly impressionistic, if breathless, compared to Elizabeth and Darcy's relatively unspontaneous, impressively rational, argument-duets. Chick lit's contemporary novels of manners lack the subtlety and ironic precision of observation that goes into the creation of Austen's heroines. Austen's dexterous use of silence—witnessed for example in *Persuasion*'s Captain Wentworth's listening to the climatic exchange between Anne Elliot and Harville—is not found in the newer form. Bridget does not match up to Elizabeth in intellect, or with either Darcy. Bridget is the product of an extreme normalizing of Elizabeth Bennet. *Bridget Jones's Diary* may succeed at lightheartedness, but this does not make for a spiritually uplifting reading experience. While through blunders she surpasses her predecessor on the point of endearing vulnerability, Bridget evokes not inspiration but merely sympathetic laughter.

The publication of Fielding's column as a novel brought to an eager audience what would quickly become stock features of chick lit. These elements, however, were not her own invention but contemporaneous with representations in notable British fiction. Specifically, *Saving Agnes* (1993), by Rachel Cusk, winner of the Whitbread First Novel Award, possesses a level of confessional detail comparable to *Bridget Jones's Diary* and, while narrated in third person, employs a dreamy, hopelessly romantic heroine who works in publishing and also keeps a diary. Though a decade younger than Bridget, the titular protagonist is equally self-deprecating. Published two years before the commencement of Fielding's newspaper column, *Saving Agnes* falls more in line with the traditional bildungsroman narrative of progress as the novel humorously relates a success story of modest proportions: Londoner Agnes Day, nearly fired from her position at a weekly newspaper because of desultory contributions, starts to buckle down, discovers she can write admirable editorial features, and begins to stand up for herself more in social situations. With this greater confidence and work ethic, she receives a promotion, becomes a homeowner (albeit jointly with two former flatmates), and acquires more discernment in matters of the heart. In a nod to romantic comedic conventions, Cusk in the text's final scene has Agnes during her bus commute to work meet a prospective suitor who initiates a conversation, their verbal rapport an indicator of physical chemistry. While Fielding drew inspiration from *Pride and Prejudice*'s love story, she may have grafted Austen's classic plot to Cusk's template, the end product joining fairy-tale romance with the novel of manners' focus on social interaction.

While Fielding has authored a modern classic through her creation of an archetypal contemporary character, she was not the first writer to create a single female protagonist who is also notably funny. The success of *Bridget Jones's Diary*, however, can be credited with inspiring a genre in which a single funny woman figures prominently. This choice of a protagonist is relatively new historically and marks a shift in representations of gender insofar as funny women have been formerly laughed at, not laughed with. The depiction of humorous single women in Anglo-American literature is largely a phenomenon of the later decades of the twentieth century. In a study of 150 single women appearing in 125 American novels from approximately 1850 to 1935, Dorothy Yost Deegan has observed that a personal sense of humor seemed noticeably lacking among single women characters as a group (81). Single women—never-married women at least thirty years of age—almost always appeared, in Deegan's sample, as minor characters. The never-married woman in Anglo-American literature has frequently served as the object of ridicule, when not depicted as a creature of pity, as in Katherine Mansfield's "Miss Brill" (1920) or Jean Rhys's *After Leaving Mr. Mackenzie* (1931), for example, or, only slightly less derogatorily, useful in matters of parochial importance. Chick lit, by contrast, foregrounds this figure as the protagonist: the never-married funny woman—whose humor contributes greatly to the genre's appeal—finds her most developed expression.

Though Fielding's novel extends sustained comic relief for the never married, the fact remains that the principal joke is on single women. We see, for instance, that Bridget's self-esteem is fragilely dependent on her status as somebody's girlfriend. Chick lit, to its credit, does not disavow feelings of deep loneliness or gnawing unrest that the novelist has traditionally ascribed to the spinster. To be sure, the novel's humor does work to critique media images of gender. Bridget, a self-identified "child of *Cosmopolitan* culture," confides she has been "traumatized by supermodels and too many quizzes" (52). Her attempt to reject this pressure is, however, hardly subversive: it doesn't go beyond spending an evening in an egg-smeared cardigan eating doughnuts. *Bridget Jones's Diary*'s parody of the culture of self-improvement and privileging of personal authenticity do not fully succeed in bolstering its hackneyed romantic conclusion.

Yet the married lifestyle is not portrayed as entirely desirable either. Several engagements and marriages are exposed as shams, not least by

Bridget's mother, who falls into adultery in late middle age. Motherhood, too, is treated satirically, as "ex-career-girl mothers" boast about their toddlers' accomplishments with cutthroat ferocity. With polite antagonism, they compare their children's genital development and make absurd claims about their infant progeny's progress in potty training. As their career growth comes to a sudden roadblock with maternity, the mothers refocus their ambition on their tots' frenetic developmental acceleration. The reader of the diary is provided, then, with neither a desirable single nor married archetype, while the swift ending accompanying Bridget and Darcy's union leaves the reader wondering if a bildungsroman-like narrative of progress in public life can coexist within the tropes and plot devices of romantic comedy.

Like *Bridget Jones's Diary*, its sequel, *Bridget Jones: The Edge of Reason* (1999), parodies the protagonist's obsessive self-development schemes and extends humorous support for the singleton on the dating circuit. It offers, however, significantly less wish fulfillment than its predecessor. Its time frame—a calendar year, as in the original (and the average time span of the main action of Austen's novels)—reveals that not much has really changed in Bridget's life. The diary entries disclose that Bridget has been unsuccessful at quitting smoking and reducing her weight, though she continues to keep tallies with the same precision. They record once again Bridget's reading and attempted application of self-help best-sellers. The number of references to relationship manuals borders on pop psychology name-dropping, though Fielding parodies not only Bridget's eager consumption but also the manuals' interchangeability: "Yes. As it says in *How to Get the Love You Want*—or maybe it was *Keeping the Love You Find?*—the blending together of men and women is a delicate thing. Man must pursue. Will wait for him to ring me" (8). The sequel often reads as a perfunctory repeat, perhaps because it employs the same structuring devices as the original. But these repetitions underscore all the more Bridget's unsuitability as a traditional *Bildungsheld*, that is, a novel-of-education protagonist.

The Edge of Reason adds a travel adventure component, perhaps to distract the reader from the essentially depressing elements of Bridget's social situation. It devotes tenuously credible sections to Bridget and company's summer holiday in Thailand and a two-week imprisonment in its penal system. A lover of Bridget's close friend Shazzer uses Bridget to unknowingly smuggle drugs through customs, and Mark Darcy makes Herculean efforts for her release. As in the original where he facilitates the release of Mrs. Jones, Darcy's legal savvy comes to the rescue and reunites him with Bridget. In the final lines Mark asks Bridget if she will accompany him to Thailand for a business matter that will occupy several months. The prospect is hardly appealing, and the sequel closes at the end of the calendar year with Bridget mulling the idea of relocation with unenthusiastic skepticism and taking comfort in a glass of wine and a cigarette.

Like the original diary, *The Edge of Reason* uses *Pride and Prejudice* as an intertext. The characters watch the BBC production of *Pride and Prejudice* on video, and Bridget succeeds in interviewing Colin Firth, the adaptation's Darcy. Readers who come to the sequel without having read the original are cued to elicit parallels between the two novels' Darcys. For many female readers, the Colin Firth interview summons the sweep of romance and gallant male virility, ideals that Bridget still holds plausible in a real-life mate after two decades of dating. The sequel, however, re-opens the tidy ending of *Pride and Prejudice* by focusing on the misunderstandings and self-doubt that accompany Bridget's relationship with Mark Darcy. For example, at a posh society party Bridget is shocked to discover that Mark usually votes Tory:

> Suddenly I felt I didn't know Mark Darcy at all, and for all I knew, all the weeks we had been going out he had been secretly collecting limited edition miniature pottery animals wearing bonnets from the back pages of Sunday supplements, or slipping off to rugby matches on a bus and mooning the other motorists out of the back window.
>
> Conversation was getting snootier and snootier and more showy-offy. (44)

Bridget Jones's Diary implicitly questions the long-term compatibility of Austen's Elizabeth Bennet and Darcy. Bridget and Mark Darcy are, like Austen's pair, challenged by class and personality differences: in Austen his austerity and her effervescence, in Fielding his borderline priggishness and her goofy joie de vivre (a trait that at moments renders her closer to Elizabeth Bennet's sister Kitty). In the penultimate chapter, Jude, Bridget's female sidekick, marries, and the reader hopes that Bridget will quickly follow, especially as Mark cuts off a rival, Rebecca, by declaring he needs not her but Bridget. Yet the conclusion's lack of closure reveals Bridget not much nearer to mistress of Pemberley than she was in the original's opening.

Neither of Fielding's novels repudiates the notion of Austen's Darcy as the ideal man. They do, however, depict a modern equivalent who heightens the Cinderella elements of *Pride and Prejudice*. In contrast to the double weddings closing *Pride and Prejudice* and *Sense and Sensibility, The Edge of Reason* presents a frustrated marriage plot.[6] We can imagine the next scene as Bridget and her urban family, half-inebriated, holding a summit on how she should best deal with the latest wrinkle in the pair's attempt at long-term couplehood; she will wake the next morning to lament the caloric intake of the night out and renew again her quest to develop inner poise. Dishearteningly, the last we learn of Bridget is that a long-term loving, committed relationship has still eluded her. Fielding's revived *Independent* column chronicled Bridget's unplanned pregnancy fathered by Daniel Cleaver, with the final column (June 15, 2006) informing us that Bridget gives birth to a boy. The healthy infant may be compensation for Daniel's lack of commitment; he is not present at the birth, though he visits her in the hospital shortly after.[7]

Perhaps the greatest irony of the *Bridget Jones* novels is, in a pathetic way, their self-help function. Bridget's ceaseless failed attempts to lose weight and general desperation make the reader's own neuroses and obsessions seem mild or moderate in comparison. In an article titled "Postfeminism and Popular Culture: Bridget Jones and the New Gender Regime" (2007), Angela McRobbie assesses Fielding's novel as working to "normalize postfeminist gender anxieties so as to regulate young women by means of the language of personal choice" (38). The texts' spoof on self-improvement culture, and its lack of self-fulfillment formulas and real advice beyond "say *pardon*," ultimately maintain the status quo: society has embraced Bridget because she is completely nonthreatening.

The film adaptation of *Bridget Jones's Diary* added yet another layer of reflexivity in its already rich intertextual connections with *Pride and Prejudice*. Numerous veterans of Austen's movie adaptations appear in the *Bridget Jones's Diary* film. Directed by Sharon Maguire, *Bridget Jones's Diary* grossed $250 million in box office receipts worldwide.[8] It broke all box office records in the United Kingdom for a domestic film in its opening weekend in 2001 by grossing nearly £7 million (Whelehan 73). Renée Zellwegger acquired a British accent and thirty extra pounds to play Fielding's protagonist. Andrew Davies, the film's screenwriter, also wrote the screenplay for the BBC production of *Pride and Prejudice* (1995), which starred Colin Firth as Fitzwilliam Darcy. Firth, obviously, became an appropriate choice for the role of Mark Darcy, as the character's identical surname with his earlier role further cues audiences to interpret the film as a modern-day *Pride and Prejudice*. In the film, the publishing house where Bridget works is named Pemberley Press (Ferriss 72). Hugh Grant (Daniel Cleaver) and Gemma Jones (Pamela) both appeared in Ang Lee's adaptation of *Sense and Sensibility* (1995). Embeth Davidtz (Natasha) played Mary Crawford in Patricia Rozema's adaptation of *Mansfield Park*. These same actors reprised their roles in the film adaptation of *The Edge of Reason* (2004). The public's association of these cast members with acclaimed adaptations of Austen's works retroactively amplified the canonical intertext of *Bridget Jones's Diary* and its sequel.

Bridget Jones and the Killjoy of Feminism

The courtship novel of the eighteenth century and its idea that its protagonist is entitled to choose a husband arose from the shift from arranged to companionate marriage. Two centuries later, in the 1970s, the Harlequin boomed parallel to second-wave feminism. The Harlequin offered, according to Ann Barr Snitow, an archetypal, fixed image of the exchange between men and women as well as a counterpoint to shifting and confusing social actualities (150). Chick lit, our latest courtship novel, has developed partly from upheavals in marriage and education demography as well as the accompanying growth of a singles culture. While Bridget Jones, and by extension, the typical chick lit protagonist, represents a limited demographic profile, the genre's engagement with single women is propelled by wider shifts in marriage, residence patterns, and singles culture. For instance, between 1970 and 2000, the proportion of unmarried women ages 20 to 24 doubled, and among those 30 to 34 the share tripled (Whitehead, *Why There Are* 25–26). Almost half of Americans are reaching the age of 30 without marrying, and the most recent decennial federal census (2000) reveals that the number of never-married Americans aged 35 to 39 increased twofold in a single generation (Hacker 25, 7). In 2005, 51 percent of U.S. women, according to a *New York Times* analysis of census results, were living without a spouse, up from 35 percent in 1950 and 49 percent in 2000 (Roberts). More than 22 million American women live alone, representing an 87 percent surge over the last two decades, and in 2003 twice as many single women as single men purchased homes (Seckler).

Chick lit is a product of the increased—in fact, all-time-high—average age of first marriage for women, documenting through fiction a situation that renders the path to the altar long and indirect, with numerous detours along the way. For instance, in 1960, the American bride was 20.3 years old, and her groom was under 23. By the year 2000, the bride's median age had risen to 25.1, the groom's to 26.8 (Hacker 15). In 2004, U.S. median ages for first marriage have been reported as 25.8 and 27.4 for men and women, respectively, an increase of 5 years for women and 4.2 years for men since 1970 (Williamson C7). For college-educated women, however, today's median age of first marriage may be closer to 27 or 28 than to 25 (Whitehead, "Plight" 75). Chick lit's portrayal of serial dating and jettisoning of the Harlequin's requisite pairing reflect a new timetable for college-educated women, a courtship pattern that joins early professional development with a delayed progression to the altar. As Bridget Jones surmises, "This confusion, I guess, is the price I must pay for becoming a modern woman instead of following the course nature intended by marrying . . . when I was eighteen" (103). Whether or not readers identify with a particular chick lit protagonist, her central conflict may mirror their own and abate the disgruntlement of not "getting it together" or of "missing the boat." The chick lit imprint Red Dress Ink's tagline "Life's Little Curves" highlights through metaphor the protagonist's circuitous and improvised journey.

Delayed marriage is a product of relaxed attitudes toward premarital sex and of continued postsecondary education for women, a phenomenon concomitant with the decline of the family wage and rising standards for a middle-class identity. The pursuit of advanced educational degrees also serves, as Barbara Dafoe Whitehead observes, as "a cushion against the likelihood of an eventual divorce" ("Plight"). Delayed marriage is also a consequence of second-wave feminism and its fight for advances in women's education and advocacy of professional achievement as liberation from compulsory marriage. *Bridget Jones's Diary* makes a direct nod to the phenomenon of delayed marriage as well as several references to feminism. The first occurs in Bridget's initial meeting with Mark Darcy at a New Year's Day turkey curry buffet, a tradition her mother forces her to attend with the idea that her grown daughter can win the attentions of Mark, an occasional playmate from Bridget's early childhood and son of a couple who have remained friends with Bridget's mother. Mark inquires if she has read any quality books recently, and the anxious Bridget scans her head but can only come up with *Men Are from Mars, Women Are from Venus* (1992), John Gray's separate spheres self-help sensation. She instead drums up not the number one best-selling relationship book of the 1990s, but *Backlash: The Undeclared War against American Women* (1991) by Susan Faludi as an answer. Faludi argues that the 1980s saw a backlash against feminism, owing especially to the spread of negative stereotypes against career-minded women. The title, Bridget believes, is a highly unlikely read for a "diamond-patterned-jumpered goody-goody" (13). Yet Mark has read the five-hundred-page treatise when it first appeared and offers the question, "Didn't you find there was rather a lot of special pleading?" (13). Feminism, then, makes its appearance as something Bridget should be aware of, but is too weighty or laborious to command a more than impressionistic investigation. Bridget, who works in publishing, puts out the title, a National Book Critics Circle Award winner, as an attempt to seem smart and with the current book scene, although the text was published nearly a half decade before their dialogue, an anachronism fitting Fielding's ironic treatment of Bridget.

That Bridget knows of *Backlash* because her friend Sharon (a.k.a. Shazzer) "has been ranting about it so much," connects the book with a chronically complaining character. Though we don't know the specifics of Shazzer's rant—whether it is directed at its message, the quality of Faludi's research, etc.—the word *rant* itself evokes the stereotypes of feminists as hostile and hectoring, and these connotations reverberate with Mark's assessment of the title. Thus, in yet another irony of Fielding's novel, Bridget co-opts feminism to appear culturally savvy enough to merit the attention of an urbane man. Or, because her first impression of Darcy is that of a pompous prig, she may select Faludi's feminist best-seller as a repellent.

Bridget Jones's Diary contains what may be chick lit's most famous reference to feminism, and from it we glean postfeminism as an attempt to ameliorate some deficiencies of second-wave feminism. Bridget observes that "there is nothing so unattractive to a man as strident feminism"— a line, like the entire *Diary*, Fielding claims she intended as ironic (18).

Yet the conservative ending of the text raises an eyebrow to this claim. It is difficult not to interpret the declaration as possessing a somewhat literal intent, especially given the closing line of Bridget's final diary entry: "Don't say 'what,' say 'pardon,' darling, and do as your mother tells you" (267). The philosophy of Bridget's mother spoken through her daughter, this entry affirms traditional values, however disjointed the gap between Bridget's mother's behavior and her actions. In an interview Fielding glossed this line by asking readers to look critically at feminism's capacity to integrate humor: "If we can't have a comic female character, if we can't laugh at ourselves without having a panic attack about what it says about women, we haven't gotten very far with our equality" ("Helen Fielding: The Making of Bridget Jones"). Fielding poses laughter as the new feminist frontier, an agenda not ignoble at that. However, Fielding's defense of Bridget's antifeminist declaration is ultimately apolitical in that it implies women readers need to take a wholly uncritical perspective on what is being laughed at. Postfeminism, it seems, aims to infuse more levity into women's perceptions of experience. In reaction to second-wave jargon such as "systemic structural change" and its connotations of pragmatic action, postfeminism validates the realm of fun and perceives nonseriousness as liberating.

While positive and direct mentions of feminism are scant in chick lit, the genre complicates liberal feminism's advocacy of personal choice, which presents a mixed blessing. Protagonists have the right to choose, but now the problem is too many choices, a dilemma that *Sex and the City*'s Carrie Bradshaw ponders on her Mac laptop and Bridget Jones's mother unsympathetically sees as a surfeit of luxury, lecturing, "You've simply got too much choice. I'm not saying I didn't love Dad but, you know, we were always taught, instead of waiting to be swept off our feet, to 'expect little, forgive much'" (169). Ultimately, though, Bridget stands as a casualty of the media and self-help industry. While we may identify with Bridget's catch-22 of choice (Natasha, the glamorous, ambitious lawyer does not get Mark either, implying a serious career woman may wind up with just her job and dwindling time left to conceive), stripped of its humor, *Bridget Jones's Diary* has a borderline alcoholic, weight-obsessed, undiscerning neurotic as its heroine. This character does not do justice to the women's movement but offers an ironic and acute deflation (or, for some, relief) of its prominent figures: the superwoman and the independent heroine. Bridget is so ham-fisted that it is hard to imagine her not blundering a serious pursuit, nor does she have the tenacity to follow through with any, whatever guffaw we would get from her maladroit effort. It is as if the supremely static nature of Bridget's character—a chief difference from Elizabeth Bennet and her acknowledgment of pride and misjudgment—offers a perverse resistance to feminism's ideals of achievement and liberation. Less harshly, we can read the novel as one that celebrates being ordinary; Bridget is not a superwoman, but she is a loyal friend who gets an alpha male or at minimum a "catch." Its message that it is OK to be average is in many ways a sensible counterargument to the self-improvement discourses that surround Bridget and that she inconsistently strives to master.

Terror Trash and the Limits of Parody

Perhaps because Bridget's lack of development was one of her hallmark features, Fielding ultimately needed new territory and, after *The Edge of Reason*, departed from her most popular character. Fielding made the first attempt to incorporate terrorist plots into the genre by merging aspects of the chick lit formula with the spy thriller genre. However timely, her *Olivia Joules and the Overactive Imagination* (2003) not only failed but yielded disturbing results. Olivia resembles the standard chick lit protagonist with her gravitation toward designer commodities; she also shares Bridget's occupation as a journalist. But her instincts, which in her career past have often reflected, in the refrain of her boss, an overactive imagination, lead her to uncover an al-Qaeda terrorist plot. While on assignment to cover a celebrity face crème launch, she becomes attracted to Pierre Ferramo, who, despite his playboy attire, non-Arabic name, and heavy drinking, she insists resembles Osama bin Laden. In contrast to her predecessor Bridget, Joules is model-thin and athletic, her figure and stylish looks catching the pseudo–movie producer's eye. Ferramo turns out to be not bin Laden but a serial killer of women and the leader of a plan to blow up the Oscars: the attack is narrowly thwarted the day of the ceremony by Joules and a CIA agent she predictably falls for. The novel, with a large neon martini glass on the cover, packages itself as a summer read; its fishbowl-like appearance complements diving scenes, crafted with technically precise detail, germane to the international espionage plot. Yet the book's cover is a jarring fit with its content; in one scene more than two hundred passengers are killed when terrorists strike a cruise liner docked at Miami Beach. The terror attacks of September 11, 2001, were still too close to the novel's publication in June 2004 for its fun action-read tone to be palatable. Released during the ongoing Iraqi conflict and recurring news of terror, lines like "*I think I'm falling in love with you,* she thought. *Even if you are a terrorist. I'm like one of those female aid workers who falls for the leader of the rebel army or gets kidnapped and falls for her kidnapper*" seem cheap (125, original emphasis). The simile, its content a common trope in Harlequins, degenerates into bad taste with Fielding using "0911" as the access code for al-Qaeda underground rooms Joules clandestinely enters.

The novel's reception is a striking example of how mixing genres—a formal component of chick lit—may brew a bewildering if not disastrous end product: Fielding in a *Guardian* interview stated that she intended the novel as a fantasy, as a spy thriller, as a work of irony, and as a comic creation ("Dumped Bridget"). Her humor fell flat when most reviewers perceived it as offensive and callous. The point is not so much that Fielding was unsuccessful in capitalizing on the new popular obsession with terrorism but that she failed to demonstrate chick lit's capacity to engage seriously with world politics. In an *Entertainment Weekly* review, one that issued the novel a rare "F" grade, critic Karen Valby argued that Fielding had birthed another genre—"terror trash."

The chick lit formula, with its lighthearted essence, was an unlikely generic candidate to integrate the events of September 11. Efforts, however, include Caren Lissner's *Starting from Square Two* (2004), which incorporates the destruction of the World Trade Center into its main story. The twenty-nine-year-old protagonist, whose husband died in a car accident a few days before the attacks, regularly attends a widows' support group on Long Island where women gather to grieve and begin rebuilding their lives.[9] The novel was additionally significant in developing the subgenre "widow lit," a category that includes *P.S. I Love You* (2004), by Cecelia Ahern, daughter of former Irish prime minister Bertie Ahern. This subset features a protagonist's attempt to reenter the dating scene after bereavement and to carry her past experiences into a hopeful and productive future. Tragedy, when it exists in chick lit, has occupied more of a subplot status— the demise of a gay male secondary character to AIDS, for example. Nevertheless, as *Olivia Joules* may have been what we thought was Fielding's swan song to, or at least a departure from, the genre she inspired, widow lit marks a widening of protagonists' marital status and transposes to a more somber register. As Fielding's *Bridget Jones's Diary* birthed a genre, her *Olivia Joules* dramatically showed its limitations.

Producing a Postfeminist Austen

Fielding can be credited with adapting one of the most beloved novels in English literary history into a comic record of a modern everywoman's dating tribulations. Seminal to her novel's global success was her creation's self-deprecating humor and her shortcomings in highly identifiable self-improvement goals. Yet the popularity of *Bridget Jones's Diary* and its sequel stems in part from its synchronicity with what Deborah Kaplan in a *Chronicle of Higher Education* editorial has termed the "Austen boon" and "Austenmania" of the past decade. The Austen boon is reflected in cinema, adult fiction, and literary studies, with selected chick lit titles contributing to the phenomenon's vitality. While facets of the chick lit formula, which *Bridget Jones's Diary* was instrumental in establishing, are more of a cultural artifact of the late 1990s and no longer in demand by publishers, chick lit survives in its influence on the more than 150 Austen-inspired women's fiction trade novels. The chick lit genre operates synergistically to repackage the Regency novelist as what Kaplan identifies as "a popular Jane Austen" (B12). This section treats these repackagings sequentially to survey how they, like Fielding's novel, produce new readings of Austen's plots and revise Austen's "author function," Michel Foucault's term for the idea that as authorship exceeds the simple attribution of a discourse to its creator, authorial heroes (and heroines) materialize and endure in part from the vicarious projection of critics and biographers, the author coming to embody a constructed persona with ascribed values.

Between 1995 and 2008 there were twelve screen remakes, on average one a year, of five of Austen's six novels. Five of these were adaptations of *Pride and Prejudice*. The BBC/A&E production of *Pride and Prejudice* drew at least 10 million viewers when it was first serialized on British television in 1995 and reached countless others when it was later broadcast in more than forty countries. Within a year of its premiere that same year, Ang Lee's adaptation of *Sense and Sensibility* had grossed more than $125 million worldwide. (Andrew Davies for PBS also adapted this novel of the social fates of two sisters, in a production that aired in March 2008.) A

Mormon version of Austen's most famous novel—titled *Pride and Prejudice: A Latter-Day Comedy*—appeared in movie theaters in 2004. *Bride and Prejudice*, a Bollywood take on the same novel directed by Gurinder Chadha, opened in the United States in 2005. That same year, Universal Pictures released its adaptation of the classic with Keira Knightley as Elizabeth Bennet and Dame Judi Dench as Lady Catherine de Bourgh.

The year 2007 saw two films that, though not adaptations, take Austen as their central focus. The first, *Becoming Jane*, starring Anne Hathaway and James McAvoy, loosely bases itself on Austen's romance with Thomas Langlois Lefroy, the Irish politician. Julian Jarrold, the film's director, comments on the film's focus and attempt to widen the idea of Austen as a prudent arbiter of propriety: "There is a stereotype of Jane as a spinster obsessed with manners. But we are looking at her when she is 21, full of life and hope and kicking against the restrictions around her" (qtd. in Hastings, Jones, and Plentl). *Becoming Jane* also aims to bring Austen to a teenage female audience. Producers deliberately cast Hathaway, who starred in *The Princess Diaries* and its sequels, a movie series inspired by Meg Cabot's young-adult chick lit series of the same title, with the idea that "many of the 11-year-olds who fell in love with her in *The Princess Diaries* are now just turning 15. They are the right age for Austen" (Hastings, Jones, and Plentl). The second, the film adaptation of Karen Joy Fowler's *The Jane Austen Book Club* (2004), directed by Robin Swicord, depicts Austen's novels as restorative, as six Californians apply Austen's insights to repair infidelity, rejuvenate crumbling marriages, and create new romantic pairings. In the adaptation of this Oprah book pick, the reading and discussion of Austen function as group therapy, with the novels serving as keys to twenty-first-century relationship challenges. Adaptations of Austen have been the subject not only for the silver screen but also reality TV in the PBS reality show *Regency House Party* (2004), described as "Jane Austen meets *The Bachelor*" (Bond 40).[10]

Austenmania has additionally manifested itself in a host of print offshoots, a surge of modern rewritings crossing multiple genres. The self-help book *Jane Austen's Guide to Dating* (2005) by Lauren Henderson culls lessons from the novelist's characters and their romantic fortunes to apply to contemporary courtship. The guide draws the clichéd "Be Prepared to Wait for the Right Person to Come Along" from *Persuasion*'s Anne Elliot and, like the *Sex and the City*–inspired self-help title *He's Just Not That into*

You, analyzes characters to prevent the twenty-first-century woman from making the same mistakes: for instance, Wickham, a "player," in modern parlance, will never settle down. Darcy Cosper's short essay "Everything I Need to Know about Romance I Learned from Jane Austen (I Just Wished I'd Taken Her Advice Sooner)" (2005) also claims Austen as a romantic savant. That Austen herself (and her sister Cassandra) never married apparently does not disqualify her as a sage advisor. Her fictional oeuvre, especially *Pride and Prejudice,* which is frequently dubbed "the mother of all modern romances," not Austen's marital status, serves as worldly credentials.[11] Austen's celibacy complements the paradigmatic chick lit heroine's singleness. The historical Austen offers implicit continuity with chick lit heroines who succeed in supporting themselves by writing or editing as well as the never-married chick lit author.

Each of Cosper's "rules," such as "Don't Expect a Relationship to Make You a Happy Woman," is followed by a relevant excerpt from Austen's novels. In diction and tone, the rules read like headlines from a women's magazine. The Austen quotes, which appear immediately below the rules, serve as corroborating epigraphs, their longer sentence structure and canonical status lending weight and credence to the modern counterpart. Featured in the nonfiction collection *Sex and Sensibility: 28 True Romances from the Lives of Single Women*—several of whose contributors are established chick lit novelists—Cosper's essay empathetically interprets Austen's view of relationships as unromantic: "Austen makes it very clear to us that love and marriage have no inherent transformative or ameliorative powers. Her portraits of marriages that have matured beyond newlywed stage range from uninspiring to downright hellish" (241).

This reading serves to align Austen's perspectives with chick lit tenets, specifically that the heroine must take stock of herself and be the catalyst of new behavioral patterns. Our world and Austen's, despite their two-hundred-year separation, work in the same way, Cosper asserts, in that each of us is responsible for her own happiness, which will not arise from love alone but from qualities of mind. Guides like Cosper's and Henderson's, in other words, assess Austen's novels not so much as meticulously crafted pieces of a bygone era but as forward thinking. Her tidy endings belie a more radical, unromantic stance, the logic follows. These readings downplay the novels' teleology of marriage for the heroine and instead emphasize Austen's satirical treatment of actual married life as well as her appraisal of women who are overinvested in securing a husband as vulgar. This observation, while valid, is argued in hyperbolic terms that verge on turning Austen's signature irony into overt moral censure, with Cosper, for example, employing phrases like "ugly and utterly contemptible" to describe Austen's treatment of grasping matrons like Mrs. Bennet (236).

While these authors have read Austen didactically, others capitalize more on Austen's name rather than her powers of drawing-room observation. "Jane Austen" becomes a selling device for genres outside of Austen's province. With the intent to attract both mystery readers and Janeites, comedy writer Laura Levine created the Jaine Austen Mysteries series. Launched in 2002 by Kensington Books, its debut title, *This Pen for Hire*, introduces Jaine Austen, a divorced thirty-six-year-old Los Angeles freelance writer, and her cat Prozac. A timid and scrawny insurance adjuster named Howard Murdoch seeks Jaine's services to attract Stacy Lawrence, a stunning L.A. Sports Club aerobics instructor to whom he has never spoken. Led to believe from Jaine's letter that Howard is the nephew of Rupert Murdoch, Stacy agrees to a date, on the night of which she is found dead in her living room bludgeoned by a ThighMaster. An unsuspecting Howard arrives for the date, finds the door wide open, enters the crime scene, and is grabbed by the police. Jaine finds herself in the middle of a murder mystery and a romance with a neighbor from Stacy's apartment complex. No brooding hero, the male love interest is revealed as the murderer. The tale's end finds Jaine again single but enrolled in the Learning Annex's "How to Be a Private Eye" course with the super sleuth at work on an idea for a Yellow Pages ad:

Jaine Austen, Discreet Inquiries
Work Done with Pride, Not Prejudice (202)

Though the comedy of manners engages Austen chiefly by surface appropriation, the gimmick enables Levine to adapt chick lit for mystery and conversely to expand the latter genre. The series employs Austen's canonical standing as a type of brand recognition and, like Cosper's essay, figures her as a formidable blend of savvy and erudition.

While chick lit has been a powerful influence on the Austen boom, it is only a segment of a larger trend in adult fiction. Titles such as Paula Marantz Cohen's modernization of *Persuasion* in *Jane Austen in Scarsdale: Love, Death, and the SATs* (2006) and her *Jane Austen in Boca* (2002), Juliette

Shapiro's *Excessively Diverted* (2002), Kate Fenton's *Vanity and Vexation: A Novel of Pride and Prejudice* (2004), and Sally Smith O'Rourke's *The Man Who Loved Jane Austen* (2006) attract Janeites by title choice and their plaiting of aspects of Austen's works into a central plot. *Persuasion*'s hero is the subject of Susan Kaye's two-volume Frederick Wentworth, Captain series (2007–). The Fitzwilliam Darcy, Gentleman trilogy by Pamela Aidan foregrounds the emotions of Austen's enigmatic hero who, despite being half of one of English literature's most famous romantic couples, we know little about beyond his £10,000 annual interest income. Aidan's best-selling series is not alone in its amplification of Austen's Darcy. Other works that promise more of *Pride and Prejudice* and point to this novel as Austen's most successful include Elizabeth Aston's *The Second Mrs. Darcy* (2007), *The True Darcy Spirit* (2006), *The Exploits and Adventures of Miss Alethea Darcy* (2005), and *Mr. Darcy's Daughters* (2003); Janet Aylmer's *Darcy's Story* (1996); Helen Halstead's *Mr. Darcy Presents His Bride* (2005); Juliette Shapiro's *Excessively Diverted* (2002); Linda Berdoll's *Mr. Darcy Takes a Wife: "Pride and Prejudice" Continues* (2004); Joan Ellen Delman's *Miss de Bourgh's Adventure* (2007), Diana Birchall's *Mrs. Darcy's Dilemma* (2004); Phyllis Furley's *The Darcys* (2004); and Jane Dawkins's *Letters from Pemberley: The First Year* (1999) and its follow-up *More Letters from Pemberley: 1814–1818* (2003). In an instance of chick lit influencing spin-offs on *Pride and Prejudice*'s hero, *Mr. Darcy's Diary* (2005) by Amanda Grange attempts to attract readers by piggybacking off the title of Fielding's novel and its intimation of confessional detail.

Darcy and his bride are the subjects of a mystery series by Carrie Bebris, the third volume of which, *North by Northanger* (2006), joins cast members of the first of Austen's novels to be completed for publication. Darcy's sister, Georgiana, receives her own sequel in Skylar Hamilton Burris's *Conviction* (2004), which introduces a new cast of characters whose fates entwine around the central plot of the protagonist's romantic adventures.[12] Those seeking a full-throttle reunion of Austen characters might consider Sybil Brinton's *Old Friends and New Fancies*, a reissue of the first of Austen sequels. Originally published in 1913, it entwines the lives of characters from all six of Austen's novels with figures of Brinton's creation. In fact, in 1996, the year *Bridget Jones's Diary* was published, at least eight sequels and spin-offs of Austen's novel appeared in print.[13] This trend in fiction appropriates, like Fielding's novel, a canonical plot for entertainment reading.

Austen's novels themselves have received renewed attention from publishers in a number of recent reissues, including new editions of *Pride and Prejudice* and *Persuasion* as well as a revised edition of *Sense and Sensibility* released by Oxford World's Classics in 2004. In 2007, Anchor Books released an annotated edition of *Pride and Prejudice*, a 739-page volume with more than 2,300 annotations. In 2005, Cambridge University Press began to release the first of three volumes in the nine-volume Cambridge Edition of the Works of Jane Austen series. To evaluate even the most dedicated Austen buff's reading skills, turn to Oxford's *So You Think You Know Jane Austen? A Literary Quizbook* (2005), by John Sutherland of University College London and Deirdre Le Fay. Should you need further remediation, the For Dummies reference series released a volume devoted to Austen in 2006. To piggyback off of the anticipated popularity of *Becoming Jane*, Penguin in February of 2007 announced it planned new editions of Austen's six best-known works with covers designed to appeal to teenagers. In May 2006, Headline Publishing issued Austen's six novels under the tag "Classic Romances" with glossy pastel covers. The Regency chick lit cover art mirrors Headline fiction editor Harriet Evans's assessment of Austen as "the archetypal popular novelist" (Van Gelder).

These forms of cultural production exist on the reified level as Austen paraphernalia. The retail catalog Signals offers an "I Love Mr. Darcy" T-shirt and sweatshirt as well as a 5¼-inch Jane Austen action figure, with her writing desk, miniature copy of *Pride and Prejudice*, and removable quill pen. There is a growing line of Austen-inspired sterling silver jewelry, as Signals featured a pendant with the quote "Where shall we see a better daughter or a kinder sister or a truer friend," from *Emma*, with Austen's initials inscribed on the reverse side, and in 2005 the catalog Bas Bleu included a cuff bracelet inscribed with an excerpt of a prayer by Austen. Bas Bleu also has available Austen note cards, a beach towel with the opening paragraphs of *Pride and Prejudice*, and a *Pride and Prejudice* board game (figure 5) in which players use game pieces representing the novel's characters paired as couples and collect tokens and answer questions about both the book and life in Austen's time; the first player to arrive at the parish church wins. These paraphernalia complemented the catalog's Austen-related nonfiction offerings. For example, *Tea with Jane Austen* (2004) by Kim Wilson includes readings of how Austen used the drink in her novels as an indicator of a character's virtue (or lack thereof) alongside of tips

Play Pride and Prejudice!

Jane Austen would delight
in this uniquely clever game.
Pick a couple from the novel
and maneuver them through
town and countryside.
Experience Regency Life,
answer questions about the book,
then race to the Parish Church
to marry and win the game.

$29 plus $8 shipping
per game

The Ash Grove Press, Inc.
P.O. Box 8564
Prairie Village, KS 66208-8564
www.ashgrovepress.com

FIGURE 5. Advertisement for *Pride and Prejudice: The Game.* (Copyright Julienne Gehrer, The Ash Grove Press, Inc.)

for brewing the perfect cup. The coffee-table book, essentially a history of English tea and a recipe collection of teatime goodies, co-opts Austen to enhance the book's appeal to Anglophiles. It appropriates connotations surrounding Austen—genteel, discerning—to figure her as a fitting chaperon or narrator of ceremonies in the reader's partaking of tea's cultural history.[14] In its November/December 2008 issue, *Tea Time* magazine presented a Jane Austen tea party menu in honor of the author's December 16 birthday. The eight-page spread included Regency-inspired recipes for rosemary crumpet sandwiches and invited readers to "raise [their] teacups in a loving toast" (Norwood 33). For complementary music, the feature might have recommended the CD *Jane Austen Entertains*, which, recorded in the author's home at Chawton in Hampshire, contains music from Austen's library. Austen's commodification is postmodern in its ubiquity, filtering into literary tourism and the etiquette industry. The guides *A Rambling Fancy: In the Footsteps of Jane Austen* (2006) by Caroline Sanderson and *In the Steps of Jane Austen: Walking Tours of Jane Austen's England* (2003) by Anne-Marie Edwards weave details of Austen's life and family with suggestions for rambles through the English countryside and trips to the beloved author's favorite haunts. The pocket-sized *Jane Austen in Bath: Walking Tours of the Writer's City* (2006) by Katherine Reeve extends Edwards's guide by focusing on a city in which Austen lived for several years and set two of her novels.

Besides serving as a source for travel inspiration and romantic counsel in a postfeminist context—new author functions—Austen continues to be co-opted as a proponent, if not authority, on decorum. For example, *Jane Austen's Guide to Good Manners* (2006) by Josephine Ross details codes on the treatment of servants to refusing a marriage proposal in the Regency era. Each rule is supported with textual evidence from Austen's novels and letters, as the guide was inspired by a correspondence between Austen and her niece Anna Austen. When Anna requested her aunt's assistance with a novel she was writing, Austen was appalled by the lack of attention her niece paid to the rules of society. A compendium of the ideal manners of polite society in the Regency era, at times the manual gently mocks the Regency upper class's dependence on hired help and highly circumscribed behavioral codes. In sum, Austen paraphernalia now extends beyond coffee mugs into a veritable secondary market for literary types and Anglophiles.

These consumer and media forms participate in what Kaplan sees as the making of "a popular Jane Austen," in which not only chick lit but also secondary readings have been forces. Kaplan surveys recent Austen scholarship to highlight how the Austen boom has had a considerable influence on scholarship about the Regency novelist, yet this phenomenon in secondary readings, she notes, has garnered scant attention. It was once typical for academics in the nineteenth and much of the twentieth century, observes Kaplan, to consider Austen's novels as the antithesis of popular culture, with Austen invoked by some academics as a symbol of the high culture that they strove to protect against the depredation of mass culture. Today, however, increasing numbers of critics see connections between her works and several types of much-loved popular entertainment such as Regency romance, detective fiction, and screwball comedies. Barbara M. Benedict's "Sensibility by the Numbers: Austen's Work as Regency Popular Fiction" (2000), for example, argues that Austen addressed her works to the novel-reading public and not just to a culturally elite circle. Austen's reputation as a highbrow writer has not been reversed, but it is beginning to be more aggressively challenged, with the collections *Janeites: Austen's Disciples and Devotees* (2000), edited by Deidre Lynch, and *Jane Austen and Co.: Remaking the Past in Contemporary Culture* (2003), edited by Suzanne R. Pucci and James Thompson, leading this critical paradigm. The contributors maintain that although Austen's view of books and taste is hierarchical, she had a regard for both "high" and "low." Kaplan, in summarizing this recent scholarship, notes that her novels demonstrate "a democratic intermingling of high and popular in the minds and worlds of her characters and depended in their own day on a readership whose cultural reference points were similarly broad" (B11). I am hesitant to claim that Austen is a fundamentally "popular" writer, but wish only to call attention to the synchronicity of this concern in eighteenth-century studies receiving greater attention at the same time as chick lit's proliferation.

The casebook *Flirting with "Pride and Prejudice": Fresh Perspectives on the Original Chick-Lit Masterpiece* (2005) is a caricatured example of the cultural trend that claims Austen as the mother of modern women's fiction.[15] The title uses diction—*flirting, fresh*—that is commonplace in media descriptions of the chick lit genre. The casebook's cover art also piggybacks on chick lit's popularity. The cover modifies the painting *In Love* (1907) by Marcus Stone to depict a bonneted period lady sitting with a suitor outdoors. On an antique table, a cup of Starbucks coffee sits next to an apple and a pink ribbon. The lady, talking on her cell phone, sits surrounded by shopping bags as her handsome suitor, wearing designer sunglasses, looks coolly in the distance. These images, then, aim to attract chick lit readers who might not jump at purchasing secondary literature on Austen. Edited by the best-selling romance novelist Jennifer Crusie, the collection's essays complement chick lit's mixing of genres and light-hearted tone. Film studies criticism on Austen movie adaptations coexist with personal narratives analyzing a crush on Colin Firth or defending Charlotte Lucas's nonromantic view of marriage. A deconstruction of the Bennet girls' dowries, suitors' investment income, and the cost of living in Austen's day is followed by a gag piece on why much of *Pride and Prejudice*'s conflict could have been circumvented with cell phones. As a title in BenBella Books' Smart Pop series, the anthology implicitly claims Austen's novels as popular literature. One piece features a screenplay with week-by-week storyboards for a *Pride and Prejudice* reality TV series in the vein of *The Bachelor*. Given the recent cultural phenomenon surrounding Austen, these tongue-in-cheek efforts, which we might call "chick-lit lit crit," cannot be dismissed as entirely spoofs. The anthology's mixing of different degrees of critical seriousness attempts to replicate in miniature how *Pride and Prejudice* has transcended the literary establishment into women's nightstand reading. Each essay's framing itself humorously reveals the influence of chick lit and may be an attempt to connect with a chick lit audience who feels that a text in the chick lit vein must contain humor.

The formal synthesis of highbrow and popular found in chick lit dovetails with new evaluations of both Austen's novels and her author function. Chick lit's product packaging may be an influence: *Sex and Sensibility: 28 True Romances from the Lives of Single Women* takes a nearly florescent color scheme with large bubbles superimposed on its front and back flap. It is plausible that aspects of chick lit—high readability, references to entertainment, and allusive titles—will be further projected onto new appraisals of Austen.

Thus the element of parody unites what the narrative traditions of the prose romance, discussed in chapter 1, and the bildungsroman, a focus here, become in these updated novels of manners. Chick lit extends the bildungsroman's plot of a protagonist's venturing into the city for a "real world" education, for preparation not only in a career but also in the experience of urban life.[16] The genre supplants the figure of the male artist-hero found in Goethe and Joyce with that of a female media professional, her reportage complementing her decidedly adult education.[17] In chick lit, the education and quest for self-definition is not limited to the young as it is in most female bildungsromans. These "contemporary fictions of female self-development," to appropriate a phrase of Rita Felski's, do not view marriage as the endpoint of the protagonist's maturation—many novels have a sequel complicating the earlier text's closure (131). While chick lit does not jettison the marriage plot—many texts conclude with a wedding or betrothal—it calls into question marriage's suitability in representing contemporary woman's desire and self-worth. Along these lines, chick lit modifies the number and type of sexual encounters the *Bildungsheld* must experience to come of age. While two love affairs or sexual encounters, "one debasing, one exalting," according to Jerome Buckley in *Season of Youth* (1974), a seminal study of bildungsroman patterns, are the minimum the male *Bildungsheld* must engage in for his emotional and moral evolution, the chick lit *Bildungsheld* alters this trope of the male hero by confessing to encounters of the first kind and conceding the rarity of the second (18). Story lines, though generally linear, present therefore a more fractured temporality of progress than the trajectory of earlier novels of formation that culminate in marriage. As many chick lit texts have been debut works, the genre has enabled women authors and their protagonists to come of age together.

Austen as Counterparadigm to *Sex and the City*?

Still, the class issues raised in *Bridget Jones's Diary* and its sequel offer a link between the other foundational chick lit text, *Sex and the City*, a focus of the next chapter, and its variants. While *Bridget Jones's Diary* has played a part in the reification of Austen, *Sex and the City* and much of chick lit dramatizes the difficulty of extricating monetary concerns and designer consumption not only from the marriage plot but also from fundamentally all human interaction. Chick lit, it appears, co-opts and vacillates between two diametrically opposed value systems, the protagonist attracted to aspects of each—the bucolic, green expanses of the English countryside offering a refreshing contrast to Manhattan's high premium for space, its smoggy Augusts and hot concrete. In an era when global warming, deforestation, and various environmental hazards make common news discourse, Austen's associations with verdant rolling landscape are heightened and attract readers wishing to circumvent dystopian narrative. Secondary individuals in chick lit are often not crafted with a distinctiveness of voice found in Austen's minor characters. Scenes move rapidly with instant-messenger-speed dialogue, the city's bustle functioning as a macrocosm of the plot's pace. The slow temporality of Austen allows time for romance and courtship, elements absent in *Sex and the City*'s hookup culture. The Regency-era garb bespeaks a genteel modesty, its understatement a counterparadigm to midriff exposure, conspicuous labels, and peeking thongs.

While Austen's milieu may evoke nostalgia, even connote relaxation, the schema is probably too dull as a permanent residence, the estates in some Austen films initially breathtaking but ultimately out of date with too much responsibility. For a calibrating effect, *Sex and the City*'s cosmos imparts a set of exciting challenges, legitimizes a drive for wealth and power, and, with a set of idioms that would make Austen blush, foregrounds a city in which rank, wealth, and power can, for both genders, be earned, lost, and rebuilt.

3   *Sex and the City* and the New York Novel

> A flame of envy lighted in her heart. She realized
> in a dim way how much the city held—wealth,
> fashion, ease—every adornment for women, and
> she longed for dress and beauty with a whole heart.
>
> —Theodore Dreiser, *Sister Carrie*

A De Beers necklace advertisement poses two abruptly personal but potentially innocuous questions: "Where'd you get that diamond?" and "Where'd you get that man?" These two queries appear in vertical print below nearly identical images of the platinum-set accessory. Before closing with its famous mantra, "A diamond is forever," in all caps, the international diamond syndicate declares, "Noticed in any size. Coveted in a ½ carat or more. Make a bigger statement." The diamond as fetish object is substitutable for man as category and consumer. Further, the necklace, not the (nonrepresented) man, is the privileged object of desire—the diamond operates as a reified phallus. The image of the necklace above the second question appears to be an enlargement of the stone and setting above the initial query. "Man" is then not only interchangeable with the adornment's visual-economic value but also a vehicle suited primarily for the procurement of luxury commodities. That a woman could purchase and bestow this accoutrement on another woman (or purchase it herself) lies decidedly outside the referential frame.

In this chapter I explore the interstices of heterosexuality, commodification, and reification that are so tellingly dramatized by De Beers. I focus on the depiction of the city, particularly New York, in chick lit and its extraliterary forms. I also present a close reading of one of chick lit's foundational works—Candace Bushnell's *Sex and the City*, the HBO series of the same title, and its movie adaptation—to situate this phenomenon within broader Anglo-American sociocultural patterns. *Sex and the City*'s three permutations merit substantial treatment in part because other chick lit novels have begun to make direct references to the HBO series in particular. It, along with Helen Fielding's *Bridget Jones's Diary* (discussed in chapter 2), has the status of a master plot.[1] My analysis of this anchoring text will be followed by readings of New York–based offshoots selected for their engagement with the novel-of-manners tradition, especially the works of Edith Wharton, and wider consumer behavior.

Candace Bushnell's *Sex and the City*

Because the title *Sex and the City* has been ubiquitously appropriated, it is first necessary to present a history of its origins. While best known as the eponymous HBO series created by Darren Starr, it began as the title of a *New York Observer* column written by Candace Bushnell (b. 1958) from 1994 to 1996.[2] The column's strappy sandal logo, modeled on one of Bushnell's own shoes, foregrounds the column's ruthless concern with surface appearance judgments among the Manhattan party-going elite. In the HBO series, the icon would become intimately attached with the column's central figure, Carrie, played by Sarah Jessica Parker. Upscale shoes, particularly the brand Manolo Blahnik, work metonymically, as an expression of Carrie's femininity and spiritual devotion to fashion. The icon also reflects Bushnell's affiliation with fashion: she served as a contributing editor to *Vogue* and once dated its publisher Ron Galotti, on whom the column's male protagonist "Big" is partly based. Galotti's favorite word is reportedly *absofuckinglutely*, decisive diction, which, in the HBO pilot episode, defines early Big's self-assurance in the boardroom and the bedroom.

In the columns, Carrie, a journalist, is both a "friend" of the narrator and an author surrogate (Bushnell, *Sex* 7). Bushnell, who shares the same initials as her heroine, has referred to Carrie as her "alter ego" (Degtyareva). She wrote the initial columns in first person but, fearing her parents might read them, decided to come up with a different name (Degtyareva). The columns were collected and published as a book with the same title in the United States and Canada in 1996 and in the United Kingdom in 1997. Shortly after, Darren Starr, who created, wrote, and produced the series *Beverly Hills 90210* and *Melrose Place*, purchased the rights to Bushnell's book for the sum of $60,000. Its status as an international best-seller came after the wild success of the *Sex and the City* TV series, which references Bushnell's collection in its credit sequence.[3]

The book, consisting of twenty-five chapters, reports on the nightlife, sexual predilections, and unspoken relationship dynamics of approximately thirty- to forty-five-year-old hip, beautiful, or powerful Manhattanites. "The city," then, consists not of five boroughs, but strictly Manhattan, with occasional reportage on corollary travel spots like Aspen and the Hamptons. Within each chapter are subchapters of a half to three pages in length, whose boldface, all-cap titles function as article subheadings. The collection as a whole extends the spirit of Jay McInerney's novel *Bright Lights, Big City* (1984) in its quick, short sentences, scenes of cocaine use, representations of the Manhattan nightclub scene, and the protagonist's romantic quest. Though Bushnell employs a female narrator, she acknowledges McInerney as an influence. Her columns share *Bright Lights, Big City*'s fluctuating tone of disillusionment and hope, as the protagonist, an aspiring fiction writer moonlighting as a fact checker, navigates the city's nonstop action. The column's varied venues, swift establishment of setting, episodic structure, and terse and rapid dialogue contained the cross-over attributes for its cable TV adaptation.

Yet what we most associate with the series—the close friendship and camaraderie of four women—is largely a creation of Starr and coexecutive producer and writer Michael Patrick King. Although the series converts several chapters into episodes with numerous lines lifted verbatim, it does not retain many character particulars.[4] For instance, in the column, Miranda Hobbes is a forty-year-old cable executive with long dark hair who appears briefly and intermittently, not the cropped red-haired lawyer Miranda (Cynthia Nixon) of the series. Charlotte York (Kristin Davis) is not the column's English journalist but a WASP Park Avenue Princess prominent in the art gallery world. The column's Samantha Jones is a movie producer, while in the series she is a PR firm owner, with the column's figure "Sarah" most closely resembling, in occupation and sexual attitude, the series' Samantha (Kim Cattrall) and her unapologetic libido.

More important, as Mandy Merck has observed, the columns contain few scenes of female gaiety: the interaction among women is "sporadic, rivalrous and often downright hostile" (49). The cutthroat climate emanates from Manhattan's well-known skewed ratio of eligible men to women. The columns' limited instances of emotional generosity extended by women evoke the dynamics of a tight marriage market like that unsuccessfully navigated by Wharton's Lily Bart. The columns' women demonstrate a superficial loyalty. Samantha Jones is identified as "Carrie's best friend. Sometimes" (110). A particular group of "girls were all 'friends,'" the column notes, "having met each other several times when they were out in the evenings, and they had even dated 'some of the same scumbags,'" the connection essentially flimsy (127). The columns foreground, if sometimes via female narrators, the opinions and credos of successful men who view women antagonistically or as trophies to showcase social prestige.

The columns feature scenes of confidences among women but not those of a long-standing friendship circle, depicted in the series in the form of Sunday brunch meetings or birthday dinners out. In contrast, when Miranda's mother passes away in season 4, Carrie immediately offers to come to Philadelphia to be of help. When Miranda has to walk down the aisle of the church alone at her mother's funeral, Carrie takes her friend's arm and walks by her side without being asked. To be sure, both the book and the television series portray female-female interactions as competitive to a certain extent; Samantha asserts in season 1 that women are hardly passive victims in a city of "equal opportunity exploiters" (1:5, "The Power of Female Sex").[5] But whereas the series depicts the women's friendship as, in the words of Lia Zneimer, "the one constant in a continually changing city," the columns lack a core group of girlfriends to provide emotional support.

Moreover, there are too many nearly identical characters in the columns, some never even introduced and others introduced multiple times. Introductions, consistently abrupt and frank, function to size up characters as swiftly as possible; for example, in the debut column—"My Unsentimental Education: Love in Manhattan? I Don't Think So . . ."—we receive on the bachelor-by-choice in question a one-sentence lowdown, "Tim was forty-two, an investment banker who made about five million a year" (1). Like Wharton, Bushnell uses neighborhoods and houses to characterize their inhabitants and respective social position. Yet gradations in the pecking order, while sometimes precisely drawn, are indicated with a relentless, bottom-line mentality. For instance, a fortyish, still beautiful, sometime TV actress reports how years back a physically unattractive suitor extended an invitation through a friend to his house in Nantucket:

> "Not on your life," I said.
> "His house is beautiful. Antique. Main Street."
> "Which one?" I asked.
> "I think it's one of the brick ones." . . .
> "If it's one of the brick houses, I'll think about it," I said.
> Ten minutes later, Dudley himself called. "I already bought your plane tickets," he said. "And yeah, it's one of the brick houses." (194)

The invitation, further, comes through a middleman, who then communicates the invitee's appraisal of the offer to the figurative seller in a dynamic that underlies the volume's connections between deal making and courtship. Bushnell's characters' blatant self-interest, together with the reification of characters in terms of real estate and upscale commodities, would become, as I will argue in further detail, a central pattern of the series.

Sex and the City's urban setting, its scenes of nightlife, its characters' preoccupation with money and status, as well as Bushnell's minxy promotion of sexy, high-end footwear in the compilation's front matter would be joined to the romantic-comedic elements and humor of *Bridget Jones's Diary* as a recipe for chick lit formula. However, it is not accurate to dub Bushnell a quintessential "chick lit author." Though she frequently receives this label, and from chick lit writers themselves, *Sex and the City* and especially Bushnell's subsequent works (*Four Blondes* [2000], *Trading Up* [2003], *Lipstick Jungle* [2005], and *One Fifth Avenue* [2008]) share more affinities with the glamour novel, discussed in chapter 2, than chick lit. Her average protagonist is decidedly not an everywoman: if not hard as nails, she is more ambitious and shrewder than the chick lit protagonist as well as older (in her early thirties at least). The social class under scrutiny has also ascended with each novel. Finally, Bushnell's depiction of men is with minimal exceptions highly unfavorable, with scenes of romance or eroticism virtually nonexistent, as if the hustle level required to survive in the city precludes this indulgence; the narrator in the initial column instructs, "Self-protection and closing the deal are paramount" (2). Money and power trump romance, with rent-controlled housing a close second.

Through her reportage on Manhattan subcultures, the journalist Carrie, albeit a flimsily disguised stand-in for Bushnell, functions as an ethnographer, a role occupied by Wharton's Newland Archer of *The Age of Innocence* (1920), a novel permeated with anthropological diction. Yet the compilation works more as a survival manual for the uninitiated Manhattanite. It does not depict a disembodiment, such as highlighted during Newland Archer's wedding to May, and an oscillating belonging to one's "tribe" that marks the protagonist's conflict. While anthropological diction may pervade *The Age of Innocence*, the locales of *Sex and the City* comprise a Darwinian universe, with taxonomy like "Toxic Bachelors" or "Modelizers" classified as deleterious specimen. Despite its high population density, the city is emotionally solitary; fittingly, parents and siblings are not mentioned. Social Darwinism sometimes peppers *Sex and the City*'s paratexts; for an issue of *Cosmopolitan* magazine, Bushnell offered career clothing tips and work-life advice for a woman's twenties, thirties, and forties, with the article's headline echoing the diction of natural selection: "So let other woman use tired tactics or lame shortcuts to hustle their way to the middle. You can play it Candace's way and stake your place on the food chain . . . on top" (qtd. in Eagleson 196). The HBO series, aiming for a more lighthearted air than the loneliness and pessimism of the columns, has in its opening credit sequence Carrie roaming around New York City habitat in a pink tutu outfit; the front of her gown is splashed with puddle water by a public transit bus. This scene of a confused party princess getting squashed provides a parody of being eaten alive in the evolutionary process.

The book's tone is cynical, harsh, and straightforward—the antithesis of romantic fiction—whereas its television counterpart epitomizes romantic comedy with its witty dialogue and optimistic undertones. Of course, if the columns were more romantic, New York audiences may not have taken Candace Bushnell seriously as a journalist. The book's epilogue ends with "Mr. Big is happily married. Carrie is happily single," giving the two protagonists approximate parity and crediting Carrie for self-sufficiency (243). Bushnell's column needed to be edgy, street smart, and fast paced, given that many New Yorkers pride themselves in being known as resilient, quick, and shrewd. The original audience of *New York Observer* readers influenced both the content and the form of the columns.

The TV adaptation of Bushnell's column debuted in 1998 and spanned six cable seasons, witnessing its finale in spring of 2004. In 2001, *Sex and the City* was awarded the Emmy for the year's outstanding comedy series, the first time that the award had gone to a cable program. Sarah Jessica Parker and Cynthia Nixon earned Emmys in 2004 for Best Actress and Best Supporting Actress in a Comedy, respectively. That same year Turner Broadcasting System (TBS) began running *Sex and the City* from its initial season. A basic cable channel lacking HBO's subscriber-only status, TBS brought the series to three times the number of cable TV viewers. The original ninety-four episodes were modified to omit explicit sex, frontal nudity, and profanity, receiving a TV-14 rating instead of an X. Commercials interrupt scenes in the edited version, since syndication relies on advertising spots. It was the first time a pay cable series had been sold in syndication to a basic cable station, and it needed to be sanitized to meet stricter language and content standards. In October 2004, approximately half a year after its final episode, the series returned to HBO for an encore presentation of its sixth season. Broadcast in two hundred countries, it is still watched in reruns on TBS by an average of 2.5 million viewers every day (Baird, Bennett, and Springen 46).

The direct influence of the HBO series and Bushnell's column on chick lit is reflected in both the form and subject matter of novels. *Chloe Does Yale* (2005), by Natalie Krinsky, reprints excerpts of Krinsky's sex column written while an undergraduate at Yale; its protagonist, Chloe Carrington, a sex columnist for the *Yale Daily News*, is clearly an author surrogate. In a reciprocal fashion, the HBO series' story lines occasionally utilize chick lit as their source. For example, the protagonist of Sue Margolis's *Neurotica* (1998), Anna, uses an at-home kit to dye her pubic zone after spotting a gray hair. She is described as setting the hair dryer to maximum heat, standing in the middle of the bedroom with her legs apart, and appearing "as if she were to deflower herself with a blast of air" (75). This intimate beauty dilemma is confronted by Samantha Jones in *Sex and the City*'s final season; when a Miss Clairol accident colors her triangle bright orange, she promptly turns to depilation. In addition to this interchange between screenplay and chick lit, *Sex and the City*'s dating plotlines entered the self-help genre with the blockbuster advice guide *He's Just Not That into You* (2004), the title of which is derived from a *Sex and the City* episode.[6] *He's Just Not That into You* then morphed into another generic form: in February 2009, a chick flick inspired by and appropriating the title of this relationship diagnostic appeared in theaters, starring Jennifer Aniston, Drew Barrymore, Ginnifer Goodwin, Jennifer Connelly, and Scarlett Johansson. The series' title is frequently a source for appropriation, as we see in reality TV programs like *Single in the City* and *Amish in the City*. It is difficult to identify a consumer or media area that the series has not permeated; for instance, Sprint PCS users can give their cell phone a makeover with the *Sex and the City* ringtone and screen savers featuring their favorite characters.

The tourism sector has, not surprisingly, capitalized on the phenomenon as well. A New York City bus tour of *Sex and the City*–related sites attracts an estimated 50,000 customers annually (Baird, Bennett, and Springen 46).[7] More elaborate, Manhattan's Tribeca Grand Hotel features a *Sex and the City*–themed package. The weekend includes breakfast in bed, cosmopolitans in the Church Lounge, and a packet of herbal tablets to cure hangovers. The package was one of twenty-five female-oriented getaways profiled in 2004 by *Budget Travel,* an article heading declaring "Move Over, Carrie Bradshaw—There Are New Girls in Town" (Boyd and Glover 84). On the opposite spectrum of price points, the film adaptation of *Sex and the City* (2008) inspired the travel company Destination on Location to offer a four-day tour in which clients, for the fee of $15,000–$24,000, are chauffeured to Manhattan's premiere department stores such as Saks and Barneys and boutiques including that of Patricia Field, *Sex and the City*'s clothing designer and stylist. In groups of eight to twelve, registrants dine at famed restaurants including Balthazar and Pastis and, in what appears to be essentially an economic stimulus scheme, choose their Saturday afternoon based on their favorite character; fans of Charlotte's patrician elegance will take a trip to Tiffany & Co. and a tour of art galleries, while those who favor the salacious Samantha will shop on Madison Avenue and visit "a high-end sex shop" (Brettell). The rising trend of "chick trips," like the series-related commodities, is an offshoot of *Sex and the City*'s popular appeal and chick lit's synergistic relationship with secondary markets.

Sex and the City and the Limits of Defamiliarization

The pilot episode of *Sex and the City* stations itself at the close of an epoch, proclaiming the "end of love." This positioning is complicated in the last season, as the finale depicts Miranda and Charlotte happily married, the fortysomething Samantha in what is probably her first committed relationship, and Carrie reunited, yet again, with Mr. Big, her first-name basis with him (we finally learn he is named John) connoting a new relationship plateau and life stage. This happy coupling, in its replication of the romantic-comedy ending, negates the initial episode's pronouncement that "Cupid has flown the co-op." While the finale portrays, then, not a farewell to but rather a reinvestment in romantic love, I wish to explore the pilot episode's declared state of endings. Just as Carrie's weekly column aspires to sexual anthropology, this section attempts to present a field report on the series' treatment of heterosexuality for the purposes of further examining a strain of postfeminism identified in my introduction as "late heterosexuality." This phenomenon is largely native to *Sex and the City*'s Manhattan locale, though the series represents the New York of late heterosexuality as a microcosm or caricature of new-millennial social values.[8]

The series implies that, at least in Manhattan, being straight and possessing a MetroCard will get you on the bus, but to make it on the marriage market there is a right but elusive heterosexuality, like the right Hamptons rental, and the latter is typically a metonym for the former. Owning a fabulous pair of Tiffany earrings earns Chivon a lay with Samantha: the luxury accessory, as critics such as Susan Zieger have observed, stands in for Chivon as the object of Samantha's desire (101–2). When Carrie discovers Aidan's purchase of a decidedly not Upper East Side engagement ring and confesses to the group the ring "wasn't good," Samantha summarily arbitrates with a "wrong ring, wrong guy" (4:12, "Just Say Yes"). Charlotte terminates a relationship because of the suitor's mismatched taste in china patterns. She weeds out a date not up to par in floral sensibility: he brings her carnations, "not flowers," but mere "filler flowers" (6:6, "Hop Skip, and a Week"). Carrie, who actually likes pink carnations, toes a bottom line in the shoe department, confessing she'd "throw away" a guy if he dared to don "docksiders, topsiders, or any of the above" (6:6, "Hop Skip, and a Week"). Charlotte finds her knight in shining armor in Harry Goldenblatt, who, short, bald, and of hirsute back, does not quite appear as a likely marital contender. Any doubts we may have had about his merit as a catch, though, are dissolved with his selection of Charlotte's engagement ring, his 5.2 quality carats rendering Trey's 2.16 Tiffany impotent. Yet the right ring does not a Sunday *New York Times* engagement announcement make: in order for the couple to make the cut, Harry needs to pose a certain way with his fiancée, seated beside her in Central Park on a Burberry blanket, the decidedly WASP, old-money artifact—however now trendy—solidifying his upper-middle-class, assimilationist credentials.[9]

These testing standards are not confined to the straight characters: gay male friends—valued members of Carrie and Charlotte's urban family—are uniformly stylish and often professional stylists. We witness Stanford questioned and then commended in a gay underwear-only club on his brand selection. The show decenters heterosexual privilege by including the gay "option" while reducing legitimate sexuality (straight or gay) to a commodity available to the gym fit, powerful, or well heeled. It is the stylishness of one's execution of sexuality, not the sexuality one chooses, that matters in late heterosexuality. The implication that one's choice of consumer goods supplants or competes with one's choice of sexual orientation is notable but hardly liberating. Late heterosexuality qualifies liberalism's tenets of self-fashioning and choice by narrowing and regulating the panoply of "looks" available.

Late heterosexuality also highlights the growing challenge of separating considerations of heterosexuality in American culture from business-based rhetoric and theoretical frameworks.[10] In late heterosexuality, capitalism levels heterosexuality's claim to naturalness in that successful heterosexuality is shown to be the product of labor or a resilient entrepreneurial esprit.[11] This attribute is a concern not only for heterosexuality studies but also for economic theory.[12] For instance, Cameron and Collins (2000), acknowledging that commercial or market considerations have long been part of the partner-matching process in many cultures and societies through the ages, apply recent economic rubrics to the study and practice of partner search (170–71). In their analysis of British matchmaking services, Cameron and Collins conceptualize relationship partners as "risky products" that require extensive search and evaluation before a decision is made; matchmaking agencies serve, in their view, as "risk reduction proxies" that alleviate the anxiety aroused when initially encountering a stranger (107, 123). Such rhetoric animates much of the contemporary self-help genre.

Women's self-help books of the 1970s and 1980s written by therapists, typically in an empathetic tone, have been replaced with a model drawn from business management theory (Mead 106). In her essay collection *The Commercialization of Intimate Life* (2003), the sociologist Arlie Russell Hochschild contends based on a review of women's advice books that postfeminism is a manifestation of the spirit of capitalism being displaced onto the intimate life. The early capitalists' activism, "their belief in working hard and aiming high, the desire to go for it, to be saved, to win, to succeed, which [they] used to build capitalism in a rough-and-tumble marketplace," is now captured in advice books that offer women strategies about how to transfer this philosophy to love in a rapidly changing courtship scene (24).[13] This form of what the American sexologist Laura Kipnis has called "labor-intensive intimacy" circulates the idea that if we work hard and network enough in our soul mate search, it will pay off, an idea touted by a self-help lecture program that Charlotte and Carrie attend in season 5 (Kipnis 18; 5:2, "Unoriginal Sin"). Though Kipnis focuses her analysis on marriage, conceptualized metaphorically as a "domestic factory," the series and these cultural phenomena corroborate her larger point that the rhetoric of the production has noticeably filtered into the language of love (19).

Samantha's assertion that the new dating field is "all about multitasking" and that none of the group can afford to fall into a "one-man-at-a-time pattern" utilizes contemporary business metaphors (one thinks of the notion of a diversified portfolio) to promote retrograde sexual politics. Playing the field is mandatory, according to Samantha's message, because the right men do exist but in sorely limited quantities.[14] Charlotte attempts to share her reading of *Marriage Incorporated: How to Apply Successful Business Strategies to Finding a Husband*, which "encourages professional women to approach finding a mate with the same kind of dedication and organization they bring to their careers" (3:7, "Drama Queens"). (This fictional self-help title may have inspired Rachel Greenwald, the author of *Find a Husband after 35 Using What I Learned at Harvard Business School* [2003], which pitches the notion that with the right marketing and product development women can succeed at obtaining a marriage proposal, even if they are chronologically challenged.) Carrie, who in the episode "Luck

Be a Lady," likens first dates to "job interviews with cocktails," comes to ponder the rationale behind speculative investment in the later episode "To Market, To Market": "When it comes to finance and dating, I couldn't help wonder why we keep investing" (5:3, 6:1). Choosing to keep her capital right where she can see it—hanging in her closet—she concludes that "after weathering all the ups and downs you could one day find yourself with nothing."

Yet the possibility of no return, coming up empty, is not enough of a deterrent for her to fold her hand. Carrie, like the sentiment of her book dedication, is hopeful, and, despite her labeling Charlotte as a "professional husband hunter" in the episode "Drama Queens," the series portrays optimism and romance alongside market considerations and dating venture capitalism (3:7). Late heterosexuality is thus marked by a postmodern contradictoriness as to the function of romance, which is theoretically opposed to monetary gain.[15] Carrie deliberates whether to conclude her book on hope or despair and, while uncertain in her own mind about love, she opts to end her book on hope, because she guesses—correctly—that hope sells.

One notable side effect of post–compulsory heterosexuality is a diminishment of the heterosexual male romantic hero's status, a phenomenon I have already commented on at length in chapter 1. In *Sex and the City* few men are named, as other critics have observed, but most are instead referred to in impersonal classifications that sometimes blur the boundaries between man and accessory (Akass and McCabe 7). Males vie with products, and in rare instances the two coalesce to the male's advantage: sporting a vodka bottle between the legs of his completely nude body, raw food waiter–cum–actor Smith Jerrod becomes a minor celebrity as the Absolut Hunk billboard sensation. He struggles with the experience of becoming a commodity and resists Samantha's efforts to contain him in a no-name identity as her role-playing partner and fuck buddy. He insists that she learn his name, but she soon changes it (from the inopportune Jerry Jerrod), replacing the girlfriend role she resists with a more familiar and powerful position as public relations manager. With the exception of Big, all of Carrie's dates compete, often unsuccessfully, with the omnipresent other man (i.e., Manolo).

It seems fitting that in the middle of the final season Carrie makes the single woman's ultimate declaration of independence and entitlement:

"getting married" to herself and registering at the Manolo Blahnik flagship store, thereby giving new meaning to "soul mate." More generally, viewers often see suitors being upstaged by the series' costume closet.[16] The four women, Carrie in particular, embrace a type of female dandyism.[17] For instance, she seems to be acting very out of character when Aidan influences her to discard some of her 1980s garb (4:13, "The Good Fight"). Resignedly attempting to make closet space for him, she throws the items to the floor with a wince, which foreshadows the union's doom.

Big, whose driver and tinted car windows imbue him with glamour and mystery, is connected in Carrie's book with classic New York, with the wealth, arrogance, and power of the "Big" Apple. In the finale episode, Big expands from a symbol of Manhattan wealth and power to one of American muscle and protection. The blatant xenophobia of the last two episodes invites the reading that Big's rescue of Carrie from Paris and her Russian lover, who slaps her, allows the restoration of American power. In the midst of the "War on Terror," Big's interception is a gesture of overt protective nationalism as he brings about Carrie's grateful return to domestic soil. His real name, John, which we learn at the close of the final episode, is also especially American. It is not insignificant that his one-time rival, Aidan, cherishes the country or that the series should depict his modest cabin and resident squirrels as annoyingly rustic, two-bit alongside Big's black Jaguar, which he drives up from the city to see Carrie at Aidan's cabin in the phonemically appropriate town of Suffren. Once again, the men are less significant as individual heroes or romantic partners than as markers and bearers of style.

Carrie's one-bedroom apartment serves as a privatized, miniature city, equal parts fashion house, Manolo showroom, and publishing company. When Aidan purchases the adjacent unit and begins to break down an adjoining brick wall, the effect is one of violation, as if bodily harm is inflicted upon Carrie's person. She sinks to the floor in a full-blown panic attack (4:15, "Change of a Dress"). A better-fitting union is witnessed in the next season when, to the accompaniment of processional music, Carrie descends a white-flower-laden staircase (5:1, "Plus One Is the Loneliest Number"). She enters not a nuptial ceremony but her book launch party, as the voice-over compares finding a publisher to becoming a bride. The series' withholding of a definite ending for Carrie and Big, coupled with Carrie's success as a writer, reaffirms narrative itself as Carrie's proper groom, or perhaps it is the city as the sleepless stimulant of narrative that is Carrie's real husband. The series creates a contemporary mythos as it chronicles Carrie's difficulty reconciling her love for the city and its sense of limitless possibility with her love of mortal man. Though not necessarily urban, late heterosexuality, as *Sex and the City* implies, has its roots in the metropolis: a setting that combines the roles of style producer, business center, and consumer emporium.

In its graphic catalog of straight sex's themes and variations, from "tea bagging" to the "to pee or not to pee" question, *Sex and the City* in the course of its six seasons (1998–2004) disclosed private conduct as being fully as eclectic as the city's dining options and the series' costume closet.[18] Viewers received thirty-minute education sessions in straight diversity, in which aspects of heterosexuality were revealed as constructed and frequently accompanied by their own set of perversities, a familiar revelation in feminist media studies and queer theory. Yet the sense of shock or amusement began to coexist with an "Is this all?" feeling, a Friedanesque though not suburban malaise, ameliorated by the series' nonstop succession of vibrant surfaces. A colleague of mine and out owner of several complete-season DVDs did not especially mourn its ending, half-asking, half-shrugging, "What are they supposed to do? Have some more sex?"

This criticism is in fact registered in the show itself. In season 2's launch, Miranda interrogates the group's limited brunch discussion parameters: "All we talk about anymore is big balls or small dicks. How does it happen that four such smart women have nothing to talk about except boyfriends? Does it always have to be about them?" (2:1, "Take Me Out to the Ballgame"). Such reflexive utterances presciently acknowledged that the series' risqué dialogue and undercover treatment of sexual trends du jour would not always safeguard against redundancy. As the series boldly depicted the spectrum of contemporary heterosexual mating rituals, judging some as more acceptable than others, frank talk about men became obligatory, if not monotonous. The limits of the series seem to indicate the worn quality of the defamiliarizing approach, reminding the feminist critic that such a methodology, however thorough, does not necessarily unmask a subversive politics or dismantle existing hierarchies and their underpinning power structures.

Sex and the City's unapologetic taxonomy of sex about town, however stylish or humorous, frequently served as a vehicle for the reconsolidation of heterosexual norms. In season 1 Samantha offers something close to a Naomi Wolf–type critique of the beauty industry when she states that we reside in a culture that promotes its impossible standards. Yet season 5 reveals her as no stranger to Botox and depicts the scorched aftereffect of her chemical peel. Carrie appraises her two-minute foray into bisexuality as a "game" that she "was too old to play," presenting this sexual orientation as not quite adult. Similarly, Samantha, calling bisexuality a "layover on the way to gaytown," dismisses it as geographically undesirable, if not a dead end (3:4, "Boy, Girl, Boy, Girl"). The positive representation of lesbianism featured in season 1's episode about "power lesbians" is undercut three seasons later in the flippant depiction of Samantha's affair with the Portuguese artist Maria. The group's use of phrases such as "the lesbian thing" and "la casa de lesbos" connotes nonseriousness and clichéd sexual multiculturalism.

In the pilot episode of the series, when Carrie's voice-over welcomes us to the "age of un-innocence," she attempts to prepare the viewer for the series' nudity and adult content, as well as its revisiting of Edith Wharton's preoccupation with women on the market and the display aesthetic. Yet the legacy of *Sex and the City* has taught us that more sexual positions do not always make for better sex or sustained audience engagement. The show's humor and effervescence ironically leave the feminist critic face-to-face with a more serious methodological issue. Is the "Is this all?" feeling the feminist media critic may have toward the series itself symptomatic of a moment within her discipline? To what extent is this "age of un-innocence" also an age of methodological un-innocence? Watching the show and reading existing commentary on it may indeed leave the feminist scholar with a vague morning-after effect. The series' luxe surfaces, like that of a dexterous conference paper, produce pleasure in the audience but fail to shake things up in any substantial way. This pleasure in the stylishness of sexual representation in feminist media studies can seem transient. Indeed, feminist theory risks running too close to the fashion pages of the average women's magazine, offering a knowing self-reflexivity along with the latest styles to bolster its glossy surfaces, but lacking sufficient critique.

Maybe the real un-innocence is that a critique of the series' construction of power systems—its classist, consumer-obsessed, and urbocentric values—has come to feel too strident and unplayful. Late heterosexuality's emphasis on style dovetails with postfeminism's move away from the more polemical, humorless aspects of the second wave. Just as Charlotte's 1950s image of marriage and home is out of date, so too is the dismantling-hierarchies trope of second-wave feminism, which exhorted scholars to investigate dully not just representations of woman but their intersection with race, class, sexual orientation, age, and location ad infinitum. This demand for thoroughness became hectoring, if not militant, and the implication that there was no time for play amid oppressions of a multiple and global nature began to weigh us down more than inspire. Yet the passing of the second wave's conscientiousness about the issue of how gender is best examined in relation to other systems of power is not necessarily something to celebrate. Postfeminism must work to marry its refreshing elements of play and style with the rigor and tirelessness of the second wave's efforts to understand the multidimensionality of power relations.

Edith Wharton and the Apparition of Lily Bart

While Austen imparts chick lit's urban period pieces with a pedigreed forebear, Edith Wharton's social observations of the marriage market further situate the genre as a modern novel of manners. Wharton's works are lightly referenced to cue the reader to chick lit's thematic continuity. Chick lit does not reflect back on as much as back-shadow Wharton's works, with Wharton as a "high culture" allusion circulating among chick lit's myriad upscale commodities.[19] The female reader can indulge in viewing herself as a descendant of a classic heroine, her situation imbued with canonical, if not quasi-epic, proportions. In this vein, Juliette Fairley's chick lit–inspired self-help guide *Cash in the City: Affording Manolos, Martinis, and Manicures on a Working Girl's Salary* (2002) devotes a chapter to financial mistakes and pitfalls to sidestep so that women readers are "not compromised as Lily Bart's character was in Wharton's classic, *The House of Mirth*" (9). Calling to mind Lily's conversation with Selden in chapter 1 on her mortal fear of dinginess ("If I were shabby no one would have me: a woman is asked out as much for her clothes as for herself"), protagonists struggle with assembling an exterior attractive to an upscale man and often incur debts for the wardrobe needed to sustain dating this type of marriage prospect (12). The popularity of this plotline in chick lit is not so much a desire to rewrite Wharton as a social reality: consumer debt, excluding mortgages, doubled from 1994 to 2004, with households averaging close to $20,000 (Loftus). The average credit card debt per American household, according to AARP, more than tripled from 1990 to 2006, up from $2,966 to $9,159 ("Plastic Appeal"). More recent sources estimate that the average adult individual credit card debt rose from $518 in 1980, to $8,650 as of January 2009 (Essig 18).[20] Chick lit parallels with Lily's class-without-cash dilemma reflect patterns in consumer spending more than trenchant intertextuality. The protagonist, though often cash poor, holds a bachelor's degree (and occasionally a master's) from an Ivy League or Seven Sisters institution. Unlike Lily, who received no substantial formal education, chick lit protagonists are professionally equipped for occupations other than society wife.

References in chick lit to Wharton's bleak social parable often seem hyperbolic because of the genre's general optimism and romance fiction lineage. The narrator of *Bergdorf Blondes* by Plum Sykes compares the ramifications of her broken engagement to Lily Bart's social displacement: "My life in New York would be ruined unless I found another fiancé. All anyone cared about in New York was who was married to whom, or was going to be. Didn't he know it was like the nineteenth century there? Didn't he know what had happened to poor Lily Bart?" (140). The number of invitations, she confides, drops off after the termination of her relationship with a successful artist, the most coveted and prestigious brand of husband in the hierarchies of the Manhattan marriage market. The climax, however, brings an engagement to English nobility with the suitor proposing in his family's ancestral estate. Although not disavowing the dating hypercompetitiveness among Manhattan society women, the royal fairy tale–like ending of *Bergdorf Blondes* eclipses the specter of Lily Bart's fate.

While *The House of Mirth* lacks comic relief or, for that matter, much humor at all, chick lit features protagonists who use self-deprecating humor as a coping mechanism amid the trials in the search for a partner. Humor additionally works to offset the protagonist's sometimes excessive self-concern. A protagonist may fail to marry, or the fear of the failure to marry may cause a gnawing dissatisfaction or loss of self-worth. Yet, perhaps because of chick lit's urban family trope and the protagonist's level of education, the stakes are not as high—certainly not a matter of life and death as was ultimately the case for Lily Bart. Chick lit protagonists internalize and share Lily Bart's risk of becoming shelved: though the protagonist may not possess the artistic sensibility of Lily Bart, she is just as picky. Yet the sexual double standard, the standard by which Lily's set erroneously judges her in the greatest irony of the novel—that Lily, at thirty-one, lives up to her namesake flower's connotation of sexual purity—is not a particular cause of anxiety in chick lit. With the exception of the Christian subset, protagonists are unapologetically sexually experienced and relish a vigorous sex life. The absence of male commentary on the protagonist's sexual history further works to give the impression that this standard is an antiquated or, at most, minor concern. The chick lit protagonist's fear of superannuating, what she perhaps shares most with Wharton's Lily, is legitimate and real because of rising standards of middle-class identity, the cost of living accommodations, and the considerable income needed to raise children, especially in Manhattan. Chick lit heroines' preoccupation with money and subsistence is normative with recent real-life social science findings: researchers such as Marian Botsford Fraser have found that the worst fear for single women—worse than having bad relationships or no relationships—is having no money (238).[21]

Chick lit's intertextual engagement with Wharton is more thematic than self-consciously and directly reflexive. However, Tama Janowitz's *A Certain Age* (1999) offers the notable exception of a novel-length rewriting of *The House of Mirth*. The protagonist, thirty-two-year-old Florence Collins, works in the estate jewelry department of a second-tier auction house. Her annual expenses are twice here salary of $26,000 a year and have been subsidized from the sale of her deceased mother's house. Florence, whose name's botanical root invites further parallels with Lily, articulates at the turn of the twenty-first century social judgments akin to the novel's source:

> "You don't get real power as a woman—you still get it being married to a powerful man. . . . At least I'm honest enough to see the world for what it is and know what it is I'm going after." (26–27)

> By high school she realized that no matter what women filled their lives with, there was still no status for them apart from whomever—whatever— they married. (76)

Her retrograde worldview narrows her choice of a partner to dangerously few prospects. Florence then makes an irreparable error by turning down a proposal of a longtime friend whom she misinterprets as being—by Manhattan standards—poor. The end of the novel reveals one mansion in the Hamptons that she admired in the novel's opening chapters as belonging to his parents. Her disastrous management of financial resources—she lets bills sit for six months before opening them—and her paucity of interests outside social climbing and shopping cast her as a worst-case-scenario caricature of a chick lit protagonist.

Further plot elements link *A Certain Age* with its source text and render it atypical in the chick lit canon. A husband of a friend, John de Jongh, functions as the Gus Trenor figure, except with darker consequences to the protagonist. Florence gives him the last $25,000 of her mother's money to invest in his friend's restaurant, but whereas Lily profits from Trenor's speculating, Florence is fleeced. Before she writes John a check, he rapes her in his Hamptons house, where his wife is hosting a party. Not only does she thus succumb to a peril avoided by Lily, but she does so before any money has even changed hands. Florence's fate at the novel's end seems bleak but ultimately ambiguous. Jobless from a layoff and homeless, she relocates precious jewels accidentally omitted from a client's inventory as they were concealed in an inner pouch pocket; because the client signed the list of items to be put up for sale without mentioning these jewels, Florence with some slight legitimacy can resell the gems clandestinely and begin to raise herself from her cindered subsistence. She does not die, yet in the social economy of Manhattan's marriage market that is her epicenter she is irrevocably impaired. In light of its source text's subtitle, *A Novel of Admonition*, Florence's financial irresponsibility and the mercenary foundation for all human interaction in the book render *A Certain Age* a cautionary chick lit morality tale.

The House of Models:
Edith Wharton's Influence on Candace Bushnell

Though she can be credited more with inspiring commercial chick lit than directly authoring it, Candace Bushnell acknowledges Edith Wharton as a major literary influence.[22] In fact, she and a girlfriend read *The House of Mirth* in their early thirties and found Lily Bart's demise harrowing. Its unnerving similarities to their own social situation in late-twentieth-century Manhattan galvanized them to adopt dating tactics that would ensure a more prosperous fate. In this class-without-money predicament characteristic of novel-of-manners heroines (Bushnell is from upper-middle-class New England stock; as a child she was a member of the Glastonbury Pony Club), the young women put in appearances at innumerable parties and spent the requisite summer weekends in the Hamptons, attending polo matches in the search for enduring romantic love and, more practically, a partner who could provide them with a safety net. Though Bushnell published in established women's periodicals such as *Ladies Home Journal*, *Mademoiselle*, and *Good Housekeeping*, her career as a freelance journalist provided a subsistence living—in her thirty-second year she earned but $8,000 and had to borrow money from a friend to pay the rent (Quinn). Bushnell's living conditions at this time were nevertheless hardly better than Lily Bart's final room, as she slept in a dreary studio apartment on a makeshift bed consisting of a piece of foam. Her twenties weren't much better, as her pursuit of modeling and acting careers were unsuccessful. The spiritual burnout from years of working very hard for little reward compounded with the realistic difficulty of living stylishly in Manhattan on her own led her to contemplate suicide (Quinn).

In the midst of this psychological and financial low, however, Bushnell, an avid reader, discovered Wharton's *The Custom of the Country* and was inspired by its deft and intricate structural architecture. Undine Spragg, in her ability to act rather than merely react, offered a flawed and static but nevertheless more engaging protagonist than the fatally passive Lily Bart. *The Custom of the Country* remains Bushnell's favorite Wharton novel, as she concurs with Hermione Lee's assessment in *Edith Wharton* (2007) that the text is Wharton's greatest fiction. A decade later *Custom* would serve as the principal influence on Bushnell's first novel, *Trading Up* (2003). This international best-seller, which has sold over a half million copies, appropriates plot elements and the mentality of *Custom*'s protagonist to update Wharton's depiction of the ascension of a new social order in which money trumps class and breeding. Spanning the late spring of 2000 and the winter of 2001, *Trading Up*, begun two days after 9/11, takes up *Custom*'s concept of New York as the final social frontier and satirizes the sense of entitlement, self-aggrandizement, and competitive consumption underpinning the professional elite of "old New York," specifically at the fin de siècle and in the bull market years of the end of the twentieth century.

Thematic continuity with Wharton's fiction—specifically, an occupation with women on the market and the navigation of Manhattan's cut-throat social milieu—is salient in Bushnell's earlier works *Sex and the City* and the short story quartet *Four Blondes* (2000). Lily's constant expenditure for the apparel and accoutrements needed to circulate in the set into which it is anticipated—and necessary—that she will marry is a concern for *Sex and the City*'s thirtysomething protagonist. As she is dating a media mogul, it is expected more and more frequently that she have an updo, or at least a blowout, and when she laments that she can't really manage this expense, her hairdresser bluntly replies, "You can't afford not to" (154). The use of fiction as an ethnography of class distinctions unites the two authors, as the narrator of *Trading Up* observes that having to carry one's own bags is a sign of middle-class status and that Manhattanites, a species chronically class observant, "sliced everything into tiny categories, and then, like diamond sorters, examined and graded each particle" (45). Bushnell's writing extends the majors topics of Wharton's fiction: at its center are the themes of single women negotiating urban space; reading hidden agendas; correlations between characters' social and net worth; and the volatility of this market system.

Trading Up deliberately employs characters' names to invite continuity with Wharton. The male protagonist, Selden Rose, a CEO of a major cable channel, senses that Janey Wilcox, the female protagonist and an aging Victoria's Secret supermodel, "needed rescuing," the phrase echoing Lily and Selden's exchange in *The House of Mirth*'s opening paragraphs (57). Bushnell's Selden, unlike his predecessor, is a man of action, as his marriage proposal does not come too late. However, Janey finds Selden's relationship to money too conservative—a complaint of Undine in her marriage to Marvell. By *Trading Up*'s end a divorce is initiated with Janey, to use a phrase of Undine's, in search of "the 'something beyond'" arriving in Los Angeles to use a *Vanity Fair* Oscar party to network for the production of her barely written screenplay. *Trading Up*, a continuation of the lead story of Bushnell's *Four Blondes*, is part social satire, part glamour novel, not, like *The House of Mirth*, an inverted rags-to-riches tale: Janey's social climbing machinations joined with flashbacks of a summer stint as a high-end prostitute render her closer to Thackeray's Becky Sharp or Defoe's *Moll Flanders* than Wharton's Lily Bart.

Yet the specter of Lily Bart flits through the novel, as when Janey, gazing out from the windows of the hotel where she resides as a newlywed onto the cold, rainy street, spies a twentysomething girl without enough money for cab fare, her designer shoes, on which she's probably spent money she didn't have, now ruined, in her attempt to meet an uptown man. Janey is reminded how for many years she was that girl, and later, remembers a date on which she got stuck with the check, her last forty dollars before payday depleted, leaving her contemplating what she would have to do for her next dinner—perhaps put out, she thinks, dishearteningly. These two flashbacks admittedly contain a pinch of the picaresque, but their note of vulnerability and absence of a female support system work to humanize a character inspired not as much by Lily as Undine and mitigate Bushnell's antiheroine's relentless narcissism.

Bushnell abandons the teasing allusions to *The House of Mirth* as parts 2 and 3 of *Trading Up* begin to substantially rework Wharton's *Custom.* Janey's passing comment to Selden, "I was telling him [Comstock Dibble, a movie industry tycoon] that he should make Edith Wharton's *The Custom of the Country* into a movie. It's never been done before and he'd be good at it," prepares readers to interpret Janey's three-month courtship, marriage, and divorce in light of Wharton's Undine Spragg (110). Plot details overlap with *Custom* on numerous points: a honeymoon in Italy in which Janey, overheated and profoundly bored, asks that if she must stay in Italy to leave the small town of Puntadellesia for Portofino or Capri; a $40,000 clothing tab while passing through Milan; a $50,000 vintage pearl choker charged to Selden's American Express card, which she rationalizes as a bargain, especially since her friend Mimi, the wife of a billionaire, picked up a $120,000 diamond necklace that afternoon at Christie's; Selden's fatigue as he struggles to keep up with his wife's social calendar and still perform in his job; and his ineffectual attempts to impresses upon Janey, that while "technically, and by nearly anyone's standards, he *was* rich," in the end he is a salaried man with most of his wealth tied up in stock options (178). Not only Selden's limited ability to enable consumption but also his relative ordinariness begins to breed dissatisfaction. Janey reaches the conclusion that "without his job [he] was really nothing more than a nice guy from Chicago . . . an average American guy from an upper-middle-class family. And while there was nothing inherently wrong with that, it was her background too—the very background she'd been trying to escape ever since she was a teenager" (95). Finally, *Trading Up*'s title complements Undine's pattern of serial marriage and shares with *Custom* what Lee discerns as expressing personal life in terms of the fluctuation of the stock market (437). The announcement of Janey's marriage, for example, is followed almost immediately by fictional financial journalism noting early signs of the deterioration of the stock market and the collapse of the dot. com boom, as if presaging the union's doom. These direct parallels work collectively to take *Custom* and Wharton beyond the quality-brand function in Bushnell's consumer-obsessed world.

Wharton's work operates as more than an invocation of high culture, as I was able to learn through an in-person and phone interview with Bushnell in May 2007 that focused on her appropriations from Wharton as well as her history as a reader. The character of Undine has fascinated Bushnell, who wanted write a novel that would "get inside the head" of a character who was a "borderline personality, a sociopath," but nevertheless a disturbingly hypnotic type that exists in real life. Bushnell spent a lot of time in the Hamptons while drafting *Trading Up* and wanted to put into fiction a type she regularly encountered there. Undine was the chief inspiration, and she strove to create a "frighteningly realistic" character "who never learns [her] lesson," "causes trouble everywhere," and "does the things we all may have thought about doing but morality kicks in." Janey was also a way to integrate the animus: her lack of a conscience a sick but enabling power, her acute self-absorption sexy in the confidence of its monogamous focus, her terrible resilience perversely admirable. Bushnell originally intended to have Janey's ego self-destruct into madness on the plane to the Oscars, but her publisher felt that the American reading public would be more accepting of a character given a chance at redemption and, in the vein of the American dream, making it, this time, on her own. In its final form, *Trading Up* moves from a satirical treatment of the tradition of the money novel to a noncondemnation of gold digging and finally to an affirmation of the divorced protagonist's half-nurtured creative drive as a media entrepreneur. Unlike her predecessor, Janey becomes not a figure of undisguised derision but a modern archetype of a "model" *pícara*.

While *Custom* may have been, in the words of Bushnell, "the big book she was studying" while writing *Trading Up*, Wharton's influence is but one of several on its composition. Bushnell's writing not only extends the New York novels of Wharton—lending the contemplative tradition of the novel of manners more action as well as aspects of the rogue's tale—but is also heavily inspired by Joseph Heller's *Something Happened*, Jay McInerney's *Bright Lights, Big City,* and Bret Easton Ellis's *Less than Zero,* the latter two authors old friends of Bushnell. To be sure, *Trading Up* does not have Wharton's elegant, mannered narration: Bushnell's characteristic short sentences and frenetic plot pace reflect a blunter, time-is-money socioeconomic system; the frequent use of ellipses at the end of sentences can border on farcical but formally mimics the more seminal point of the city's flux and the need for its inhabitants, unable to stand still in perpetual search of the "next," to keep moving to be interesting.

Despite her creator's amused contempt for Janey, three years after *Trading Up*'s publication, Bushnell would step into a role that her protagonist approaches more substantially in the text's closing scenes, toying naively with the pursuit of being a screenwriter and movie producer. A TV series based on Bushnell's latest novel, *Lipstick Jungle* (2005), debuted February 7, 2008, on NBC, with Bushnell as executive producer, and aired for two seasons. Her choice of a marriage partner, however, was a romantic contrast to the machinating Janey: in July 2002, at forty-three, she married in a Massachusetts beachside ceremony Charles Askegard, a dashing principal dancer for the New York City Ballet, six foot four and a decade her junior. Fifteen years after her initial reading of *Custom,* much has changed for the author, now a woman of wealth and international repute with a dynamic media career. She is the winner of the 2006 Matrix Award for books (other recipients include Joan Didion and Amy Tan). The first of two volumes of the prequel to *Sex and the City, The Carrie Diaries,* a young-adult treatment of Carrie's senior year of high school and her first year in New York, appeared in April 2010. This project, an attempt to tap into the lucrative "tween" market and a way to bridge this audience with the phenomenon's adult fan base, follows the popularity of Cecily von Ziegesar's Gossip Girl series, whose initial volume echoes *The Age of Innocence* in its opening scene of a free-spirited young woman mysteriously returning to New York. In an Amazon.com interview, Bushnell advised women that "it really is about becoming your own Mr. Big and finding all of those things in yourself," and her life appears to have lived up to this recommendation.

Yet the book she read in a bleaker time lives on as a source of inspiration and architectural model. Bushnell continues to reread the first chapter of *Custom* and studies it and the book as a whole for lessons in structural economy and condensation. She looks to Wharton for how to do "big scenes" without sliding into melodrama. She is especially impressed by the craftsmanship and multipurpose functions of *Custom*'s Mrs. Heeny and confided that her ideal would be to create a secondary character that could connect scenes and traverse settings as seamlessly. Without difficulty it can be said that Bushnell's engagement with Wharton has resulted in a success story for author and character—her first book, in title at least, saw its movie adaptation with a world premiere in London on May 12, 2008, four years after the HBO series finale in 2004, and with a release in the United States on May 30, 2008.

Labels or Love?

In the *Sex and the City* movie, directed and written by Michael Patrick King, the TV series' lead actors reprised their roles after three years of news media rumors about the film's status. The successful film adaptation of *The Devil Wears Prada* (directed by David Frankel) in 2006, which earned more than $320 million at the box office worldwide, renewed interest in the *Sex and the City* movie. While receiving mixed reviews at best (Anthony Lane wrote in the *New Yorker* that it needed a subtitle—"The Lying, the Bitch, and the Wardrobe"), it was an unequivocal commercial hit; its debut weekend earnings of $55.7 million gave it the most successful opening box office to date for an R-rated comedy and for a movie with a female-led cast.[23] Its premiere was tops for a film adaptation and, according to an *Entertainment Weekly* box office report, the number five opening for an R-rated film (Rich). Its gross earnings of approximately $415 million worldwide justified a sequel, which was released in May 2010.

Though technically outside the time parameters of this study, a discussion of the film is useful for examining the evolution of Bushnell's *New York Observer* column and the status of style and form in this international media phenomenon. With two costume changes per minute, the film upped the ante of late heterosexuality's element of compulsory style: set three years after the season 6 finale, the film in its running time of 2 hours and 22 minutes depicted more than 300 costumes changes for the four women, including 81 for Sarah Jessica Parker, its coproducer. We witness a scene in which Samantha is criticized by Anthony Marentino (Mario Cantone) and then taken aside for a group therapy session for gaining fifteen pounds, her forty-nine-year-old abdomen protruding a paunch in probably at most size 6 pants. Harry, Charlotte's doting attorney husband, makes a call to

Carrie to ask why his wife, pregnant in her forties after established fertility challenges, has stopped her daily running. While the call is most likely an act of sincere concern, we cannot help wondering if part of his rationale is to ensure she stays slim. A swimsuit-clad Miranda is reprimanded by Samantha for "growing a forest" between her legs, internalizing the depilatory oversight that she reads as Samantha's siding with her husband, Steve, who, as he reveals, has a one-night stand as a result in part of his wife's pinched availability. Between her full-time job as an attorney, the raising their son young Brady, and the care management of her mother-in-law who has Alzheimer's, she has put sex on the back burner for the past half year. While the status of style was complicated in the HBO series, with designer goods and the institution of marriage ascribed mixed messages, the film is almost pathologically double voiced, with the word *love* (whether typed hesitantly on Carrie's Mac or in the cursive form of her assistant's gold key chain) feebly competing for air time against the heavy hitting of upscale commodities in a recession economy.

Alternating between discourses of antiromance and the Cinderella story, the film draws on the HBO series' scenes of female camaraderie and leisure to offset the misandrist or putzlike representation of men and the fragility of marriage. In an attempt to break their sexual dry spell, a thrusting Steve tries to prolong intercourse with Miranda, an endeavor deflated by her plea to "get it over with." At the rehearsal dinner, a wiseass colleague of Big's comments on his multiple marriages with snipes like "Three times a charm." Samantha, reaching the five-year mark with Smith, is afflicted with monogamy-induced ennui: feeling diminished managing his TV career for the past two years, she vents frustration and curbs the urge to cheat by overeating. She resorts to adopting a perky dog, who despite castration, engages in frequent pillow-humping, affording its new owner vicarious pelvic action. It is not hyperbole to estimate the straight men have about only 2 percent of the lines in the film, with more than 50 percent of these being "I'm sorry" or "I know I screwed it up" or variations thereof.

Luxury goods are no less valuable per se than in the series. Items from previews such as small technology goods make appearances in the film itself. The film's heavy use of product placements call to mind Jameson's observation that a characteristic of the postmodern era is the diffusion of goods into entertainment and news media as part of their content: reading the TV series *Dynasty* (1981–89), he notes, "It is sometimes not clear when the narrative segment has ended and the commercial has begun" (275). Samantha needs no time to think about accepting Smith's offer to let her keep a $55,000 cocktail ring when she tells him she needs to end their run. Carrie's assistant, Louise (*Dreamgirls'* Jennifer Hudson), is ecstatic to receive for Christmas a Louis Vuitton that she regularly rented on BagBorrowOrSteal.com ("Netflix for purses"). When she is given a purse of this brand, Louise is united with her homophonal second half. Her luck continues when she becomes engaged to her estranged boyfriend back home in St. Louis, proudly proclaiming to Carrie her diamond solitaire is "not rented." Yet such products are also depicted as compensatory mechanisms (the back of Samantha's white Mercedes-Benz GLK is loaded with Gucci and other premiere designer bags in a retail binge) and blinders to direct communication.

Specifically, after three more years of dating, Carrie and Big, revealed in full as "John James Preston," decide to cohabit, the financier effortlessly purchasing a Fifth Avenue penthouse suddenly available after "a nasty divorce." Carrie's relationship milestone is undercut, however, by a jump cut to a jewelry auction for the waitress-model-actress girlfriend of a billionaire, who after ten years of dating (the length of time Carrie has been with Big) arrives home one night to find the locks changed and herself on her own. As she and Big are not married, Carrie raises the question of the status of her apartment, suggesting to Big that she sell it and apply the money to the purchase of the penthouse so she is not without legal rights to the residence. Big then asks Carrie if she wants to get hitched, and, in a scene devoid of physical contact, let alone romantic diction, she accepts his proposal, answering his question as to whether he should get her a ring in the negative and instead negotiating for a custom-built closet—the apartment's lack thereof, she reasons, being a contributing cause of the former occupants' separation.

In a *Vogue* shoot for its annual "Age" issue in which Carrie represents the forties (the last age the editor deems appropriate for a woman to be photographed in bridal), a magnificent slideshow of Carrie in gowns distracts viewers from the couple's history of breakups and appeases fans hoping to see Carrie in bridal couture. Yet the litany of designers ("Vera Wang, Carolina Herrera, Christian LaCroix, Monique Lhuillier, Christian Dior, Oscar de la Renta, Vivienne Westwood") is hardly talismanic: Big stands Carrie up at the altar. (He tells his driver to turn around in the limo after he pulls away and intercepts Carrie and the bridal party in an attempt to convey he's now ready to walk down the aisle, but she's understandably had it.) Carrie comes to learn that one reason for his jilting her was that she "let the wedding get bigger than Big," the guest list spiraling out of control and her planned headpiece consisting of a bright stuffed bird. And though the film is ambivalent on who is the casualty, Miranda during the rehearsal dinner has a run-in with Steve and comments out of anger toward Big that he has to be crazy to get married, as, in her reasoning, "marriage ruins everything." Carrie and the bridal party retreat to Mexico, as she had pre-paid the honeymoon as a surprise to Big, and, in a strained middle section of the film, her friends nurse Carrie back to passable functionality.[24]

The film's attempt to represent a multicultural Manhattan also produced competing discourses. With the exception of Charlotte's Chinese daughter, Lily, the few immigrants or people of color represented are in service positions, from Carrie's black assistant to Miranda's Ukrainian nanny. A Sikh taxi driver is represented parodically, nodding like a cheerful robot while listening in on a conversation between Carrie and Miranda on the value of forgiveness; Miranda, during her search to find acceptable accommodations for herself and Brady after separating from Steve, uses the ad hoc philosophy "follow the white man with the baby" as a navigational strategy. On the vacation abroad Charlotte eats only prepackaged chocolate pudding from Poughkeepsie "because it's *Mexico,*" the couple of drops of shower water that enter her mouth corroborating her xenophobia.

The ultimate union of Carrie and Big is no less consistent. When he proposes again, he reasons that the engagement failed the first time because it was "all business, no romance then," yet nearly immediately he adds, "So that's why there's a diamond—you need to do something to close the deal." In a scene conjoining the Cinderella myth with commodity fetish-ism, he, kneeling, makes do by putting a $525 Manolo she hasn't yet worn on her foot. (Earlier in the film, Carrie, reading the Cinderella tale to Lily, tells her the ending doesn't happen in "real life," but the enchanted pre-schooler nevertheless asks to hear it again.) Carrie elopes to city hall wear-ing a labelless vintage suit, and she and Big meet the group for a recep-tion at a generic diner, the script implying that the eschewal of labels has enabled Carrie to get back to some platonic origin. In reality, the white crepe suit was neither labelless nor vintage but part of Dior's 2008 cruise collection. Singer Cristina Aguilera was photographed wearing the suit, which retailed for $6,000, to a New York City Dior show two weeks before the film's U.S. release. Replicas of Carrie's Vivienne Westwood gown became available on March 30, 2009, through online retailer Net-a-Porter for $9,875 and sold out in hours. Because the longevity of Carrie and Big's union has been called into question so many times, the film smartly cuts to Samantha's girls-only fiftieth birthday bash, where the only single woman in the film, rejuvenated through her decision to live independently, toasts to another half century with the group, sealing the toast with a signature cosmo.

While scrutinizing the idea that marriage and long-term coupling are no guarantees to happiness, the script tries to offset the deglamorization of marriage and monogamy with female banter and laughter. Beset by Montezuma's revenge, Charlotte, crapping in her Pilates pants, offers relief for Carrie's malaise as well as the film's comedic climax, or at least its upturn, one at best hokey. The closing images depict a younger generation of stylish women on the streets enjoying Manhattan nightlife, poeticizing Carrie's quest as an archetypal rite of passage. The women's commitment to their friendship is the grounding and only consistent element amid the film's pyrotechnic eye candy. For viewers who followed the series, by the end of the movie the women are bonded as deeply as blood sisters. Michael Patrick King has commented that he never wanted to show Carrie's parents because of the idea that the women were "purely creations of New York," and Miranda, Charlotte, and Samantha were "grown-ups who made family of one another" (qtd. in Bellafante). While it would be imprudent to use the four women's bond to make a broader statement about female relationships in postfeminism, the group retains and takes very seriously, if only at the privatized, local level, the second-wave feminist slogan "Sisterhood Is Powerful."[25]

The closing credits roll to "Labels or Love," a hip-hop song performed by Fergie also featured in the film's opening sequence. The lyrics' unflagging confidence in retail therapy annihilates the film's gesture to return to a prelapsarian state through the renunciation of conspicuous consumption. The song begins with the couplet "Shopping for labels, shopping for love / Manolo and Louis [Vuitton], it's all I'm thinking of" and mentions more than ten designer brands, most of whose logos make appearances in the film or are mentioned in dialogue. The rapper refers to her heavy credit card spending as an "addiction," and acknowledges that this practice is partly rooted in the disappointments and frustrations of dating; yet she stresses the interchangeability of men, who are and inferior to high-end retail goods, and links their availability to a procession of runway models and new fashion seasons. Though this bookend to the movie jars, lyrically and acoustically—the sound is less than euphonic, shall we say, and a movie video for the single was never issued because of the song's poor performance—I cannot stress how many viewers the two times I saw the film in the theater looked radiant exiting, and those who came with groups of other women seemed elatedly proud to be another woman's friend. The first hour after seeing the film was among the best I've felt in five years, and I've had a pretty good life. Maybe it was that spring had fully blossomed in Philly and weatherwise it was a perfect day; maybe it was that total strangers, in line or waiting seated for the film to begin, started focused conversations predicting what would happen to Carrie. Once the movie came up as I was advising a student on a paper topic during office hours: a young woman who, though naturally intelligent, wasn't tops in the gravitas department, looked me in the eye and said, very slowly, "It was a great day." I couldn't really disagree with her. Despite its mixed messages, the film conveyed with brave honesty the four women's ability to ride out highs and lows with a spiritual tenacity, their commitment to each other a permanent core value in a tide of seasonal or rented accessories.

What, then, are we to make of these paradoxes? In the climate of late heterosexuality, female ambition and the desire for autonomy coexist with a blunt entitlement via the pockets of a man and participation in exacting, slavish standards of self-presentation. With its excessive materialism and preoccupation with surfaces, late heterosexuality is hardly an advancement over the feminist project, though it reveals a blind spot in radical feminist thought. A tenet of second-wave feminism was that containing the power of female sexuality was necessary to preserve the dominant system of patriarchy. Yet, as Laura Kipnis notes, what was not foreseen was the ease with which female sexuality could be commodified; as she writes, sexuality was "packaged and sold back to women in the form of pricey accoutrements: the bad girl lingerie, the kitten-with-a-whip wardrobe, the fuck-me heels, and the regular bikini waxes" (*Female* 64). The relaxed constraints on female sexuality—an effect of the sexual revolution, feminism, and widespread availability of the pill—opened a new market that, harnessing the power of print and electronic media, upped the ante on standards of sexual desirability.

In consequence, part of many women's increased earning power is absorbed by the cost of assembling a sexy or at least youthful look for the purposes of self-pleasure, sexual confidence, and, of course, marriageability. Postfeminism works in tandem with the rapid growth of cosmetic dermatology, medi-spas, salon facials involving expensive extras like Alpha Beta peels and microdermabrasion, plus the normalization of tooth whitening procedures, bikini waxing, photo facials, and laser hair removal. With sexual "freedom" has come more work and a new master, if this time more self- and media-imposed. For all its concern with appearances, late heterosexuality is a far from glamorous cycle. Fueled by captiousness with style/self-help experts as handmaidens, it operates through the spending of money that serves not so much men as a new god, Style. It feeds off insecurity and self-derision, a large basis for competitiveness, if not jealousy, among women. To return again to the film, when announcing to Charlotte and Miranda that she will be living with Big in the two-terraced penthouse, Carrie expresses aloud disappointment that Miranda, judiciously suggesting that she hold onto her apartment, "can't feel jealous" for her.

Given this oscillating line between self-development, narcissism, and self-loathing, it is not surprising that a double standard may accompany woman's partner search, as professional women report seeking vicarious financial security while aiming to retain the respect of an equal. In 2000, *New York Times* journalist Felicia Lee interviewed single professional New York women in their twenties, thirties, and forties and found that most admitted to a nagging little voice inside their heads saying that they want a man to take care of them and that, though it's acceptable for a man to marry down, a "catch" for women is a "financial powerhouse." Mr. Right allows them to continue their careers but leaves the door open to leaving, providing a safety net that doesn't have to assume responsibility for all the bills but could. Lee observes, "We seem stuck between the 50s paradigm of marriage and the feminist fantasy, between being repulsed by the implications of a show like *Who Wants to Marry a Multimillionaire?* and captivated by its possibilities."[26] A television executive in her thirties confessed to Lee, "When a man takes me out to dinner, I sure feel good. It's oh, I'm going to be a girl today. I get tired of wearing the pants. Maybe we haven't come quite as far as we think we have. Or maybe we've come far enough and we want to turn back." Along these lines, *New York Times* journalist Ruth La Ferla has conceded in a feature titled "They Want to Marry a Millionaire" that the label "gold digger" has lost much of its sting. While many chick lit protagonists can be ascribed this moniker, others cannot.[27] All, however, are acutely conscious of the high and increasing cost of urban living. According to the U.S. Department of Agriculture, raising a child born in 2004 from birth to the age of seventeen may cost more than a quarter of a million dollars (Karbo 70). These costs can swiftly escalate when a child enters college: a College Board report in 2006 revealed not only that tuition and other costs at private and public universities rose faster than inflation, but also that since 2001, tuition and fees at public institutions had risen more than at any other time in the past thirty years, increasing by 35 percent, with tuition and fees at private universities increasing by 11 percent over the same period (Glater). In this light, we may wish to consider postfeminism an effect of the relative reduction of the family wage, escalating housing and education costs, and the economic fact that a double income is increasingly needed to raise children in a middle-class lifestyle, a cost compounded by rising standards for this social rung.

Chick lit does not disavow journalist Lori Leibovich's observation that "the knight in a pin-striped suit is a potent fantasy for many women" (192). The protagonist of Karen Templeton's *Loose Screws*, stood up at the altar like Carrie Bradshaw, along these lines confides, "And right now, I don't have the energy to be a feminist. I'm having enough trouble dealing with being a woman" (70). Similarly, the protagonist of Jane Green's best-selling *Mr. Maybe* (1999) analyzes her near marriage of convenience to a priggish millionaire by asking, "How can they understand that, despite my independence and so-called career, I was swept away by a fantasy, seduced by a lifestyle, and that I am evidently far more shallow than even I ever dreamt?" (400). In this mythology, the knight figure operates as an entitled payoff for investments in early career development and delayed marriage. Manhattan singleton and social critic Katie Roiphe tenders a like-minded affirmation: "We are a generation of strong women looking for even stronger men" (85).

If we accept the fantasy components of chick lit's renditions of the success story, perhaps its greatest hoax upon the reader is the plotline that centralizes a protagonist's conflict between choosing an affluent man she can passably tolerate and a barely solvent sensitive soul. When she chooses the financial underdog, it is quickly revealed he has just signed a publishing deal or lucrative contract. Plotlines of this type conjoin romantic elements with monetary aspirations and attempt to buffer a protagonist's drive for class ascendancy. Ultimately, the phenomenon of *Sex and the City,* and chick lit's commercial success, leaves the feminist scholar to ponder the degree to which a female bildungsroman with a heterosexual protagonist can dissociate itself from the marriage plot, and the marriage plot from the pleasures of acquisition.

4 The Legacy of Working-Girl Fiction

> It appears to me the problem is this: how to create
> a body of writers who are, artistically, to serial
> literature what Dostoyevsky was to Sue and
> Soulié or, with respect to the detective story, what
> Chesterton was to Conan Doyle and Wallace.
> With this aim in mind, one must abandon many
> prejudices, but above all it should be remembered
> . . . that one is faced with a formidable organization
> of publishing interests.
>
> —Antonio Gramsci, "Problems of Criticism"

THERE IS A TEMPTATION for the literary critic to award points to popular fiction with canonical masterworks as intertexts, as if the use of allusion logically lends gravitas to the popular. The reflex to highlight a pedigree is in part a defense mechanism against suspicions about the relevance of the endeavor to the established canon and the implication of questionable taste, the critic reasoning, consciously or not, that an elucidation of intertextuality may offset accusations of "slumming it" or, especially for junior faculty, dubious time management. While mindful of the motives spurring gestures of this sort, I aim to detail how chick lit's high readability belies a more intricate genealogy, one extending beyond Jane Austen and Edith Wharton, the most commonly named antecedents. While indebted to the Harlequin and the novel of manners, it also appropriates significantly from the career-girl novel. Because chick lit's ancestors date back to our first novels and span three centuries, a comprehensive catalog is beyond the scope of this project.[1] My sample focuses primarily on twentieth-century urban fiction with working women protagonists because they are nearest in setting and character. I have deliberately selected both canonical and lesser-known titles in order to mark chick lit's adaptations from a diverse set of narrative traditions.

As we revisit earlier heroine-centered literature, I must pause to acknowledge that the act of naming texts as antecedents to the chick lit genre replicates marketing tactics that capitalize on the popularity of the phenomenon; at worst, it implies a telos in which chick lit is the culmination rather than merely one incarnation of the heroine-centered novel. The media's overuse of the chick lit label has claimed texts as chick lit retroactively though they may contain only a few facets of the formula. The *chick lit* appellation labels, sometimes erroneously, the work as entertainment reading and its writer as commercial and invokes the negative values charged to this classification. The critic who wishes to present a taxonomy of this popular genus confronts a daunting categorical concern: the task raises the question of what recent fiction by women featuring a female protagonist or a cast of women characters is *not* chick lit.

In the past five years, chick lit has filtered into the mystery, young adult, cookbook, and self-help genres and has spawned the subsets "mommy lit" and the unflatteringly named "hen lit," the latter for the over-fifty reader. Though *Sex and the City* and *Bridget Jones's Diary* focus on the dating travails of thirtysomething women, chick lit has expanded to include the phases of a woman's life from adolescence to menopause. Protagonists now need not be writers or employed in the media sector. Though protagonists are employed in largely middle-class, white-dominated occupations, not all who work in media industries are Caucasian. For example, *The Accidental Diva* (2004) by *Teen People* beauty director Tia Williams spotlights an African American beauty editor of a leading, white-oriented fashion magazine. The definition of the label *chick lit* is further complicated by the fact that it is occasionally written by men.[2] As chick lit continues to evolve and may no longer confine itself predominantly to the city, core attributes might become less definite. In delineating a genealogy some texts or sub-genres of fiction show overlap in certain areas but not others: an earlier novel's rising and falling action may reveal similarities with chick lit but may vary in tone and form.[3] At minimum, tracing chick lit's lineage makes assumptions about a core set of generic characteristics and raises questions as to what elements of the genre we wish to foreground.

This chapter works alongside Imelda Whelehan's study *The Feminist Bestseller: From "Sex and the Single Girl" to "Sex and the City"* (2005), which analyzes American feminist fiction of the 1970s and concludes with the suggestion that in British chick lit we find the germ of the legacy of the consciousness-raising novel. Whelehan skillfully examines popular fiction and related self-help from the end of the 1960s through the 1980s more through the lens of feminist debates than with a literary or stylistic focus, and her analysis of chick lit in her concluding chapters is mostly confined to British texts. The protagonist's mixed-sex urban family re-places, I believe, the same-sex consciousness-raising group of second-wave feminism, and the issue of subjective fragmentation found in earlier feminist fiction such as Doris Lessing's *The Golden Notebook* (1962) is not as trenchant a theme. Nevertheless, chick lit takes up the consciousness-raising novel's negotiations with the assembling of a unified subject by focusing, often obsessively, on self-presentation and the reconciliation of the creative woman with glamour. This chapter supplements Whelehan's pioneering scholarship by expanding its historical chronology, examining texts from literary high culture, and identifying overlooked popular fiction within Whelehan's time frame. The growth of chick lit into further subsets may render this genealogy dated or, worse, foster the pattern of labeling all fiction by women or fiction focusing on courtship, marriage, and female urban living as chick lit. While chick lit and its penetration into second-ary consumer markets may lend the impression of ubiquity, it should be viewed as a subset of mainstream fiction whose sanguinity and ties to the comedic tradition adumbrate social critique.

Respect and the City

Chick lit protagonists are a composite of gendered presences associated with the modern city and, in particular, the working girl and female shopper. As observers of urban life, protagonists share salient characteristics with the flaneur. Although protagonists, however bourgeois, do not necessarily possess the unqualified leisure that is by definition the flaneur's, as a producer of sociological commentary on city life, they have characteristics that David Frisby (2001) has identified in the work of Walter Benjamin as allied with *flânerie*. Benjamin associates the flaneur, and the activity of *flânerie*, not just with observation and reading but also production and deciphering. In addition to merely an undirected, ambling observer, the flaneur can also be for Benjamin a producer of literary texts (including lyrical and prose poetry as in the case of Charles Baudelaire), a producer of illustrative texts (including drawings and paintings), a producer of narratives and reports (including journalistic and sociological writing) (Frisby 29). A journalist and stroller of the city's avenues, the chick lit protagonist conjoins *flânerie* with a validation of the department store.

This chapter aligns itself with endeavors in literary scholarship, particularly, the work of Deborah Parsons (2000) and Janet Wolff (1985), which complicate earlier feminist criticism and cultural sociology's tendencies to support the masculine definition of the urban observer. If we accept Frisby's formulation that *flânerie* can be associated with "a form of looking, observing . . . reading the city and its population (its spatial images, its architecture, its human configurations)," the novels discussed in this section, set in the late 1920s and 1930s, portray the obstacles that arise when protagonists attempt to negotiate the unmediated experience of city life with recreational and monetary consumption (28–29). They offer a darker modernist representation of the conflict the chick lit protagonist usually emerges from successfully and predate the genre's attempt to reconcile solitary *flânerie* with the pursuit of a committed pairing.

Dawn Powell's debut novel *Whither* (1925) ultimately stands as a bildungsroman manqué yet depicts a female world of urban modernity whose themes and exuberant tone predate the chick lit genre.[4] Best known as a novelist who satirized the middle class, especially New York's intelligentsia and café society, Powell (1896–1965) also produced dramas, musicals, screenplays, and hundreds of reviews, the latter to support her fiction writing. Her papers were not easily accessible until the mid-1990s, and until 1989, all of her books were out of print (Rice x). Renewed interest was sparked in 1987 with the publication of an essay on Powell by Gore Vidal in the *New York Review of Books*. A National Public Radio piece marking the release of *Dawn Powell at Her Best* (1994), a collection of two novels and several short stories, furthered the recovery effort. In 1995, John Updike contributed to Powell's renaissance with an essay published in the *New Yorker*. Tim Page has been most influential in reviving Powell's work through the publication of her diaries and letters, in 1995 and 1999, respectively. In 2001, the Library of America released a two-volume anthology, with notes by Page, which reprinted nine of her fifteen novels.

Powell began *Whither* approximately four years after her arrival in New York upon her graduation from Lake Erie College in Painesville, Ohio, in 1918. Among her lesser-known novels, it focuses on twenty-two-year-old Zoe Bourne's landing in New York from Albon, Ohio, and her immersion in the manners of urban life. Powell's early letters reveal autobiographical overlaps with Zoe: in her olive complexion, diminutive stature, bob haircut, and bit part in a movie, the freshly minted city girl, as Marcelle Smith Rice has noted, resembles the author's young self (142). Zoe, an aspiring playwright, secures housing in a ladies' residence and obtains a position as a filing clerk. She moves up to a copywriter, but the city's material lures and the influence of her stylish, prodigal housemates—mostly aspiring actresses or singers too proud to audition for chorus or minor parts—lead her to live beyond her means. Her bright youth and literary yearnings attract the attention of a married boss and advertising mogul, Mr. Kane, with whom she shares a quasi date. She abruptly quits the position out of embarrassment when a supervisor, who spies them out, reprimands her for walking arm in arm with Kane, the public display a liability to Kane's standing with clients. The fast-paced novel comes to an even faster, tenuously credible close. Zoe accepts Kane's invitation for a good-bye lunch when she learns from a coworker he has accepted a position in London. In the outing, Zoe and the freshly divorced Kane declare their love, marry that afternoon, and leave on a steamer for overseas the next day.

Zoe's express marriage does not entirely stop her commercial writing: *Vanity Box*, a society gossip puff weekly for which she oversees a section, asks her to write a monthly foreign letter. The relocation abroad indicates a final drying up of any artistic literary endeavors, perhaps implied in the title's homonym, *wither*. The interest in nightlife and fashionable clothes quickly trumps Zoe's yearning to write drama. *Whither*, despite its ingenuelike overuse of exclamation points and frequent repetition of utterances like "This now, was New York!" is not a satirical novel, either in its representation of a fledgling's proverbial "desire to write" or in Zoe and her housemates' narrow concerns and accruing debts (37). In light of Powell's long and prolific career, it is, however, ironic that Zoe relinquishes trying to write plays after half a day's work—she quits after barely two lines of the list-of-characters page. Zoe's invitation to write a travel column for *Vanity Box* places her on the continuum of chick lit protagonists, yet her questionable ability to stand on her own feet with any money she earns renders her a dwarfed figure.

Zoe Bourne's enjoyment of cosmopolitan pleasures is shared by the protagonist Lynn Harding of Faith Baldwin's *Skyscraper* (1931), though Baldwin's character exhibits a greater work ethic than Zoe. Described in her *New York Times* obituary tribute (1978) as a "doyenne of American light fiction writers," Baldwin's career spanned seven decades and produced over sixty novels ("Faith Baldwin" 283, qtd. in Hapke 251). Feminist Press reissued *Skyscraper* as one of the premier titles of its Femme Fatales: Women Write Pulp series. The series, launched in fall 2003, marks the press's endeavor to bring greater scholarly attention to pulp fiction of the mid-twentieth century: despite the pulp revival of the past decade, women-authored pulp writing has been virtually ignored (Tenzer and Casella xi). While editorial director Livia Tenzer has assessed the social values of the chick lit as "retrograde," it is not implausible to connect the Women Write Pulp launch with the popularity of chick lit.

The adversities of the early 1930s empowered the character type embodied in Baldwin's protagonist, a hardworking business girl of middling origins (Hapke 252). This reemerged bachelor maid figure differed from her predecessors in that she is excited by rather than fearful of a workplace she and her creator are determined to navigate (Hapke 252–53). The novel, originally serialized in *Cosmopolitan* and published in book form as a Dell Romance title, chronicles Lynn's rise up the ranks of New York's fictional Sea Coast Bank and Trust Company during the early Depression years. Comfortably employed in sales research, Lynn lives in a ladies' residence uptown before obtaining a flatshare with a sleek model, Jenny. Lynn's dark curls contrast with her roommate's fair locks, the latter's behavior as a mistress to a businessman and growing haggardness foiling Lynn's virtue, freshness, and self-reliance. To save Lynn's industriousness and high morals from coming off as goody-goody, Baldwin introduces the career romance plot, with a rakish high-profile lawyer courting Lynn and failing to win her hand. Married, dashing, and verbally dexterous, David Dwight wins a divorce from his wife but fails to win Lynn's heart, as his involvement in inside trading is exposed by Lynn's supervisor, Sarah Bennett, a discarded lover of Dwight's, Lynn's godmother, and mentor.

The Baldwin plot adapts the career romance story line from the pulp writer Laura Jean Libbey, whose virtuous clerical heroines achieve upward mobility through marriage to their bosses by virtue of their comeliness and character. The page-turner *Skyscraper* concludes with Lynn's marriage to Tom Shepard, an entry-level financial analyst who worked in the same building as Lynn before becoming a radio-broadcasting technician. Though Shepard is of modest means, his hard-earned and honest income works as an obvious contrast to Dwight's surface wealth and growing debts. The closing paragraphs of *Skyscraper* celebrate not matrimony per se but the couple working together in the city. The skyscraper, intoned histrionically in Baldwin's closing lines, affirms itself as iconic of man's potential for progress and the newlyweds' conquering of personal obstacles.[5]

The romance plot is not enough, however, to connect us with well-mannered and earnest Lynn. While she is an admirable figure, her absence of moral flaws and personal shortcomings make for borderline sententiousness. Unlike most chick lit protagonists, Lynn is financially conservative—a saver, not a spender—despite the city's material lures. Lynn's nose, refreshingly, is not always to the grindstone: she smokes, albeit sparingly, takes advantage of the city's entertainment, and is not afraid to indulge herself in a cocktail. In a protofeminist vein, she resists Tom's demands to cease working upon marriage and maneuvers chains of command to ensure she is not laid off once wed (as was common during the Depression era, when working married women were viewed askance especially if their husbands could provide for them). In contrast to the vast majority of chick lit characters, sexually Lynn is squeaky clean. Lynn's virginity is compulsory, according to Susan Hapke in the novel's afterword, in order to diffuse the long-held cultural suspicion that young women were not fit to work amid the carnal temptations the clerical-boss relationship present (253). The Baldwin plot, despite these differences, lends a noncanonical entry point into chick lit's origins.

The Mental Illness Story

"Neurotic" is a label often applied to the chick lit protagonist by media commentators to characterize her conflicting needs and wants, compulsive list keeping, or dating hyperactivity. The media's loose usage of the medical classification in this context is not entirely surprising, as novelists, conduct-book writers, and social psychologists have often linked the figure of the single woman with mental illness, depression, or sexual dysfunction. Even *Sex and the City* at one point connects the protagonist with mental degeneration: in an attempt to give readers a more developed ending to Carrie and Big's relationship, Bushnell in 2001 added two chapters, one in which Carrie, in her final line of direct dialogue, phones Big at his office asking to be admitted into a mental asylum. We don't know how much of her crying stems from being single and how much from a substance abuse problem's effects on the nervous system—in the last third of the text she drinks heavily on top of regular cocaine use. Nevertheless, she pleads to be able "to lie in a white room and watch TV, and maybe make potholders," the last request perhaps deflating the severity of her affliction (241).

With few exceptions, however, chick lit reflects a departure from this trope.[6] The heroine may think that she will "just die" if she fails to find a husband or boyfriend but frequently is gratified with a romantic union; if she isn't, she comes to the realization that she can still live a reasonably good existence, with works like Lisa Cach's *Dating without Novocaine* (2002) concluding on the protagonist's thirtieth birthday and her awareness that marriage is but one of many possibilities in an already satisfying life. Chick lit appropriates, though, elements of black comedy present in some women-authored works of contemporary mental illness fiction with career-girl protagonists. Critiques of heterosexual institutions in the mental illness novel resurface in chick lit yet are contained or subdued in a romantic ending or the protagonist's self-acceptance. The mental illness story's celebration of childhood and accompanying nostalgia is jettisoned in chick lit, as childhood is seldom mentioned, and when it is, is attached to associations more neutral or negative than positive. These mental illness stories' reformulation of the bildungsroman's developmental trajectory, however, presents an antecedent to the chick lit genre's tension between the marriage plot and a narrative of individual accomplishment.

Sylvia Plath's *The Bell Jar* (1963) is one of literature's finest representations of a breakdown as well as biting commentary on inadequacies in mental health services of the 1950s. The novel remains a staple text of high school and undergraduate English classes, where it is examined in the bildungsroman tradition; it is also included in psychology courses for its vivid descriptions of life underneath the figurative bell jar, whose concave projections fragment the protagonist Esther Greenwood's sensory world into disturbing and unintelligible pieces. This first-person account is well established as highly autobiographical, recounting Plath's guest editorship experience with *Mademoiselle* in the summer of 1953, for which she introduced the August college issue. *The Bell Jar,* published under the pseudonym Victoria Lucas, chronicles with bitter honesty Plath's first mental breakdown, to which many read the details of her own suicide ten years later as an epilogue.

The protagonist's apprenticeship as a media professional reveals that the *Bildungsheld*'s expected progress and fruition isn't for women a full-fledged possibility. Her accumulation of scholarships and straight A's will end in a developmental stillbirth. Marriage and motherhood are presented as female essence and not a matter of choice: her boyfriend's mother's analogy—"What a man is is an arrow into the future and what a woman is is the place the arrow shoots off from"—defines the heteroscript as a natural law, in the same vein as real-life commentators of the period (58). For instance, in 1955 alone there were more than three hundred pro-marriage tomes directed at single American women (Israel 190). In 1951, almost 60 percent of all American women were married—with one in three of them having wed by age nineteen (Israel 184). By 1957, 14 million girls were engaged at age seventeen, and the majority of them were mothers at twenty-one; in 1958, 97 out of every 1,000 girls between the ages of fifteen and nineteen gave birth (Israel 184). To opt out of marriage is presented as treason, and to stress this connection, the novel begins with a reference to the Rosenberg execution. Esther Greenwood's name itself seems to imply a connection with the Rosenbergs, whose electrocution foreshadows her shock therapy treatments; "Esther" is similar to "Ethel," and her surname is a variant of Ethel's maiden name "Greenglass" (and the surname of her brother, David, who supplied documents to her husband, Julius, from the Los Alamos National Laboratory). Like many protagonists of early female novels of development, she is without reliable parental guidance; her father is deceased, and her well-meaning but conformist mother attempts to teach her shorthand. Peer models also seem deficient, as *The Bell Jar* offers a cast of women she could become yet each individually is in some way inadequate. Her boss, Jay Cee, whose name's gender ambiguity connotes her all-business personal style, is a walking time clock who schedules in emotional commitment for her plotted office plants. The glamour girl, Doreen, exudes in excess Jay Cee's deficiencies, her overripe femininity finding an objective correlative in the musky smell she secretes.

The novel's status as a classic lies in its sustained acerbic sharpness and Esther's astute identification of the narrow range of acceptable choices afforded to women in the 1950s. Yet the character's plight evokes more interest than sympathy, especially as she is grateful to no one. We sense she will never be satisfied; while not snobbish, she judges nearly all with a sneer, and she wants it all, yesterday. Despite being a neophyte to city life, she is prematurely jaded and unable to begin to imagine a more socially accommodating world. While the novel successfully conveys caustic humor, the comic relief, unlike that in chick lit, is rarely self-deprecating. Esther takes everything seriously to the point that we doubt whether she can laugh at herself, an assessment compounded by her inflated sense of professional and material entitlement.

Yet as Plath through Esther channels feminist anger into pathological self-derision, she weaves in an accessible novel an intricate associative network. *The Bell Jar* contains rich imagery and symbolism, literary devices typically absent in chick lit. The latter's clothing references work as product placements and markers of social status, whether actual or coveted, yet do not aspire to the density of canonical works such as Plath's (or, alternatively, Jean Rhys's). Particularly engaging is *The Bell Jar*'s use of clothing as reflective of Esther's changing mental states. Her new wardrobe in New York represents a transition into a world of success, sophistication, and appearances, a universe where she "was supposed to be the envy of thousands of other college girls" (2). They become an expression of her changing self and of uncertainties and insecurities in Manhattan, with the city depicted as a glittering but overwhelming universe of choice.

She readies her departure by ritualistically throwing her entire closet into the night wind, thereby dramatizing her inability to make the transition into a more glamorous identity and her distaste for the city's excessive concern with surface appearance. Indeed, the adjective "imitation" occurs frequently in the New York section, underscoring that its material allure fails to satisfy her inner drive toward creativity. In the novel's final mention of clothing, a description of Esther's outfit for her exit interview with the sanatorium staff, apparel operates as a synecdoche of her descent and recovery as well as her successful assembly of a sanctioned persona: "My stocking seams were straight, my black shoes cracked, but polished, my red suit as flamboyant as my plans" (199). The reader who derives pleasure in tracing morphing imagery or values ascribed to a symbol will in this regard find the chick lit genre deficient.

Esther attempts to be a creator and be cared for. The cold war climate in which she resides does not accommodate both. Chick lit protagonists struggle with inhabiting both roles, yet as beneficiaries of the women's movement, they have a viable chance of succeeding. Consequently, they tend to view their future with more optimism and faith; their ties with the romance tradition often lend tentativeness toward social criticism. *The Bell Jar*, though, is a novel of female development that does not treat marriage as a panacea and, more importantly, begins to complicate the unilinear development of the *Bildungsheld*. In Esther's social climate the female artist-hero confronts a succession of images of confinement and thwarted growth.

Gail Parent's *Sheila Levine Is Dead and Living in New York* (1972) extends *The Bell Jar*'s black humor and looks to suicide as an escape from the failure to conform to prescribed gender roles. Identified by novelists such as Jennifer Weiner and Melissa Senate as a founding text of the chick lit genre, this first-person account chronicles the titular protagonist's attempts to find satisfying work and a husband in a hypercompetitive dating locale armed with less-than-average looks. A best-seller of the 1960s, *Sheila Levine Is Dead* employs sustained self-deprecating humor to buffer an extreme dramatization of compulsory heterosexuality and de rigueur marriage.

Sheila's earliest memory is of lying in her crib and hearing her mother beam that one day her baby will be a lovely bride. Her mother's refrain

"When you're married . . ." pervades her Long Island middle-class child-hood and adolescence. After graduation Sheila takes an apartment share consisting entirely of alcoves and hopes the city's bustle will bring her in contact with a suitable husband. But weeks turn into years, with Sheila's apartments moving up the East Side and then regressing to a no-frills East Twenty-sixth Street unit, and no husband. With not much to show for ten years of trying to survive in the city, Sheila decides at thirty that living has become gratuitous and so begins to arrange the details of her burial. She takes a bus out to South Orange, New Jersey, to decide on a cemetery plot: "It's like looking at a new apartment and, thank God, I won't have to move again" (161). Even there married privilege confronts her: the undertaker informs her that it is a family cemetery that doesn't cater to single people and, out of sympathy for her purported terminal illness, offers her a double plot at a discount. Particulars of the shopping expeditions for her burial clothes have the novel ultimately serve as a lengthy suicide note.

Yet, because the novel is a comedy, Sheila, swallowing a bottle of sleep-ing pills, does not die. The ending compromises realism as her mother, after calling her apartment, senses something is wrong and contacts the emer-gency squad. In recounting her rescue, Sheila takes pride that she remem-bered to give the doorman a quarter before blacking out in the ambulance. *Sheila Levine* chronicles the ill-fated adventure, romantic disappointment, and rebirth of one gal Friday in a children's record company. Simultane-ously, its integration of demographic data into the fictional protagonist's story provides a social anthropology about dating and New York City on which chick lit continues to base plotlines, documenting, for instance, the city's disadvantageous male-female ratio—today approximately 81 single men for every 100 single women (Stanger and Mandell 75).[7]

Parent's black comedy, despite its refusal of a conventional tragic con-clusion, falls into a case study of desperation. The protagonist never real-izes that she makes herself too sexually available, thinking she has to com-pensate for being slightly overweight, if she is even that, by sexual favors to uncommitted partners. She settles for regular sex, as most men never take her anywhere. Naturally generous, she offers money to a boyfriend in jail for nonpayment of alimony, who then convinces her to obtain pot, which she mails to him. Later he demands cocaine, which she promptly ventures into the East Village to obtain. The humor sadly masks a low self-esteem that grows lower as friends from her early twenties marry and lose contact. In the epilogue Sheila's regained resilience strikes us more than ever as a sickness. Yet again trying to answer to her family's hopes that she find "a nice Jewish doctor," on her hospital bed in Bellevue she sizes up her chances of dating members of the floor's medical team: "It was those men in white coats that made me want to live. They're all attractive, and they're all concerned, or seem to be. They smile at me. All I need is one out of the six" (22). Sheila's drastic measures to opt out of the marriage market operate through hyperbole to diffuse single readers' feelings of hopelessness or anxiety much in the same way some chick lit novels caricature micromanaging behavior in otherwise normal women. Yet *Sheila Levine*'s riotous laughs belie a dark undertow. In the end, not much has or will change for Sheila. The novel's implicit message that after a certain age an unmarried woman is as good as dead remains the same.

A leading comedy writer for four decades, Parent's credits for TV include the *Carol Burnett Show; Mary Hartman, Mary Hartman;* and *The Golden Girls.* More recently, she wrote the screenplay for the 2004 hit movie *Confessions of a Teenage Drama Queen.* As is common in the chick lit genre, the book's author bio begins by mentioning the similarities and differences of creator and character. Parent, like her heroine, attended Syracuse before earning a bachelor's from New York University. Unlike Sheila, she married one week after graduation. Sheila's failure to obtain a husband is further underscored by paratextual elements, as the blurb swiftly differentiates between its successful married author and the suicidal singleton.

The Edible Woman (1970) by Canadian author Margaret Atwood presents a female bildungsroman not as humorous as Parent's novel but with a protagonist who shares a similar conflict over socially sanctioned developmental paths. Atwood's first published novel, written when she was twenty-four, features a conventional college grad as its protagonist and encompasses many chick lit tropes. Twentysomething Marian McAlpin earns her living by revising market research questionnaires written by psychologists to make them more accessible to the general public. Workload variations include licking envelopes and taste-testing canned rice pudding flavors. Despite Seymour Surveys' dingy brick with small windows, formulating questionnaires for razor blades and dehydrated dog food beats her roommate Ainsley's job testing electronic toothbrushes. The two reside on the servants' quarters floor of a house in one of Ontario's more genteel districts. Shifts in point of view parallel Marian's attempts to define her existence and mirror the tug-of-war between conformity and self-acceptance.

The novel, written in the spring and summer of 1965, predates the women's movement by a few years but, like *The Bell Jar,* comments on the absence of appropriate models for young women wishing to combine marriage and career. Marian's friend Clara doesn't finish college and quickly has three young children. Her roommate doesn't believe in marriage and deliberately gets pregnant by a virtual stranger to satisfy her need for a child. Coworkers around her own age are confined to "the office virgins," a band of chaste fresh faces angling to meet a financially fit bachelor on their lunch break. Male peers don't remedy her lack of an adequate social support system: while conducting beer surveys she meets a graduate English student, Duncan, who occupies his time outside class with obsessive-compulsive ironing. Granted, aspects of the novel are now outdated—the landlady is repulsed when a male suitor stays the night, and Marian will be terminated from her job shortly after marriage—but contribute to the protagonist's narrow social and professional options.

The Edible Woman can be read as a protofeminist case study of societal forces, namely compulsory heterosexuality and the marriage imperative, that mimic adjustment disorder symptoms in Marian. The lack of challenges at Seymour Surveys enables us to trace Marian's malaise, and her boyfriend, Peter, a handsome junior lawyer, offers not much more emotionally than security. Trepidations of being caught and caged permeate parts 1 and 2: on a group date she takes off and flees in the night streets, and at another social gathering she hides under a low bed, like Esther Greenwood, who walls herself in the subcellar crevice. Part 1's first-person narration gives way to third person in part 2, mirroring the dissolution of Marian's ego upon her engagement and a self-detachment. The shift marks the beginning of the novel's central and sustained metaphor of eating: Marian starts rejecting certain foods until she finds eating lettuce cruel to the leaves. Finding marriage hard to swallow, she starts crying out one night with Peter and friends, and her antipathy toward eating culminates in when she abandons her engagement party. The metaphor reaches its deepest expression when she bakes a cake woman for Peter, its face "doll-like and vacant except for the small silver glitter of intelligence in each green eye" (298). The symbolism is too obvious; nevertheless, consuming the cake enables her to begin to undo Peter's and society's attempt to assimilate her. Part 3 reverts to first-person voice with Marian informing us she has broken off her engagement. Yet another cake partaken of by a former sexual partner allows her to move forward by seeing the relationship as ephemeral. Resuming healthy calorie intake and cooking indicate a more integrated ego and a new beginning.

In this way *The Edible Woman* performs a revisionist function to what cultural historian Lynn Peril has identified as "fatty fiction" (51). Fatty fiction plots, which flourished from the 1950s to the early 1980s, focus on the female protagonist's weight-loss struggle. The denouement occurs when the character reaches her goal weight, and along the way, emotional and social problems are resolved, the consequence of her weight loss. Atwood's novel predates the chick lit genre's rewriting of this body image trope. For instance, works such as Jennifer Weiner's *Good in Bed* (2001), Wendy Markham's *Slightly Single* (2002), and Jackie Rose's *Slim Chance* (2003) dissociate unnaturally obtained slimness from heterosexual success; the chick lit heroine's weight loss often coincides with an emotional nadir, a financial low, or the fallout of a significant romantic relationship. In *Slightly Single*, a novel that chronicles the protagonist's forty-pound weight loss and the painful dissolution of a three-year relationship with a self-absorbed aspiring actor, the breakup offers freedom from a plotted teleology. The protagonist, who "always needed to know how books end," discards a novel into a public trash can, the gesture complementing her realization that learning to live with suspense holds more possibility than stagnation in a one-sided relationship (270). Similarly, at Atwood's novel's close, Marian is back to square one but can approach life more on her own terms. *The Edible Woman*, though less humorous than most chick fiction, stands as an ancestor to its reformulation of the bildungsroman's trajectory.

Chick lit reads as an intermediary between the success story and the mental illness narrative, especially as much of the "early" chick lit of the late 1990s did not conclude with a romantic ending. Chick lit of the late 1990s has been referred to as "dump literature" by Barbara Defoe Whitehead, as the novels concerned themselves chiefly with the fallout of a breakup and the protagonist's attempt to come to terms with it through writing ("Plight"). Best-sellers like *Animal Husbandry* (1998) by Laura Zigman and *In the Drink* (1999) by Kate Christensen, though sardonically witty, have a much more depressive tone than standard chick lit fare. Such often semiautobiographical tales serve as vehicles to write about the trials if not traumas of modern courtship. In a dating climate often described by women as "brutal," chick lit does not entirely jettison modernism's split subject of failed romance but displaces anxiety through humor.

Proto–Chick Lit and the Urban Sophisticate

Depicting the city in more positive, less fragmented terms than those of the mental illness story, the twentieth-century works discussed in this section celebrate camaraderie between heterosexual single women or affirm possibilities of singleness. Their figure of the upper-middle-class, independent career woman witnesses its evolution in the chick lit genre. Though not uniform in tone, collectively they anticipate chick lit's vivacity, its less-than-romantic representation of sex, and its repudiation of a compulsory male-female union.

The protagonist of Rona Jaffe's *The Best of Everything* (1958) imbues *Skyscraper*'s Lynn Harding's work ethic with a nascent A-list flair. A precocious child, Jaffe attended the Dalton School in Manhattan and graduated from Radcliffe College when she was nineteen. Curtailed by the societal judgment of the 1950s that respectable girls should not take up house alone, she returned to Manhattan and moved back in with her parents. But she yearned to be free, and after working in publishing for a while, she signed a contract with Simon and Schuster, based on the first fifty pages for her debut novel. She then persuaded her father to help her get her own apartment. Feeling liberated by her escape, Jaffe, then twenty-five, wrote *The Best of Everything* in just five months and five days.

The blockbuster best-seller began to establish Jaffe as one of the foremost chroniclers of relationships in the modern age. It presents the most developed contemporary prototype of the chick lit genre. Its resemblance to the chick lit of four decades later is uncanny, so much so that it reads in hindsight as a writer's guide to chick lit tropes.[8] Not coincidentally, Penguin in the summer of 2005 published a new edition, the reissue reborn as retro or "classic" chick lit.[9] Its epigraph, from an ad in the *New York Times*, offers a manifesto to chick lit protagonists:

YOU DESERVE
THE BEST OF EVERTHING

The best job, the best surroundings,
the best pay, the best contacts.

The opening scene, however, foregrounds how the attainment of "the best," is hardly glossy like the ad in which the copy appears. The protagonist, Caroline Bender, is among the hundreds of girls who file out of Grand Central Station one midwinter morning in 1952. The scene offers a panoramic view before the novel focuses on the stories of five young women, begins to delineate distinctions, and then discerns a common thread:

> They carry the morning newspaper and overstuffed handbags. Some of them are wearing pink or chartreuse fuzzy overcoats and five-year-old ankle-strap shoes and have their hair up in pin curls underneath kerchiefs. Some of them are wearing chic black suits (maybe last year's but who can tell?) and kid gloves and are carrying their lunches in violet-sprigged Bonwit Teller paper bags. None of them has enough money. (1)

While focusing on twenty-year-old Caroline Bender's rise from a secretary in Fabian Publications' typing pool to a successful fiction editor four years later, the novel intertwines her story with those of the lives and marriage market fortunes of the other major characters also employed in the city's media and entertainment industry.

The Best of Everything not only offers one of the first women-centered insider's peeks into the office rungs of the Manhattan media world but holds its audience through a careful balance of the glamorous and mundane. Details of Caroline's status as a young worker dovetail with that of the standard chick lit protagonist. While "more than a pretty girl," for her first day on the job she is attired in her college dress-up suit, her attaché case holding women's magazines and commuter tickets. The novel predates chick lit in both the attributes it assigns to its heroine and its subplots. For instance, Caroline's coworker Mary Agnes Russo occupies sizable sections with minutiae of her wedding planning and related festivities, much like the protagonist of *Diary of a Mad Bride*. Caroline's seriocomic resolution to start making a list of all the money she has given out for weddings and baby showers so she can be sure to get it all back in the event she marries intersects with chick lit's satire of wedding-related expense, a topic discussed in chapter 5 at greater length.

Chick lit's coupling of editorial promotions with romantic success or advancement as a writer obtained as consolation for relationship disappointments finds precedent in Jaffe's novel. The novel begins a few months after the protagonist has endured a broken engagement the summer earlier and ends leaving her with three options, none of them ideal: an engagement with an adoring but boring lawyer; a liaison with her married ex-fiancé; and a whirlwind affair with celebrity actor John Cassaro, who whisks her away to Las Vegas for Christmas. She meets Cassaro, one of Hollywood's "most notorious bedroom athletes," through work when she is assigned to have him endorse a paperback novel published by a Fabian imprint (436); the endorsement will in turn help him promote his new film. The closing scenes withhold a pat romantic ending and affirm the protagonist as newsworthy. Her ex-fiancé, buying an evening paper and magazines in an airport, spies Caroline's picture on the front page, the story reporting that while described by the heartthrob as "an old friend," she refused to comment or to pose for photographers, and locked herself in her room, next door to Cassaro's. Caroline's position as both a producer of media and its subject, on top of her set of romantic choices, is the pinnacle of success in chick lit, comparable to and even surpassing that of a married ending.

Jaffe's mother grieved over the success of her daughter's novel—it went on to sell 7 million copies—because an identifiable career would put a damper on her chances for marriage (Israel 206). Yet Jaffe's life narrative reads as a chick lit success story. A publishing sector employee in her early twenties, she drew on autobiographical experience to craft a novel that would begin a long and lucrative career. Her fifteen novels and one children's book have sold more than 32 million copies worldwide, with The *Best of Everything* being adapted as a movie featuring Joan Crawford as Caroline's tyrannical boss. Jaffe's writing enabled her to directly support the production of women-authored literature: The Rona Jaffe Foundation, which she established in 1994, annually offers literary grants to American female writers.

A harbinger of the sexual revolution and figurative how-to guide to the best of everything, Helen Gurley Brown's *Sex and the Single Girl* (1962) stands, in title and spirit, as a foundational predecessor to the chick lit genre. Its reprint by Barricade Books in 2003 restyled the original cover to appear as a chick lit self-help tome: a woman's full and fuchsia lips appear on a hot pink-and-yellow background, the front cover proclaiming, "Before there was *Sex and the City* there was. . . ." On the back cover, a blurb from *Sex and the City*'s Kim Cattrall attests to its influence on her life, mind, and libido. The bombshell classic, on best-seller lists for a year, has been published in twenty-eight countries and has been translated into sixteen languages. *Sex and the Single Girl*, published three years before Brown began her thirty-two-year reign as *Cosmopolitan*'s editor in chief, was also made into a movie starring Natalie Wood and Tony Curtis. Its matter-of-fact frankness, particularly its discussions of premarital sex and affairs with married men, was found shocking. Risqué aspects aside, its rejection of the cultural myth that every girl must be married and its directives for having a fulfilling and romantic, if not enviable, life as a single woman underlie chick lit. Thousands found Brown's central message and sassy prose style a welcome contrast to Betty Friedan's best-selling feminist classic *The Feminine Mystique* (1963), which, published shortly afterward, disclosed the suburban malaise beleaguering white middle-class housewives.

Some aspects of *Sex and the Single Girl* are now outdated; for instance, quoted salary figures are those of the 1960s, while Brown's take on gay men—living in "an arrested state of sexual development" and bearing "tremendous emotional problems, which presumably respond the least of any to psychoanalysis"—at the very least unenlightened (30). Brown's penchant for italicizing—"And can you think of *anybody* who needs her glossy hair, waxen skin, stalwart nails, shiny eyes, peachy cheeks . . . *more* than a single woman? What you eat has only just *everything* to do with them"—comes off as a hard sell, if not annoyingly emphatic (167). Yet chapters devoted to the practicalities of apartment furnishing, wardrobe selection, and financial management still read as highly contemporary. So too does Brown's assertion that the single woman is "the newest glamour girl of our times," with the chick lit phenomenon signaling a broader cultural moment in the status of career women, a new wave to what Brown identified forty years earlier (5).

Brown's life, like that of her contemporary Rona Jaffe, reveals a nearly mythic success story with Brown a chick lit heroine archetype. She was born in 1922 in rural Arkansas to two schoolteachers; her father died when she was ten, and treatment for her sister Mary's polio quickly devoured the insurance money. In the 1940s she answered fan mail at a radio station for six dollars a week while learning shorthand. She worked seventeen jobs before becoming a secretary to an advertising executive who later let her write copy, and she quickly rose to the ranks of the country's highest-paid ad copywriters in the early 1960s. She married for the first time at thirty-seven to motion picture producer David Brown, whose best-known credits include *The Sting*, *Jaws*, *A Few Good Men*, and *Driving Miss Daisy*. (Of course, as Whelehan has astutely noted, the fact that Brown's platform of the wife of a top movie producer ironically enabled her affirmation of aspects of singleness for women to be taken seriously [30].) *Sex and the Single Girl*'s second paragraph informs us that the pair has two Mercedes, one hundred acres of virgin forest near San Francisco, a Mediterranean house overlooking the Pacific, and a full-time maid. Paragraph three shifts gears by emphasizing her lack of remarkable qualities, a profile summed up in her term "mouseburger": like many of the genre's protagonists, "not beautiful, or even pretty," "not bosomy or brilliant" (3). In spite of a self-confessed severe case of acne, her prodigious work ethic and sense of style led her to both personal and professional success. Besides leading a jet-set life for four decades with her husband, she increased *Cosmopolitan*'s circulation from 750,000 to 3 million. In 1988, she was inducted into the Publishers Hall of Fame and was listed five times by *World Almanac* as one of the twenty-five most influential women in the United States. Brown developed *Cosmopolitan* into today's best-selling magazine on college campuses and the best-selling monthly periodical on the newsstand. After passing the U.S. edition's editorial torch to Bonnie Fuller in 1996, she became editor in chief of its fifty-nine international editions, a position she still holds today.

    Cosmopolitan's current editor in chief, Kate White, author of the best-selling career guide *Why Good Girls Don't Get Ahead—but Gutsy Girls Do*, extends Brown's legacy to the chick lit genre. Born in 1950, White got one of her biggest breaks in her twenties when she was a junior writer at *Glamour* in charge of turning out short pieces for a section called The How to Do Anything Better Guide. A former editor in chief of *McCall's*, *Child*, *Working Woman*, and *Redbook*, she started her career at *Glamour* after winning its Top Ten College Women Competition. In order to establish herself as an important player in the editorial department, White realized she needed to write a major feature. Most of the articles in *Glamour* at the time were reporting pieces along the lines of "Dating and Mating: How Much Have the Rules Changed?" (White, *Why Good Girls* 48). Yet she decided to try to break the mold with an essay, the genre and its first-person voice not standard in women's magazines of the mid-1970s. Seriocomic and autobiographical, it related her thoughts on living as a single woman in a shabby apartment in New York, her often lackluster social life, and her vulnerability, sometimes terror, in living alone in the city. After it appeared she received dozens of letters from readers who instantly connected with the piece, and the managing editor gave her carte blanche in her choice of essay topics. Its success foreshadowed not only chick lit appeal but also White's natural flair as one of its admired authors—in 2002, White's debut novel, *If Looks Could Kill,* described by *Publishers Weekly* as "Bridget Jones meets Nancy Drew," began her best-selling Bailey Weggins murder mystery series.

Brown's mixed take on the status of living single parallels the chick lit genre's tug-of-war between liberal feminism—its tenets of autonomy, choice, and control—and the desire for conventionality, security, and routine. In the introduction to *Sex and the Single Girl*'s reprint, Brown exhorts women to get over "celebrity bank-account envy or trying to acquire capital through his" and advises women to ask for raises as well as allocate earnings into an IRA, mutual fund, and savings account (xviii). This proactive approach to financial responsibility and wealth is depicted, however, as hardly glamorous: the next paragraph tells of a CEO of a small electronics firm who confides to Brown that she is stretched so thin from being a dynamo that she is thinking of announcing a baby that she won't really have—an "escape baby," as she puts it—so she can go home, care for two children already there, and live like a normal human being. Chick lit, like Brown's nod to the glamour novel's figure of the successful climber, addresses a larger fallout moment in the women's movement. While many protagonists acquire their own column or receive promotions, career advancement without adult human intimacy—or, ideally, the resolution of romantic longing—leaves characters half full. With heroines caught between suburban domesticity and liberal feminist ideals of androgyny that no longer appeal, self-deprecating humor is offered as the interim solution.

Ramifications of the Chick Lit Label

Journalists' attempts to establish a canonical lineage for the chick lit genre have often evoked the ire of fiction writers who maintain that the "proto–chick lit" label assesses their work inadequately. Erica Jong's landmark novel *Fear of Flying* (1973) earned her the "mother of chick lit" title in a *New York Times Book Review* article commemorating the novel's thirtieth birthday and New American Library anniversary edition release. In print in twenty-seven languages, Jong's best-known work has sold over 12 million copies globally. Yet the author adamantly rejects the chick lit label, denouncing the genre in a *Newsday* interview as "nothing more than the contemporary version of the 'How to Get Married Novel' invented by Charlotte Bronte and Jane Austen—and done much better by them (needless to say)" (Jacobson).¹⁰ While *Fear of Flying*, she maintains, "details the disappointments of marriage and the search for freedom and individuality," chick lit, in contrast, is "a retro form that details the search for and nabbing of a husband, any husband." Today's twenty- and thirtysomething women, she declares, are looking for the antithesis of what their mothers looked for: "Their mothers sought freedom; they seek slavery. They want The Ring, The White Wedding, The Bugaboo Frog Stroller." (The comparison is interesting in light of her daughter Molly Jong-Fast's writing; author of the autobiographical novel *Normal Girl* [2001], she penned in 2004 a personal essay series for *Modern Bride*.) Many chick lit protagonists are fixated on matrimony, yet the novels involve a larger search for identity beyond a male love interest. Nevertheless, the connections between Jong's 1970s classic and the newer genre are not entirely improbable. Twenty-nine-year-old Isadora Wing's "contradictory itches" and her status as a budding writer invite parallels (11); so too do the text's first-person narration, frankly nonprocreative sexuality, and confessional mode.

Jong is but one of many writers whose work has retroactively received the chick lit label now that naming established authors as chick lit elders has become a media trend. Numerous chick lit novelists have cited Jane Eyre as a paradigmatic heroine—she is ordinary looking, she falls in love with her boss—but do not take into account Rochester's attempted bigamy or his maltreatment of his confined West Indian wife. (Jane, a textbook match with readers' identification with an everywoman, is a reoccurring name in the genre.)¹¹ Less innocuously, *New York Times* critic Janet Maslin named Larry McMurtry the "father" of chick lit, as his novel *Terms of Endearment* (1975) and its hit film adaptation anticipated the Bridget Jones heroine. In his novel *Loop Group* (2004), sexagenarian women spout chick lit aphorisms—and clichéd at that: "It's not about age, it's about attitude," declares the protagonist's travel companion. In a July 2005 *New York Times* feature article by Felicia Lee on popular black women writers, novelists Terry McMillan, Connie Briscoe, and Benilde Little were dubbed "midwives of chick lit." In the article McMillan laments that too many publishers have used her phenomenal sales as a yardstick to judge emerging women writers, asking them to write novels like her megahit and critically acclaimed *Waiting to Exhale* (1992). This replication hampers them, she says, from developing their own style and stories. Further, for McMillan, Briscoe, and Little, in their fifties, chick lit's man-chasing focus does not reflect where they are in life. McMillan herself passionately detests the term *chick lit*, calling it a cheap shot, "because most women writers write about the heart and matters of the heart, and that can encompass a lot of things." McMillan argues her work carries a more universal significance by setting it against the traditional version of the chick lit formula.[12]

Naming texts as chick lit prototypes or analogues can perpetuate misreadings, add undue importance to factual elements (such as the narrator's or protagonist's being a young female), and homogenize tonal differences. An Amazon.com list, "Girl Time! Great Chick Lit and Movies," by Florida-based "Allison" seems to dub works as chick lit primarily because of the central character's gender, no matter whether the text is a comedy or tragedy. The list includes novels by best-selling authors Sophie Kinsella, Lauren Weisberger, and Emily Giffin alongside literary fiction such as Tolstoy's *Anna Karenina* (1873–1877), an Oprah's Book Club pick, and thus straddling the realm of the literary and popular, but more significantly, a novel whose titular protagonist commits suicide by throwing herself in the path of a train. Also featured is Ian McEwan's *Atonement* (2001), whose protagonist's complicity in a false rape accusation leads to her sister's and her lover's deaths in World War II. Another item, Alice Sebold's bestseller *The Lovely Bones* (2002), employs a first-person omniscient narrator addressing the reader from heaven to retell the details and aftermath of her rape, murder, and dismemberment by a neighbor at fourteen. The inclusion of Nobel Prize–winner Gabriel García Márquez's *Love in the Time of Cholera* (1985) may also raise an eyebrow: the suicides of two secondary characters bracket the novel, and it carries the less-than-upbeat idea that lovesickness is a literal malady, an affliction comparable to cholera. Its well-developed protagonist, Fermina Daza, and her romantic reunion in old age with a suitor she once rejected in her youth, could conceivably qualify the novel as "hen lit." All in all, still macabre stimuli for "Girl Time!"

Employing a bit more uniform criteria for selection, the Amazon.com list "Great 'Chick Lit' Fiction for Black Womyn" by "renaynay," a self-professed "Avid Reader and Chick Lit Expert" includes seventeen items by black women authors. The majority of the titles involve a protagonist coming to terms with her lesbian identity, where the coming-of-age story is overlapped with the coming-out narrative. Others, like Ann Allen Shockley's *Loving Her,* tell a tragic story about same-sex interracial love between a black musician and a white writer. The list's alignment of the selected work with chick lit is odd given that very few chick lit novels feature lesbian characters, and imprints such as RDI do not yet consider manuscripts with lesbian protagonists.[13] The list is, granted, well meaning, and while more of a recommended prowomen reading list than a scholarly comment, its inclusion of Audre Lorde's *Zami: A New Spelling of My Name* (1982), a second-wave feminist classic, would raise eyebrows among many feminist and queer studies scholars. A popular selection for Introduction to Women's Studies, Lorde's memoir explores the intersections of race, class, and sexual orientation in a manner chick lit has not been able to do in a trenchant or sustained way. While not grave in tone, neither is it humorous. The "biomythography" employs mythmaking to affirm the protagonist's search for origins and the creation of a symbolic genealogy: she renames herself *Zami,* a word from Grenada's Isle of Carriacou for women who work together as friends and lovers. Though scenes of female bonding and friendship communities are plentiful in chick lit, the genre is, at present, homosocial and not lesbian.

While canonical works have been retroactively labeled chick lit, new fiction by women is sometimes erroneously classified as such, whether through blurbs or cover art, in an effort to take advantage of the genre's popularity. As publishers scurry to cash in on variants of *Bridget Jones's Diary,* recent fiction by women is sometimes inappropriately pegged. Publishers' opportunism, argues Margaret Weigel in a *Women's Review of Books* review essay on recent novels by women, will leave a "non-Bridget nugget of a story" overlooked in the "general gold rush" or, yet worse, "force [novels] to dress up in Jones's clothes" to be enlisted as "foot soldiers in the *Bridget* army" (34). Such is the case with Stephanie Lehmann's *Thoughts on Having Sex* (2003). While its protagonist attempts to cope with the memory of her older sister's suicide, it is classed among the *Bridgets* because, like Laura Zigman's *Animal Husbandry* (1998), it explores the fallout of a significant sexual relationship. For all its disparagement by journalists, chick lit has increasingly become the yardstick by which women's novels, particularly debut novels, are measured. Weigel's generic neologism "anti-Bridget," in an attempt to distinguish new literature from formula fiction, ultimately concedes this classificatory trend.

Older women writers such as Beryl Bainbridge and Doris Lessing have publicly decried chick lit as George Eliot dismissed her century's contemporary romance fiction—their condescension toward popular fiction aims to prevent their own novels from being classed one day as beach reading. As chick lit has expanded to portray women of color as well as married, divorced, and widowed protagonists, its wider inclusion may compromise the canonical standing of other women-oriented texts. Amazon.com lists' liberal naming of chick lit elders at worst implies that the term *chick lit* may be cycling back to its original usage of twenty years ago. Chick lit has inspired reprints of best-sellers like Helen Gurley Brown's *Sex and the Single Girl* (1962), yet the edition's chick lit cover art—a woman's fuchsia lips on a hot pink-and-yellow background—many would find inappropriate on women-centered works like *The Color Purple* or *The Women of Brewster Place,* two titles the Amazon.com list mentions. While we wish to keep in mind Rita Felski's assertion that, "given the diversity of feminist positions, it is in fact impossible to draw any once-and-for-all line between the 'feminist' and 'woman-centered' text," we need to exercise discernment in claiming titles as chick lit because they are female-oriented, employ first-person narration, or are set in a city (132). Chick lit should be viewed primarily as a comedic genre deliberately written for women, whose light-heartedness and optimism upstage social criticisms.

Chick lit's general status—or lack thereof—as entertainment reading frustrates the feminist critic who hoped the genre would not just reflect but transform society. The genre will not provide feminism's "fourth wave." Nor will it provide prize fiction. At this juncture, chick lit has transitioned from an offshoot of the 1990s American literary avant-garde to entertainment reading characterized by a vigorous interchange with media and consumer forms. Its success affirms the permanence of light reading with vicarious wish fulfillment its modus operandi.

5 Theorizing Postfeminist Fictions of Development

Paradoxically, then, the term [*postfeminism*] signals both failure and success, both an anti-feminist critique of the misguidedness of feminism and a pro-feminist nod to feminism's victories.

—Astrid Henry, *Not My Mother's Sister: Generational Conflict and Third-Wave Feminism*

ALTHOUGH Cris Mazza and Jeffrey DeShell did not intend to promote the commercial, entertainment reading now associated with the label "chick lit," their anthology title, *Chick-Lit: Postfeminist Fiction* (1995), abetted the practice of interpreting mainstream chick lit as a pointer to a postfeminist age. This volume of contemporary American women's avant-garde fiction directly inspired theoretical formulations of postfeminism and catalyzed media coverage that would attach the unhyphenated *chick lit* to this milieu. A review of the anthology by journalist Margaret Quamme highlights, if by reverting to stereotypes, icons germane to three conceptual phases of women's history:

PREFEMINISM	FEMINISM	POSTFEMINISM
kitchen	protest march	psychiatrist's office
shirtwaists	power suits	lots of leather
white rice	brown rice	sushi
Donna Reed	Gloria Steinem	Madonna
I Remember Mama	My Mama, My Self	Deconstructing Mamma
man and woman	woman and woman	man/woman
romantic	heroic	ironic (Quamme 6G)

From this key-word register, one glimpses that postfeminism retains second-wave feminism's desire for empowerment while distancing itself from the second wave's rally for collective and public political action. The list item "Deconstructing Mamma" hints at the influence of postmodern theory, especially its characteristic pastiche on postfeminism. The entry "irony," while surely not associated exclusively with postmodernism, is often a trait. Still, Quamme's list of key words, while an intriguing start, leaves the theorist much wanting for clarity.

The appearance of the terms *chick lit* and *postfeminist* in the title of Mazza and DeShell's anthology, however, may have led commentators to ascribe the term to what would become the mainstream fiction form. The most salient example is journalist James Wolcott's and *New Yorker* editorial "Hear Me Purr: Maureen Dowd and the Rise of Postfeminist Chick Lit" (1996). By naming his editorial this way, Wolcott manipulated the anthology title, as discussed in chapter 1, to suggest to the New York literary scene the idea that postfeminism can be found in mainstream chick lit and that chick lit is a condition of postfeminism. Wolcott's derisive title and his scorn for what he calls the "flirtational" type of voice found in recent women's journalism initiated the judgment of chick lit as a manifestation of a decline of the fighting type of feminism, particularly, its unhesitating assertion and debate. In this shift from feminism to postfeminism, Wolcott maintains, the old polemical edge, argumentative zest, and sense of political seriousness were exchanged for cuteness and a nearly desperate affirmation of desirability.

Because Wolcott attempted to discredit the original artistic and social intent of the anthology, I wish to note several important differences in the two types of chick lit. The edgy and in some instances sardonic quality of the narrators in Mazza and DeShell's anthology differs significantly from the confused though upbeat temper of the commercial counterpart. While the experimental volume featured a wide gamut of sexual and bodily acts, mainstream chick lit's representations of female sexuality are largely heterosexual. Both types of women's writing reject or complicate the figure of the Superwoman, yet the original version does not share commercial chick lit's capitulation to the marriage plot and investment in romantic ideology. Although both strands of chick lit repudiate identification with "victim" or separatist politics, the original version does not supply a prototype for the chick lit protagonist's gravitation toward fine consumables and profligate tendencies. This "second wave" of chick lit has reached wider audiences in part because of its greater proximity to conventions of mass fiction, such as verisimilitude, chapter demarcations, and linear plotting.

In a gesture analogous to Quamme's use of Mazza and DeShell's anthology to name signifiers of a postfeminist milieu, I wish to examine chick lit as an implicit commentary on feminism's gains and deficiencies. This aim, I should point out, has been identified as a postfeminist theoretical practice (Yaszek 3). Postfeminist theory attempts to make sense of feminism's legacy and blind spots to identify an epistemological shift, to mark a new theoretical juncture, or to arrive at a blueprint for the future. In productive frictions between ties to the romance and the bildungsroman's emphasis on individuation, chick lit yields social observations that work concomitantly with feminist philosophy and critical heterosexuality studies. This variance between autonomous development and heterosexual coupling, monetary gain and romantic sentiment, is a classic female dilemma as well as a locus of postfeminist affect. Through chick lit, we can glean that postfeminism is not so much a social agenda or critique of power hierarchies but operates instead through defamiliarization. Postfeminism maintains a more ambivalent view on independence than second-wave feminism and, in its most historically recent manifestation, is propelled by twenty- and thirtysomething women negotiating the tensions between feminism and femininity. Chick lit replicates in its formal structures and generic amalgamations the quandary of multiple and contradictory meanings confronted in a taxonomy of postfeminism.

Historicizing Postfeminism

While we can discern how the term *postfeminism* originally came to be attached to chick lit, the theoretical implications of the term are more slippery. The multiple and contradictory meanings ascribed to postfeminism reflect feminism's growth beyond a unified political agenda and its fracturing into competing, sometimes antagonistic, strands. The *OED* definition isn't especially helpful; the term, hyphenated, is defined as "an ethos of the period following the feminism (and improvement in women's status) of the 1960s and 1970s, characterized by further development of or reaction against feminism, especially in acceptance of masculine ideals or of aspects of the traditional feminine role." The definition allows for a reading of postfeminism as both an extension of second-wave feminism and a backlash, though connoting the reconsolidation of a separate-sphere mindset.

While theorists Sophia Phoca and Rebecca Wright (1999) suggest that postfeminism should not be seen as a distinct ideology but instead part of an evolution of the search for a discourse to express sexuality identity, many scholars of postfeminism themselves admit an understanding of the term and its purpose has been less than satisfactory (170–71). In her essay "'I'll be a postfeminist in a postpatriarchy,' or, Can We Really Imagine Life after Feminism?" (2005)—its title quoting a familiar bumper sticker slogan in New Zealand in the mid-1970s—Lisa Yaszek begins by confiding that postfeminism's meaning has been "somewhat hazy" for many thinkers, even college-level instructors of gender studies such as herself.[1] Yaszek wished to gain a more nuanced understanding of postfeminism's meanings when invited by *Electronic Book Review* to contribute an essay theorizing postfeminist writing, so she began by attempting to locate the term's primary use. Yaszek encountered in the course of the research seven origin stories. Her delineation of postfeminism's meanings reveals that while the 1990s saw the rise and popularization of the term in both the media and the academy, periods of postfeminism have both predated second-wave feminism and flourished with "third-wave" feminism.[2]

Because confusion may exist between postfeminism and the "third" wave, and these two moments in social history share some overlap, a delineation of the latter term is useful. Third-wave writing has been largely the product of women under thirty-five who are sometimes referred to as "the New Feminists." The phrase "third-wave feminism" was initially used in a *Ms.* magazine editorial written by Rebecca Walker, the daughter of Alice Walker, in 1992. (Walker is also a founding member of the Third Wave Foundation, a national activist, philanthropic organization for girls and women ages fifteen to thirty, established in 1996.) In an interview with Sangamithra Iyer, Walker contends that she and her cofounders (Catherine Gund, Dawn Lundy Martin, and Amy Richards) were responding to critiques of the second wave with the goal of greater diversity, insisting also that social change agents should be remunerated for their labor to prevent burnout and to cultivate young women to be in a position to be philanthropists themselves. On this emphasis of inclusiveness in the organization, she states, "It was important to us . . . that Third Wave be, at its very core, multi-racial, multi-ethnic, multi-issue, pan–sexual orientation, with people and issues from all socio-economic backgrounds represented." The third wave's best-known works are Walker's anthology *To Be Real: Telling the Truth and the Changing Face of Feminism* (1995), Merri Lisa Johnson's edited collection *Jane Sexes It Up: True Confessions of Feminist Desire* (2002), Paula Kamen's *Her Way: Young Women Remake the Sexual Revolution* (2002), Naomi Wolf's *Fire with Fire: The New Female Power and How It Will Change the 21st Century* (1993) and *Promiscuities: The Secret Struggle for Womanhood* (1997), Susie Bright's *Sexual State of the Union* (1997), and Jennifer Baumgardner and Amy Richards's *Manifesta: Young Women, Feminism, and the Future* (2000). This phase of feminism exhorts women to seize their sexual power in a way that is individualist, not for the purposes of serving a feminist or political agenda. Unlike radical feminism, it does not see heterosexual and feminist as incompatible identities and distances itself from the theoretical formulations of heterosexuality put forward by antipornography feminists such as Andrea Dworkin and Catherine MacKinnon.

The third wave perceives itself as more voluptuous, more unapologetically libidinous than its second-wave mothers and, like the chick lit protagonist, aims to manipulate power to its advantage within the dominant social system as opposed to the radical feminist advocacy of a separatist culture. Chick lit's insistence on the right to female sexual pleasure dovetails with the third wave's prosex attitudes. Third-wave thinkers, zealous to affirm their sexual appetite and command, do not sufficiently acknowledge theories of women's capacity for pleasure, as seen, for instance, in the manifesto-type writings of French philosophers Hélène Cixous and Luce

Irigaray. The third wave should be seen not as a stage prior to postfeminism but as recent feminist nonfiction produced by social theorists. In the third wave's value system, popular culture is not inherently an instrument of female objectification and patriarchal control; on the contrary, writers look to pop culture as a way to make sense of their lives. The third wave dovetails with the chick lit protagonist's critique of and simultaneous fascination with popular media as well as her attempt to acquire power through the skillful production of popular media itself.

The third wave identifies itself as part of feminism's ongoing struggle to address gender inequality even if it achieves this in part by distancing itself from earlier feminisms. While it does not, unlike chick lit, eschew *feminism* as a label (Walker, though, prefers instead "the movement for the eradication of discrimination based on gender difference," as feminism, she believes, no longer galvanizes or unifies ["Riding"]), the third wave's sense of the second wave as out of date is consistent with postfeminism. While it may problematize aspects of previous feminisms, it still acknowledges itself as a daughter, if with the caveat that many women of color do not feel an affinity with the term *feminism* and are reluctant to embrace the position of woman as victim.

To return to the chronology of postfeminism itself, in what might be the first documented use, an American women's literary group called "Judy" described itself as "post-feminist" in 1919, and articulated in its journal the term's philosophy: "We're interested in people now—not men and women" (qtd. in Henry 19, 190n11). This meaning, its call to focus on human sociology, may be the first instance of the prefix *post* employed to point to a temporality after feminism. *Postfeminism* in this context denotes an era when feminism is no longed needed precisely because its goals have been accomplished (Henry 19). This denotation complements an origin story that Yaszek reports, one that erroneously claims the term *postfeminism* first appeared in the *New York Times Sunday Magazine* during the mid-1970s, where it celebrated women's newfound equality in the public sphere and the completion of all feminist reform. Along these lines, the term *postfeminism* has frequently signified periods when feminism and women's movements are in decline or abeyance. In "Notes on Post-Feminism" (1982), one of the earliest theoretical investigations of postfeminism written in English, Mary Russo identifies this cultural shift in the writings of Julia Kristeva, a Bulgarian-born philosopher and major "French feminist," though she herself does not identify with this tag, and Maria-Antonietta Macciocchi, a Parisian-based intellectual and prominent member of the Italian Communist party. Coming out of France in the late 1970s and affected by the student revolutionary movement of 1968, continental postfeminism perceives the women's movement as orthodox and narrow and advocates a more fluid economy to transcend identity politics grounded in biological gender. A distrust of binary oppositions (especially that of male-female, the basis arguably of second-wave feminism) as well as a deconstruction of the concept of "patriarchy" characterizes postfeminism and link it to postmodernism in the latter's scrutiny of master narratives.

The idea of postfeminism as signaling an end of feminism is not necessarily indicative, though, of failure, nor does it suggest that feminism is passé. Postfeminism, as the New Zealand theorist Ann Brooks (1994) contends, expounds on feminism's interstitial quality with elements of cultural theory, its intersection with postmodernism, poststructuralism, and psychoanalytic theory, as well as with the theoretical and political debates around postcolonialism, with the goal to "establish a multivocalism for both feminist theorists and practitioners" (188). Postfeminism, for some theorists, is not a wholesale rejection of second-wave feminism but instead the current state of feminist thinking—the culmination of a number of debates within and outside feminism (7). Conversely, some theorists deem the practice of identifying a postfeminist milieu a deliberate strategy to counteract and dismiss the achievements of the women's movement. Tania Modleski begins her book *Feminism Without Women: Culture and Criticism in a "Postfeminist" Age* (1991) with a reading of a 1987 *New York Times Magazine* article, "Literary Feminism Comes of Age," to argue that texts proclaiming or assuming the advent of postfeminism are really engaged in undermining the feminist project. For Modleski, postfeminism is characterized by male literary and cultural critics' appropriation of the female subject position for reactionary purposes (3). Modleski theorizes postfeminism, then, as a type of misogyny intended to direct American society back to a prefeminist world.

Postfeminism has also been theorized as a marketing scheme, one pitching a feminism à la carte, so to speak, and often targeting a young demographic. In their article "Work, Family, and Social Class in Television Images of Women: Prime-Time Television and the Construction of Postfeminism" (1993), Andrea Press and Terry Strathman analyze the representation of women in popular television programs such as *The Cosby Show* (1984–1992), *L.A. Law* (1986–1994), and *Designing Women* (1986–1993) to discern that "mass media's commercial packagings sandwich whatever thin slices of feminism might survive in the finished product between thicker slices of commercial femininity" (11). Postfeminism, seeing capitalism as a vehicle for self-fashioning, aligns itself, some theorists maintain, with consumption targeted at girls. Since the 1990s it has facilitated the emergence of girl discourse, manifested, for example, in the commodified girl hero. This discourse, Sarah Projansky (2007) contends, "contributes to and sustains postfeminism," as its turning toward girls is a means to keep postfeminism fresh in the context of corporate commodity culture (44, 46). Consumption (and its cousin, leisure) is central to postfeminism as a strategy and to some degree its connection with liberal feminism's tenet of personal choice.

In one of the most sophisticated analyses of postfeminism, Yvonne Tasker and Diane Negra (2007) identify the following mechanisms and shortcomings of postfeminism, a formulation they perceive as white and middle class by default: as postfeminism "commodif[ies] feminism via the figure of the woman as empowered consumer," it "tends to confuse self-interest with individuality and elevates consumption as a strategy for healing those dissatisfactions that might alternately be understood in terms of social ills and discontents" (2). While one may certainly wish to press harder on their assertion that a penchant for consumption is limited to white, middle-class women, Tasker and Negra are not alone in highlighting postfeminism as "presiding over an aggressive mainstreaming of elaborate and expensive beauty treatments" (3). Drawing women further into commercial culture by commodifying wrinkle-, cellulite-, hair-free sleekness as a type of benchmark, postfeminist media market this aesthetic as the contemporary standard of female middle-class presentation.

The term, then, has had positive, negative, and neutral meanings in popular and scholarly discourses. Though first used in a women's literary group's revised mission statement to mark a shift in interest from binary formulations of gender to liberal individualism, *postfeminism* has been utilized to signify temporal economies suggesting the completion, suspension, or waning purpose of earlier feminism as well as a futuristic sense of going beyond it.

From Journalism to Autobiographical Fiction: Chick Lit as Postfeminist Memoir

In a Women's National Book Association panel, Sessalee Hensley, head fiction buyer for Barnes and Noble stores, has said of chick lit, "If it was serious it wouldn't be chick lit. It would be memoir."[3] This distinction, while exaggerated, points not only to the humorous function of chick lit but also to the high frequency of autobiographical parallels between author and character. For example, Michelle Curry Wright's desire for a different life after indulging career dreams in New York led her to the flat southwestern plain of Telluride, Colorado, where she has resided for more than twenty years. Similarly, the titular protagonist of her second novel, *Miranda Blue Calling* (2004), leaves behind the frenetic pace of New York City for the small town of Otnip, Colorado. The protagonist of *The Girl Most Likely* (2003) has a Vegas marriage, returns home to Australia to pack up, but ends up very quickly separating from her husband, then to move back in with her parents and attempt to recalibrate—experiences all shared by its author, Rebecca Sparrow. The name of the protagonist of *Getting over Jack Wagner* (2003), Eliza, echoes that of author Elise Juska. The female friendship circle of Jennifer Weiner's *Little Earthquakes* (2004) was based in part on the author's own experiences with her prenatal yoga classmates. The protagonist of *The Perfect Manhattan* (2005) is a bartender in Manhattan and the Hamptons, the cash flow occupation of authors Leanne Shear, a journalist, and Tracey Toomey, an actress. The writing team met their literary agent, in fact, while tending bar. In this way chick lit complements the assertion of the protagonist of Lessing's *The Golden Notebook* that "literature is analysis after the event" (196).

Sarah Mlynowski, who wrote at the age of twenty-three *Milkrun* (2001), a novel with a twenty-four-year-old heroine, confides, "My friends are in their mid-twenties, I date guys in their mid-twenties, my financial and relationship concerns are those of someone in her mid-twenties" (qtd. in Carlyle, "Have Dress"). Paratexts often draw attention to similar author-protagonist parallels. The front matter of Karen Templeton's *Loose Screws* (2002) acknowledges that the author's twentysomething years in New York City provided fodder for her protagonist's experiences. *Diary of a Mad Bride* (2002) and *Diary of a Mad Mom-to-Be* (2003) author Laura Wolf admits to sharing with her creation Amy Thomas the compulsive writing of to-do lists. Observing that the author bios of chick lit texts emphasize the similarities between the authors, and their characters, Caroline Smith points out that Melissa Bank (*The Girls' Guide to Hunting and Fishing* [1999]) highlights her single status, noting that she "lives in New York City with her Labrador Retriever, Maybelline" (*Cosmopolitan Culture* [2008] 6–7). Kayla Perrin, a *USA Today* best-selling novelist, makes no pretense as to a real distinction between author and protagonist, affirming frankly, "The chick-lit heroine is me" (Baratz-Logsted 75).

Many chick lit novels exhibit overlap between the protagonist's occupation and the career history of their authors and thereby offer figurative reportage acquired from the production of factual reports. Sarah Dunn, author of *The Big Love* (2004), was a columnist for Philadelphia's *City Paper* and was raised as a born-again Christian; her protagonist is a columnist for the fictional alternative newspaper the *Philadelphia Times* who struggles with integrating her evangelical Christian upbringing into her premarital sexual relationships. Alisa Valdes-Rodriguez, author of the international best-seller *The Dirty Girls Social Club* (2003), was a staff writer for the Calendar section of the *Los Angeles Times*, where she was the first American reporter to cover the Latin music industry as a full-time beat and was twice nominated for a Pulitzer Prize in feature writing; the novel presents a Latina reporter. Anna Maxted was a consistent contributor for the British edition of *Cosmopolitan*, writing articles in the late 1990s, before publishing *Getting Over It* (2000), a novel with a protagonist who works for a teen magazine (C. Smith, *Cosmopolitan Culture* [2008], 9,147n18). Jasmin Rosemberg, author of *How the Other Half Hamptons* (2008), bases her novel on the Hamptons sharehouse column she penned weekly for the *New York Post*. Kavita Daswani has worked as a fashion journalist and editor; the protagonist of *The Village Bride of Beverly Hills* (2004) works her way up from receptionist at a celebrity gossip magazine to a staff reporter with a regular interview feature, while the protagonist of her debut novel, *For Matrimonial Purposes* (2003), is in the PR area of the New York fashion industry.

In convincing the protagonist to commit to a pseudonymous column on male sexual inconstancy, a character in Laura Zigman's *Animal Husbandry* anticipates the success of chick lit authors who were former journalists: "It's the ultimate revenge fantasy. You get rich and famous writing about something you're already obsessed with. If nothing else it'll be cathartic"

(223). This assertion finds a case study in author Sophie Kinsella (1969–). A philosophy and economics graduate from Oxford University, Kinsella, previously "Madeleine Wickham," was working as a financial journalist on a pensions magazine when she wrote her first novel, *The Tennis Party* (1995). She adopted the name Sophie Kinsella to complement the effervescent, faster-paced novel *Confessions of a Shopaholic* (2000). *Confessions* has since spawned a series that to date consists of five novels, has sold more than 13 million copies, and has been translated into more than thirty languages. It features a protagonist who, in the first volume, works as a finance writer. Kinsella, with her behavioral proximity to her characters, appears to play a *fort-da* game between biographical history and media persona. The back cover bio for *Confessions of a Shopaholic* notes Kinsella's status as a former financial journalist, the heroine's occupation, and asserts that the author has an "excellent" relationship with her bank manager, as she is "very, very careful with her money and only occasionally finds herself queuing for a sale." The acknowledgments immediately preceding the back cover, however, express gratitude toward a friend who taught Kinsella how to shop. Thus, Kinsella employs paratextual elements to affirm the pleasures of consumption while establishing herself as an experienced finance writer and fiscally responsible adult. Admissions of similarities between author and protagonist are a paratextual trope in the chick lit genre and serve as an amplification of a "relatable" protagonist.

That chick lit novelists are, like their protagonists, often journalists sometimes influences compositional form. For example, Allison Pearson, a columnist for the *Evening Standard*, followed the advice of her editor at the *Daily Telegraph* to write her novel as a column. As she had not written a novel before, the column format helped the working mother of two get started, and after six months she began pulling them together. The product, *I Don't Know How She Does It* (2002), discussed at greater length below, became an international best-seller and "mommy lit" classic. Less acclaimed, Natalie Krinsky's novel *Chloe Does Yale* (2005) reprints excerpts of her sex column written while an undergraduate at Yale. Its protagonist, Chloe Carrington, is a sex columnist for the *Yale Daily News*. The protagonist of Dunn's *The Big Love*, a 2004 *Library Journal* best book pick, interrupts the narrative to apologize on its tenuous transitions: because she is used to writing short columns—like Dunn—in which she keeps everything moving forward, she isn't acclimated to a transition's backward glance.

Chick lit took off in the late 1990s in part as a result of editors' interest in reading fiction with characters in media-related occupations, and sometimes blurbs from publishing titans—such as *Vogue* editor in chief Anna Wintour's endorsements of *Bergdorf Blondes* (2004) and *The Devil Wears Prada* (2003)—work as an editorial stamp of approval. Chick lit's characteristic occupational setting may be a result of following the "write what you know" adage, and as authors publish follow-up novels we may witness heroines' careers branching out. The journalism background of many chick lit authors complements the novels' sociological impulse and in medias res analysis of modern courtship behavior.

In an allusion to the popular second-wave feminist consciousness-raising slogan, Barbara Defoe Whitehead remarks on the genre's focus on the bourgeois individual: "In chick lit, the personal isn't political. It's personal" (*Why There Are No* 45). Whitehead's observation on the "personal" quality of chick lit can be extended to encompass its life-writing function. Novelist Deanna Carlyle compares the functions of reading and writing chick lit to those of violent DVD games for teenage boys, confiding that "the laughter releases hurt, anger and catty competitive feelings about 'getting the guy.'"[4] Generically chick lit may be best appraised as semiautobiographical tales of upper-middle-class urban women; it would not be entirely inappropriate to label chick lit, especially authors' debut works, as "postfeminist memoir." Its emphasis on individual quirks and the process of self-fashioning renders a compendium of semiautobiographical coming-of-age reports.

"The Gorge Factor": Postfeminism and Late Heterosexuality

Some, though not all, of chick lit is distinguished by another overlap between author and character—with respect to physical appearance. That many of authors are above average in appearance and frequently physically resemble their stylish heroines may account in part for critical sneers toward the genre, with journalist Scarlett Thomas's epithet *chickerati* a denigrating testament to their glamour. For instance, Candace Bushnell bears physical resemblance to HBO's Carrie Bradshaw as played by Sarah Jessica Parker (figure 6). Author and screen character share the same initials, lithe body type, fair skin, blue eyes, and medium-length blonde hair.

FIGURE 6. Author
photo of Candace
Bushnell (b. 1959) for
Trading Up (2003),
by Jon Ragel. (Image
supplied by Corbis
Images.)

Jennifer Weiner, herself a large woman, features plus-size heroines in her
first three novels. The cover art of Pamela Ribon's *Why Girls Are Weird*
(2003) features a young woman with pigtails; the "About the Author" notes
tell us that Ribon "has been known to wear pigtails." Christian chick lit
author Kris Billerbeck takes the pattern of authors physically resembling
protagonists to the next level: the novelist's signature colors, bright pink
or lime green, deliberately match her book covers (Cote 13). Such physical
resemblances add a visual texture to such texts' autobiographical quality.

On the other hand, this phenomenon of doppelgangers can be blamed
for promoting the idea that the female author, particularly the debut author,
needs to be glamorous in order to garner positive attention. By extension, the argument arises that publishers' and self-marketing efforts highlight chick lit authors' youth and beauty to bolster mediocre writing. Or
younger women writers of fiction with chick lit themes may feel compelled
to appear as fashionistas. Such is the chosen persona of Bushnell, a former

Vogue contributing editor who maintains friendships with numerous leading designers. At a book party for Bushnell's *Four Blondes* (2000) hosted by Donna Karan in her Manhattan flagship store, the author's attire, a garnet-colored leather-and-cashmere ensemble designed by Karan, matched the one-serving-size red glass bottles of Piper-Heidsieck champagne guests sipped from straws. At a reading and book signing for *Trading Up* held in the Philadelphia Free Library on July 8, 2003, an audience member during the Q&A session asked if the author has summer shoe recommendations, as if Bushnell were Carrie Bradshaw herself, to which Bushnell responded without a blink.

In journalism on chick lit, compliments to the author on her fashion sense seem to stand in for literary praise, with the author's physical persona and consumer choices often receiving the foreground. This pattern has emerged most prominently in writing about Kinsella. For instance, an Associated Press journalist interviewing Kinsella in London for a CNN entertainment section article titled "Confessions of a Shopaholic Enabler" described the then thirty-four-year-old author as possessed of brand savvy commensurate to her fictional Becky Bloomwood: "Kinsella was wearing a flowered summer Cacharel frock, Jasper Conran kitten heel shoes and fondling a light pink leather holdall 'picked up on a European holiday.'" An author photo accompanying the article of Kinsella strolling boutiques in greater London further emphasizes the connections between the protagonist and her creator, who confirmed forays into retail therapy and defended her right to shop: "I once bought a ring I wore for the evening and next day—and never again. . . . I could have drunk some alcohol, I didn't do that; I could have smoked some cigarettes, I didn't do that; I could have taken some narcotics, I didn't do that; or I could have stuffed my face with cholesterol, I didn't do that. I bought a ring, it didn't bankrupt me, it was huge and shiny and at that moment it hit the spot." The defense's parallel construction ironically renders the jewelry purchase a type of druglike fix, a narcotic for the nonuser. In her declaration concerning personal minutiae the author represents herself in the confessional style of the series. In this context, Kinsella's sales success justifies her own consumption, and the chick lit author serves as an endorsing voice for consumerist behavior.

Media descriptions of Kinsella offer an entry point into other narrative patterns in journalism on chick lit. Journalism implying the close behavioral proximity between writer and character sometimes borders on parody in its construction of the female author; it additionally replicates the vicarious wish-fulfillment readers of chick lit expect as stock fare. The following excerpt from a *San Francisco Chronicle* article on Kinsella by Laurel Wellman titled "Confessions of a Queen of Chick Lit," for instance, casts the novelist as stylish and confused like her protagonist, with a comparable shopping appetite:

> I found Sophie Kinsella looking somewhat forlorn, sitting alone on a banquette behind the bar at the Rotunda restaurant, surrounded by what seemed to be her worldly possessions—her tote, her purse, and a Marc Jacobs carrier bag.
>
> "Is that the new Banana Republic coat?" a woman next to her asked, admiringly.
>
> Actually, the coat was Burberry, and it was too heavy for the 70-degree day outside—but Kinsella was . . . partway through her North American book tour, and confessed she hadn't known what to pack for all the different weather she'd faced. Also, [Golden Gate] bridge traffic had meant the usual author's escort hadn't been able to meet her at the airport, so she'd gotten a cab straight to Neiman Marcus and left her suitcase downstairs at the Jo Malone counter.

The description begins by presenting Kinsella as a gauche bag lady, her excess of bags klutzy and style-cramping in an upscale restaurant, where she is found sitting like a wallflower. Yet her stock ascends as the last bag is distinguished as designer, while an external presence validates her coat, which the interviewer reveals to be even more expensive than it seemed on initial observation. The bulky bag toting is symbolically forgiven through the mention of a shopping foray in which the author quickly ditches the luggage. Instead of simply placing it with the store baggage check, she claims it is deposited at a cosmetics counter whose London-based beauty and fragrance products have found in recent years a following among the well heeled. The description of Kinsella appearing lost assuages the descriptions of materialism, while details that close the interview section are crafted to imply that Kinsella exceeds the sum of her accoutrements. Wellman notes her "huge brown eyes," "shoulder-length dark hair," and that Kinsella "didn't seem to be wearing makeup," the latter a compliment to either her art in appearing not made-up or to the fact that she doesn't need any.

Media commentary and author publicity highlighting the chick lit author's appearance, in which looks compete with or upstage any substantial
literary considerations, seem to be part of a wider marketing impetus in
contemporary publishing. "Looks sell books," reports Linton Weeks in
a *Washington Post* article titled "Judged by Their Back Covers": "It's a
closed-door secret in contemporary American publishing, but the word is
getting out."[5] He details a growing "clamor for glamour" as highly competitive booksellers compete for author appearances, readings, and signings. Such attractiveness keeps writers on extensive book tours and assists
at nearly all stages of the publishing process. Novelist Lolita Files, herself physically attractive, concedes in the article that not only do today's
authors have to be salespeople, but they also have to "be sexy," emanating "something that makes people want to know something about them."
Freelance publicist Camille McDuffie echoed Files, frankly stating, "If
the author's great-looking, we've got a better shot at *Glamour* or *GQ*."
And across the Atlantic, British publishers openly admit that the "gorge
factor"—whether a new author is seen as gorgeous or not—has become a
principal consideration in deciding whether a book receives an aggressive
marketing push.[6]

The gorge factor began to receive media attention in 2001 when Helen
Richardson, publicity chief of Orion Books, sparked debate at the London
Book Fair by accusing agents of "touting their new discoveries around
publishers in a well-run beauty pageant" (Gibbons). Her claim came as a
band of elder novelists, led by Deborah Moggach, Margaret Drabble, and
Anita Brookner, chastised the new "ageist and lookist" attitudes among
publishers. A band of young and attractive writers, led by the novelist Nick
Blincoe and united under the designation "the New Puritans," lamented
that they are tired of being marketed as cool and trendy, strategies that
have prevented them from garnering recognition as serious and authentic
voices of their generation. As publishers are seldom giving authors the
luxury of three or four books to find a readership, a culture of promoting photogenic young faces has permeated the industry, with writers being
judged on the number of features they might generate in newspaper and
lifestyle sections.

Even deceased but perennially best-selling authors are not immune. A
New York Times feature titled "Pretty Words, Jane; Would That You Were
Too" reported in April 2007 that Wordsworth Editions, a British publisher,

decided to Photoshop the portrait of Austen by her sister Cassandra, a dour scorning image, but accepted by many Austen scholars as the only portrait taken from life, for the cover of a reissue of a memoir of Austen by her nephew, James Austen-Leigh. Austen "wasn't much of a looker," Helen Trayler, the managing director of Wordsworth, told reporters in Britain. "She's the most inspiring, readable author, but to put her on the cover wouldn't be very inspiring at all." The new image presents a Pre-Raphaelite Austen with cherubic blush and, in the words of the article's author, Charles McGrath, removes "the frumpy headgear [of Cassandra's sketch] and giv[es] Jane some hair extensions." Trayler added that she was also considering making over "George Eliot, who was frumpy, and William Wordsworth, who was pretty hideous." Though McGrath ostensibly perceives Trayler's comments as shocking in their irreverence or at least misguided in their privileging of cover over content, he himself concludes with the assessment that "the dreary spinster of the Cassandra sketch isn't anyone we recognize," suggesting that the airbrushed Austen does better justice to her novels' romantic current.

The increasing emphasis on compulsory glamour has implications beyond publishers' marketing strategies for the chick lit niche. We cannot help but speculate that chick lit's physically attractive female author invites the idea in younger or less experienced writers as well as women writers of different genres that trying their hand at chick lit will imbue them with glamour, sophistication, or sexual desirability. Or interested writers may be discouraged if they do not fit the stylish, youthful chick lit author image. The "gorge factor" is an application of Naomi Wolf's beauty myth—both publisher-directed and self-imposed. While not limited to women authors, it seems requisite for the chick lit circle: I have never encountered an author photo that represents the chick lit novelist as unattractive, even average-looking, or at minimum less than well groomed. We cannot help but wonder if "the gorge factor" is also a condition of late heterosexuality in its discourses of style upstaging content.

Patterns of self- or media representation of the chick lit author raise the question as to whether earlier feminism's lack of a chic aesthetic has become the justification for physical narcissism. A variant of this argument has been introduced by Maureen Dowd in *Are Men Necessary? When Sexes Collide* (2005), a compilation of the Pulitzer Prize–winning journalist's *New York Times* columns. Dowd contends that the women's movement has been overcome by vanity, the aggressive growth of cosmetic dermatology in the past decade, and the media's touting of this industry's potentialities for eternal youth. In her words, "Whether or not American feminism will be defeated by American conservatism, it is incontrovertibly true that American feminism was trumped by American narcissism" (150). Dowd's assertion finds support in that cosmetic surgery in the United States has increased by 846 percent since 1980, with 90 percent of cosmetic-surgery patients female (Essig B10–B11). From the case of chick lit, we can glean that postfeminism replaces the stereotyped physical image of a second-wave feminist—Birkenstocks, unshaved legs, no makeup, natural hair—with that of the glossier working-girl fashionista, her valorization of high heels a decided contrast to earlier feminism's stance toward an instrument of oppression.[7] Along these lines, Debbie Stoller in *The "Bust" Guide to the New Girl Order,* a compendium of *Bust* articles, writes, "Unlike our feminist foremothers, who claimed that makeup was the opiate of the misses, we're positively prochoice when it comes to matters of feminine display" (qtd. in Goldberg). Employing tongue-in-cheek allusions to earlier feminist key words, Stoller in self-confident rhetoric and with a penchant for alliterative/assonant triads makes explicit the link between the new feminism, beautification, and entitlement: "We're well aware, thank you very much, of the beauty myth that's working to keep women obscene and not heard, but we just don't think that transvestites should have all the fun. We love our lipstick, have a passion for polish, and, basically, adore this armor that we call 'fashion.' To us, it's fun, it's feminine, and, in the particular way we flaunt it, it's *definitely* feminist." Chick lit articulates that strands of postfeminism participate in the commodification of femininity, while trying to integrate what Rachel Brownstein in her British literature study *Becoming a Heroine* (1994) differentiates as a "heroine of the mind" as opposed to a "heroine of the body."

"I'm not a feminist, but . . .": The "F-Word" in Chick Lit

Feminism's direct mention in chick lit is infrequent, a fact unsurprising in a genre intended as popular fiction. As we see in *Bridget Jones's Diary* (discussed in chapter 2), *feminism*'s mention is usually derogatory or linked with negative consequences. For example, a beloved Delhi-based sister of the protagonist in *The Village Bride of Beverly Hills* was a women's studies major and volunteers at a battered woman's shelter, but because of her outspoken feminism (and lack of interest in cooking), she is "not even a candidate for wifehood" (180). *Diary of a Mad Bride* (2002) by Laura Wolf treats the minor character of a gender studies major with condescension. The climax of *Neurotica* (1998) by Sue Margolis unmasks the fraudulence of a Harvard feminist academic named Rachel Stern, referred to by the protagonist as "some mad American feminist" (308). Stern, who established her career as an author with a book-length diatribe against cosmetic surgery, receives national publicity for her proadultery tome *The Clitoris-Centered Woman*. The British protagonist, a media professional, confronts her on a TV program and in a bloody brawl outs Stern's earlier elective cosmetic surgery, which is leaked through one of the protagonist's lovers. The feminist's fraud is used to distance the proadultery stance of her book from the protagonist's own adulterous behavior. The protagonist's coming clean about her adultery in a print article is set up as a foil to Stern's breach of integrity. The protagonist, then, attacks a feminist theorist to purge herself of adulterous behavior and resultant guilt.

The characterization of the fictional Stern is a bit dicey: Stern's first book is conceivably on the continuum of critical analyses of the Western female body in contemporary times (the work of Susan Bordo or Emily Martin, for example), but the title of her *The Clitoris-Centered Woman* seems more promasturbatory or homoerotic, like a mainstreaming of radical lesbian feminism, than proadultery. Further, while various feminists and radical feminism in particular, have critiqued marriage as a patriarchal institution, there is nothing especially "feminist" in Stern's advocating adultery.

The mother of the protagonist of *Sex and Sensibility: The Adventures of a Jane Austen Addict* (2005) by Rosemarie Santini is a feminist who writes a book similar to Stern's. In a radical feminist vein, the book exhorts women to leave their husbands. Later it is revealed that this prominent feminist author was abandoned by her husband and has become more a lonely figure than a celebrity author. She is also remembered as a cold mother, with the protagonist confiding that she would call her "silly" and "stupid" when she cried as a child (47). The protagonist's relationship with her mother is vexed but not entirely negative. What is uniformly depicted with disapproval is the mother's sense of style. Her theatrically heavy makeup is atypical of a middle-age feminist, but negative nonetheless; some of the products she uses ("purple-blue eye makeup" and "porcelain pancake") are associated with the 1980s and elderly women (86). Her clothing is a peculiar amalgam of sleaze and retro kitsch, as a "tight red leather skirt" and "low-cut satin top" are paired with a floppy hat (86). It is disclosed that she owns a feathered turban and a tweed skirt decorated with sequins, a wardrobe in general that the protagonist can only "routinely describe . . . as 'odd' " (149). Thus, the mother—and her feminism—are depicted as a sociovisual liability, with postfeminism privileging sleeker models.

At best neutral in its representation of feminism is the chick lit roman à clef *The Nanny Diaries* (2002) by Emma McLaughlin and Nicola Kraus. A scene chronicling the protagonist's attempt to secure employment outside of her capacity as a nanny to the Manhattan elite portrays a group inter-view with a fictional South Bronx conflict-resolution team for city schools. The interviewer's exceedingly unprofessional behavior compromises the scene's verisimilitude. After speaking for an hour about his professional accomplishments, misguided childhood, and attempts to quit smoking, the male interviewer notices from the protagonist's résumé that she is minor-ing in gender studies. He asks for clarification, quickly interrupts her re-sponse, and bluntly asks, "So, you're not a feminist bitch, then?" (186). The protagonist, working to retain her patience, attempts a weak laugh: she neither rejects the label of feminist nor defends it.

McLaughlin and Kraus's next novel, *Citizen Girl* (2004), features a self-identified feminist protagonist-everywoman, albeit with negative and mixed representations of older feminists. "Girl," a twenty-four-year-old Wesleyan grad (public policy major, gender studies minor), is at the novel's beginning employed at the fictional Center for Equity in Commu-nity among a "menopausal sea of the waistband-and-ironing board ad-verse" (2). Her hemp and Nubuck-clad boss fires Girl at the end of chapter 1 (titled "Doris Mindfuck") when she stands up for herself after her boss essentially steals her research report of a year and a half's work, reneging on her promise to let Girl herself present the report at a feminist confer-ence. Girl believes she has found a mentor in the elegantly dressed Julia, who operates out of a well-appointed Manhattan apartment a Magdalene-type outreach for refugees of sexual slavery. Yet she is ultimately shown to be only marginally better than Doris, as she accepts a million dollars from Girl's next employer, a progressive Internet startup that Girl resigns from when it transitions into a Web porn company. The fact that Julia is aware that the company is employing former international female-trafficking victims to "perform" in violent porn doesn't prevent her from eagerly accepting the check offered in the company's attempt at a veneer of public outreach. Girl's story is a search for feminists to collaborate with, and the postlapsarian realization that more established feminists are capable of exploiting her labor.

In comparison to *The Nanny Diaries,* a number one *New York Times* best-seller and the longest-running hardcover best-seller of 2002, *Citizen Girl* tanked. The novel's dilemma of morals versus lucre did not, I suspect, offer enough comic relief, with Girl appearing too serious to elicit sympathy and too overworked to inspire. In her interactions with her quasi boyfriend, Buster, she appears bossy and strident, and while the feminist may applaud her tested commitment to social justice, the novel, with its tendencies toward polemical dialogue on Girl's part, did not succeed in bridging the chick lit formula to a narrative with feminism at its foreground. McLaughlin and Kraus, who travel around the country speaking to young women about gender issues in American corporate culture, are alone in their pioneering attempt to craft with commercial appeal an overtly feminist chick lit protagonist.

With minimal exceptions, then, in chick lit the women's movement is taken for granted as an unquestioned birthright, if not directly treated with hostility.[8] And in the case of *Sex and the City* HBO series, Beth Montemurro observes that even though HBO is no stranger to "strong" language, *feminism* appears to be on the "do not use" list, as if it were the show's one taboo word. While chick lit may work in tandem with third-wave feminist writing to probe female sexuality and its psychic dimensions, chick lit does not share this writing's polemical and manifestolike functions. It also is oblivious to or chooses to ignore works of second-wave feminism that focus less prescriptively on the complex interactions surrounding sexuality, such as Carole Vance's classic anthology *Pleasure and Danger: Exploring Female Sexuality* (1984). From the genre's general avoidance of the word *feminism* and the characters' hesitation (or outright refusal) to identify themselves as feminist, the feminist critic can infer that the term *feminism* still stigmatizes and, for today's generation of young women, has connotations of unflattering fashion. Chick lit characters recognize the gains of feminism but distance themselves from a formal affiliation to avoid being perceived as dowdy, hectoring, or shrill.

It is plausible that the less politically wrought undercurrent of antagonism that sometimes exists in passable, even pleasant, mother-daughter relationships is being projected onto the "bad mother" figure of the feminist. Susan Faludi, commenting on third-wave feminists and postfeminists, ponders, "It seems to me it's a much more internalized struggle that these women are projecting out onto an older generation. It's not clear to me what the older feminists did that was so terrible that incurred their distress" (qtd. in Goldberg). While I do not wish to make light of mainstream postfeminism's gross simplification of the women's movement, the clash between the two camps may in part be a more ancient battle of young versus old: a friction seated in the multiplicity of life-career paths now available to younger women as a result of the efforts of their "mothers," and the postfeminist consciousness of each lifestyle paradigm's trade-offs.

Chick Lit and the Burden of Liberal Feminism

Chick lit is characterized by a vexed feminism, appropriating certain strands as it does narrative traditions. Its embrace of women's rights but eschewal of the feminist label mirrors the most common response of young women toward feminism today (Scott 8). Chick lit's affirmation of the individual as an agent borrows from liberal feminism. Its cover visuals emphatically maintain sexual difference and suggest gender essentialism rooted in women's gravitation toward the omnipotent magnet of apparel and accessories. In its pattern of heroines garnering literary recognition through editorial promotions, columns, or book contracts, it extends cultural feminism's attempts to recover and create a literature of its own. These intersections, however, typically operate within the marriage plot's telos, one in which married heterosexuality, specifically moneyed, is held as the prize, a column of one's own a consolation or close second. Novels such as *Bridget Jones's Diary*, for instance, present a trenchant examination of heterosexual privilege but nevertheless capitulate into a wedding primer. Others, such as Kate Harrison's *The Starter Marriage* (2005), foreground the psychological aftermath of divorce but conclude with the protagonist romantically paired. More often than not, critiques of married privilege are balanced, if not contained, by the protagonist's search for Mr. Right. The best-selling chick lit novelist Caren Lissner, who, as a journalist, edits a string of weekly newspapers, views the challenge of her characters as a fictional exploration of the pressures of choosing wisely: "Ultimately, people—no matter how liberated they are—don't want to be lonely. So how to find a man you want to make compromises for without compromising the things that are most important to you?"[9]

The best-seller *I Don't Know How She Does It* (2002) by Alison Pearson dramatizes this conflict, as the *Concise Oxford Dictionary*'s definition of *juggle* prefaces the novel. This Oprah's Book Club selection catalyzed the mommy lit subset within the chick lit genre, an offshoot that focuses on a protagonist's difficulties with balancing family, particularly young children, with her career and scraped-out "me time." Pearson's novel performs the postfeminist work of deflating without entirely burying the Superwoman ideal. To her coworkers, thirty-five-year-old protagonist Kate Reddy is a wonder with as much pep as her surname. A hedge-fund manager at a major London investment firm, she manages to find the time to bake mince pies for her daughter's carol concert in her stately Victorian home. While mommy lit heroines such as Reddy share the high energy level of the genre's twentysomething childless protagonists, they adopt a less optimistic tone toward the work-life balancing act, measuring the "having it all" ideal against sober experience.

The mommy lit protagonist experiences conflict between self-development and her responsibilities toward the family unit. Kate tells a friend debating whether to abort an unplanned pregnancy that if she could pick only two days from her life, they would be the days of the births of her two children. Nevertheless, she confesses the demands they have made on her time and energy. She pays a nanny as much to take care of her children as her architect husband earns, but fairy tale–like vignettes of Kate in "The Court of Motherhood" intersperse the domestic and workplace scenes, formally mirroring the guilt she feels when her daughter asks each morning before work if she'll be home to put her to bed. Marital relations have become yet another item on her Christmas to-do list: "I take time brushing my teeth. A count of twenty for each molar. If I stay in the bathroom long enough Richard will fall asleep and will not try to have sex with me. If we don't have sex, I can skip a bath in the morning. If I skip the bath, I will have time to start on the e-mails that have built up while I'm away and maybe even get some presents bought on the way to work" (8). Kate's alcoholic father, like that of the glamour novel's stock heroine, walked out on his young family, leaving his daughter to move up in the world on her wits, at which she succeeds. Yet breaking through the glass ceiling has left her with no time, as "husband" becomes an entry on her "Must Remember" lists that appear at each chapter's end.

Work enables Kate Reddy to feel in control of her life when the rest of it seems a mess. At times it is therapeutic, a soothing contrast to her daughter's ceaseless questions; as she observes, "I love the fact that the numbers do what I say and never ask why" (18). But when her husband leaves a throw-in-the-towel note that the nanny has to read over the phone to Kate, who is away on overseas business travel, the juggling act becomes impossible. To make matters worse, her daughter Emily's headmistress in a parent-teacher conference judges the girl not sufficient in extracurriculars to secure a place at a good London secondary school. She suggests an instrument (the clarinet is less common than the violin and has plenty of personality) and one of the more unusual sports (rugby for girls, she believes, is gaining in popularity), to which Kate responds, "Emily needs a CV at the age of six?" (238). Before Kate decides to leave her position to become a full-time mother, the text attempts several feminist gestures: Kate heads a benchmarking survey measuring gender parity and diversity in the workplace, she helps a top-performing junior colleague (Momo Gumeratne) bring to the company's attention a supervisor who manipulates the young woman's face onto pornographic digital images. The penultimate entry on her "Reasons to Give Up Work" list—"Becoming a man is a waste of a woman"—affirms sexual difference by latching on to essentialisms (341).

A move from the city to a more modest country residence helps mark the protagonist's new life stage. The novel ends not with uncomplicated domestic bliss but with strategic planning that may ultimately let Kate have it both ways. Kate receives a call from her sister, saying that the dollhouse factory her sister does piecework for has suddenly gone bust. Kate dons Armani armor, visits Companies House to look at their accounts, and begins to mull over ideas on how to develop and diversify the business. The final pages reveal Kate beginning to network with a small-business-owner female friend on securing financing and with Momo on the possibility of wooden dollhouse frames being made by workers employed by a Sri Lankan aid agency she has been advising.

Pearson's debut novel presents a not fully satisfying medium between the glamour novel with its all-powerful heroine and the working mother chronically on exhaustion's brink. On one hand, it can be read as a conservative text, with Kate's exit from the workplace to salvage her marriage retreatist. Such is the choice of the lawyer protagonist of G. Pearl Mak's *Frozen Pancakes and False Eyelashes: One Imperfect Woman's Quest for Peace, Balance . . . and Maternal Mojo* (2007), who, like Kate Reddy, is her household's primary breadwinner. After an unplanned pregnancy, the protagonist returns to work after a three-month maternity leave to quickly discover she can't juggle breast-feeding, commuting, and clocking 2,400 billable hours for the firm, let alone a sex life with her husband. To transition to full-time motherhood, she borrows on her cottage home and trades her BMW sports sedan for a generic minivan. She finds happiness in the arrangement, especially as she's retained one indulgence, eyelash extensions and their upkeep. The novel concludes cyclically, with the discovery of a second unplanned pregnancy. The text's privileging of stay-at-home mothering correlates with what Negra identifies as a key strand of postfeminism discourse in the early twenty-first century: a 2003 front-page *New York Times Magazine* article, "The Opt-Out Revolution," by Lisa Belkin gave a name to the phenomenon of celebrating, or at minimum defending, the choice to leave the workplace, represented as a "white-collar sweatshop," in favor of full-time child caring.

At the same time, the final paragraphs of *I Don't Know How She Does It* depict a nascent all-female business team, with Kate musing that if they develop a range of store buildings instead of a traditional Georgian townhouse, her husband could design them. The gendered space of the dollhouse is not a prison of enforced docility as it is for Ibsen's Nora but a commercial opportunity that may afford a happy medium between a serious career and stay-at-home motherhood. The ending is not entirely fantastic, as we've seen three hundred pages of evidence that the protagonist has the savvy and stamina to pull it off. The mommy lit subgenre, then, retains the humor of standard chick lit—when dark roots overgrow Kate's highlighted blonde hair, her daughter asks if she has a hat on—yet addresses workplace politics, sexual harassment, and the double burden. Comedy in mommy lit functions to mitigate anxiety and guilt about professional ambition and to make a successfully high-achieving protagonist more relatable. The genre advocates neither a retreat from the workforce nor a uniform condemnation of this retreat; instead, humor and the protagonist's finding potential or actual solutions work to fortify the reader with confidence that her chosen path and goals are achievable and not selfish.

Responding to Beryl Bainbridge's assessment of the chick lit genre as "a froth sort of thing" in the *Guardian*, the international best-selling author Jenny Colgan came back the next day with the retort, "We know the difference between *foie gras* and Hula Hoops [a type of sugar-laden cereal], Beryl, but sometimes we just want Hula Hoops." Colgan defends chick lit through a liberal feminist defense. She asserts that women readers can distinguish the genre from "serious literature," but this statement does more than defend. Often quoted as a sort of chick lit fan's credo, it declares that women have a right to choose their own reading and that the pleasures of popular literature are equal to if not greater than those effected by more classic, culturally revered works. It is a guilt-purging admission that accomplished women may deliberately choose light reading, like readers with graduate degrees who choose Harlequin romances, despite a variety of headier options. In its readerly functions and in its social implications, chick lit is not progressive but operates as affirmative bibliotherapy: its self-help functions impart a sense of calm, optimism, and identification, if only temporary and half-grounded in the pleasures of fantasy.

A Qualified "I Do": "Bride Lit" and Marital Ambivalence

The coexistence of grounded hope and consumer whimsy finds its fullest—and most caricatured—expression in chick lit's subset of texts that focus on a bride or fiancée's story. This subset, often called "bride lit" or "bridezilla lit," combines wish fulfillment with astute social observations on the wedding industry, estimated in the United States by the Condé Nast Bridal Group at $83 billion dollars annually (Mead 26).[10] Bride lit not only has a synergistic relationship with the wedding industry but also is arguably chick lit's richest source of theoretical commentary that informs postfeminism.[11] Its defamiliarization of marital ritual also works alongside recent cultural studies projects and feminist theorizations of the wedding.[12] Most of chick lit, but especially the bride lit subset, works to affirm and contest, sometimes simultaneously, feminist thought that perceives the female as a nonsubject, her value always already determined by a male order in which she functions as an object, her value solely as real or social barter. For instance, Gayle Rubin's "The Traffic in Women" (1975) protests the phallocentric order in which women function as transferable commodities circulated exclusively for male consumption. Luce Irigaray similarly asserts in her classic polemic "Women on the Market" (1978) that woman's value lies only in her ability to be exchanged. The chick lit genre refines Rubin's and Irigaray's theses by locating value not only in woman's circulation but also in her ability to get others to exchange currency. Irigaray's statement that as "commodities, women, are a mirror of value of and for man" is revised by chick lit authors, who present protagonists whose value is affirmed both by men and the sellers of commodities, commending the protagonist on her ability to stimulate exchange between the literal and heterosexual marketplace (177). More typically, though, the protagonist works to negotiate her subjectivity as a commodity on the marriage market, her desire to be a commodity, and her self-assessment, in line with chick lit's romance roots, as a creature beyond a price, one with value independent of exchange.

Sophie Kinsella's *Shopaholic Ties the Knot* (2003) belongs to the chick lit subset of New York–area wedding farces. The third title of the Shopaholic series, it presents a campy satire of wedding planners and Manhattan society weddings: protagonist Becky Bloomwood's "Magic Forest" Plaza Hotel ceremony is modeled on the *Doctor Zhivago*–themed wedding extravaganza that Joan Rivers designed with her daughter, Melissa, in 1998.[13] When Becky discovers it is permissible to register with more than one store—she registers with more than five—the text works to corroborate feminist analyses of American weddings (Ingraham 1999; Geller 2001) as consumer-acquisition events. This corroboration is encapsulated in *Modern Bride* editor in chief Antonia van der Meer's editor's letter proclaiming engagement a full-throttle shopping period: "Get ready to shop! What is the engagement period if not an intensive 18-month shopping spree?" *Shopaholic Ties the Knot* implicitly represents the betrothed woman's value in her ability to have others circulate capital around her: Becky gives Alicia, her archfoe, the "Manhattan once-over" and with clandestine smugness observes that her ring is slightly larger (143); the Tiffany employee who helps her register squeezes her arm and gives her a "well done" on the performance of her registry list: "You're right up there with our top brides" (265). Variations on this link have been extolled by the wedding industry. J. Daniel Brock, for example, publisher of *Elegant Bride*, informs subscribers to his magazine that market research has determined that their "spending potential" is "exceptionally high." We can imagine

Becky as a likely reader, as the novel's concluding page consists of a mock prenup stipulating the couple's shopping protocol:

5.1 The joint bank account shall be used for necessary expenditure on household expenses.

"Household expenses" shall be defined to include Miù Miù skirts, pairs of shoes, and other items of apparel deemed essential by the Bride.

5.2 The Bride's decision regarding such expenses shall be final in all cases. (n.p.)

Chick lit's general endorsement of consumerist behavior and meticulous descriptions of dress and fashion distance it, in contrast, from the treatment of commodities in the Austenite tradition. Austen is terse, too, in her descriptions of characters' dress, and typically singles out for mention female accoutrements only to satirize those characters, such as *Pride and Prejudice*'s Lydia Bennet or Lady Catherine, who expend more energy on adornment than the cultivation of inner qualities. Juliette Wells writes, "In Austen's moral universe, an extreme focus of externals—whether beauty or clothing—betrays superficiality of character, a damning characteristic indeed" (63). Against this grain, *Shopaholic Ties the Knot*'s protagonist cashes in her registry gifts for two first-class tickets around the world for a year-long extended honeymoon–spending spree and informs her boss at Barneys that she "may or may not" return to work (325). It appears that Becky, Barneys' best personal shopper, should she decide to return, will do so in the position of a pampered client.

Suzanne Finnamore's *Otherwise Engaged* (1999) expresses more ambiguous feelings about the bridal role, while not disavowing the pleasures of wedding-related consumption. The debut novel overlaps with the self-help genre in offering anxious brides-to-be sympathetic identification with the protagonist, Eve. The novel exposes hierarchies within heterosexuality—the protagonist notices how her status as a fiancée elevates her socially among friends and acquaintances—and criticizes mouthpieces of the wedding industry such as *Modern Bride* magazine. *Otherwise Engaged* focuses on what we can call "the engagement mystique" and works in tandem with feminist analyses of marriage, specifically, Jaclyn Geller's concept (2001) of "the marriage mystique":

There was a fantasy that the moment we got engaged, we would be invari-ably happy. That all the conflict we had up until this time had been about commitment, and that with commitment would come contentment. But lately I feel fatigued and resentful. I considered how I labored to put on this Great Woman act so he would ask me to marry him. . . . For eigh-teen months I was patient and dressed provocatively and entertained his friends and listened to him go on about Cormac McCarthy and about how he wished he lived in the forties so he could wear hats every day.

For eighteen months I made him soup and rubbed his neck and per-formed really sincere fellatio and now I'm tired. There's a backlash of con-fusion, now that it's finalized. Like, why did I have to do all this? And even, sometimes, why did I want this? I've won, but what have I won? (79–80)

Finnamore problematizes courtship's teleological aspect, its mandate to progress, as not a natural evolution but a passive-aggressive orchestration on the part of the female demanding a payday: the novel opens with Eve deciding after six months of living together with her boyfriend Michael that the "free introductory period was over" (4). Her performance of man-catching heteroscripts is effective—and not entirely insincere, as her love for Michael is credibly evidenced—but the victory alternates between resentment, emptiness, and triumph: "The truth is now that I've secured him I feel like I can really tear ass" (80).[14] When Michael says that he's unsure about still wanting to marry Eve at the engagement period's mid-point and Eve demands clarification, she is self-conscious of the dialogue's formulaic lack of spontaneity: "We are reading directly from the script. It protects me, I think, from going completely insane. The script is good for that" (92). The novel, however, ultimately serves as a metaheteroscript: the set phrases, though made self-conscious, advance Eve's desired telos, as the novel closes with a joyous October wedding.

Otherwise Engaged represents the engagement period, particularly the ring purchase, as a composite of a luxury consumer entitlement, repara-tions for the ills of the past, and a sweepstakes win. Eve looks at a ring in Tiffany's that whispers *"Hey girl. You really deserve me. . . . I am the IT ring"* (12, original emphasis). At a more middlebrow vendor, she selects a .81 carat in the couple's ring budget, and as Michael "forks over" $7,000, Eve feels she "had just won a game show," and must restrain herself from skipping down the aisle (13). When she later purchases Michael's wedding band, he jokes aloud, "Congratulations. You've just purchased your first husband. With the proper care and maintenance, he should last a good ten years," and Eve silently muses to herself on the economies of the transaction: "I was thinking how great it was that his ring cost me eight hundred dollars and my ring cost him seven thousand" (158). She decides that the next day she'll return to the store to buy a Raymond Weil watch that he admired, calculating that she'll still "be way ahead" (158).

In this respect *Otherwise Engaged* is typical in chick lit's representations of diamonds, which appear frequently as icons of social ascendancy or as markers of a nonmalicious but disheartening divide between single and married women. Most typically, they serve as confirmation of progress on courtship's teleology. The protagonist in the epilogue of *See Jane Date* (2001) by Melissa Senate reports that Valentine's Day found her wearing "small, sweet diamond stud earrings from Tiffany's," a gift from her boyfriend, while her recently engaged friend has arrived in a more impressive way: "We're talking two carats," is the especially New Yorker–style appraisal (281). Conversely, the protagonist of *Milkrun* (2001) by Sarah Mlynowski views herself as "practically engaged" because a suitor proposes a $200-a-ticket play for a first date (66). She judges his boisterously rakish behavior during the performance to warrant reparations for her offended sensibilities: "He is so going to have to invest in a huge three carat to make up for this night" (75). After experiencing his good-night kiss as a tongue attack, the protagonist sighs, "I'm going to have to give him back the three-carat ring," lamenting not so much his smoocher shortcomings as much as the loss of the imagined knuckle duster (76). An attribute of postfeminism, then, is a self-fashioning through participation in commodity culture, an inversion of radical feminism's goal of dismantling capitalist structures. These postfeminist marriage plots portray their protagonists as transferable capital and agents of capital acquisition and make apparent, without necessarily critiquing, the economic underpinnings of marital union.

Some titles in the wedding subset, however, contain polemical undercurrents. Cara Lockwood's *I Do (But I Don't)* (2003) merges the wedding farce with meditations on the increasing inability to dissociate the wedding from consumer activity. The protagonist, Lauren Crandell, a divorced Texan wedding planner, meets Nick Corona, a firefighter, when a groom in one of her weddings gets stuck in a tree through a botched ceremony-entrance attempt. In another farcical moment, a client is caught during the wedding rehearsal making out in a church vestibule with the groom's brother, by whom she has conceived a child after failed seduction attempts on Nick. Nick's fortitude in spurning the blonde beauty's ardor makes him for Lauren the obvious hero. Soap opera elements coexist with an identification of what Geller has named "marital entitlement" as the chick lit protagonist becomes a vehicle for social critique:

> It's odd, really, that so many people who don't strive for perfection in any other area of their lives (professional or personal) have no qualms about demanding a flawless, magical ceremony celebrating (more often than not) a rather imperfect union, witnessed by two less than functional families. It's a universal truth that relatives will not be on their best behavior just because you've spent ten thousand dollars on food. (If that were the case, then psychologists would prescribe surf and turf instead of Prozac.) (2).

The protagonist remarries in a small yet well-appointed wedding, a contrast to that of the client's in the opening pages. However, in an interview appearing in the back matter, Lockwood addresses the reader directly on the nearsightedness of the courtship teleology and the wedding as an elaborate orchestration of girlhood and consumer fantasies: "There's a real danger in seeing a wedding as a goal rather than as the start of a journey. Weddings should be fun. They shouldn't be status symbols, or an excuse to indulge yourself beyond what's unreasonable" (n.p.). Though romantic comedy ultimately upstages these polemical instances, Lockwood's critical scrutiny of wedding-related expense is a new trend in women's fiction and a new, antiromantic element in the popular romance.

In its stance toward consumption, the postfeminist marriage plot presents a mixed message: it offers the reader vicarious enjoyment of commodity culture through the protagonist's compulsory participation while extolling the idea that romantic love needs no accessories. For instance, Carole Matthew's romantic comedy *For Better or Worse* (2000) presents a related-outsider's view of a megabudget American wedding from the perspective of a recently divorced Londoner, Josie Flynn. Like Senate's *See Jane Date*, it details bridesmaid expenses and apparel as the thirtysomething protagonist must don lilac chiffon for her cousin Martha's Long Island wedding extravaganza. The use of a foreign protagonist enables Matthews to defamiliarize wedding rituals and new trends. The novel treats the idea that a wedding, however capacious its budget, is no guarantee of a happy day, let alone a happily ever after (HEA). Despite peacocks in cream silk bows and a fireworks display on the program, Josie catches Martha fornicating in the bridal dressing room with the best man. A transatlantic best-seller, *For Better or Worse* examines how the high cost of a wedding can prohibit a reconsideration of marriage, as Martha the day before confides to a suspecting Josie, "I can't stop it. . . . Not even if I wanted to. Everything's booked" (81). Martha departs with her pompadour in the middle of the reception, leaving a devastated groom in the wake. In the meantime, Josie's ex-husband Damien crashes the wedding bearing a £20,000 "re-engagement ring" and hoping to win Josie back. When Josie realizes the costly gesture is provoked by "not wanting [her] to be happy with anyone else" rather than by love or concern for her well-being, she casts the ring in the reception venue's pond, where it is quickly swallowed by a duck (266). From her Fifth Avenue hotel getaway Martha—out of guilt, out of love, out of slavery to the conventions of romantic comedy—decides to return to jilted Jack, who takes her back as the cleaning crew sweeps up the wedding debris.

The wedding farce exists concurrently with the love story. The protagonist unites with a recently divorced rock journalist seated next to her on their flight to JFK, and after a mere few dates, the couple declare their love. Despite its skilled use of realistic wedding-related detail and its view of the wedding as a constructed, performative act, the novel ultimately positions itself in romantic comedy's clichés. The closing scenes depict Josie and Matt hugging "each other tightly in an unspoken promise to have and to hold from this day forward. For better, for worse" (344). The duck, confiscated and released by customs officials, simultaneously passes Damien's ring with a happy quack and a great sense of bowel relief (344).

Laura Wolf's *Diary of a Mad Bride* (2002) similarly explores the towering cost of Manhattan weddings.[15] The middle-class protagonist, Amy, must operate on a $10,000 wedding budget, a sum that will not even cover the site fees for her first-choice reception venues. Amy opts for an at-home wedding, has her mother's gown restyled, and forgoes a limo, but her dreams of a lobster risotto and pumpkin bisque sit-down dinner for 115 are deflated when a local caterer suggests she call Chef Boyardee and Little Debbie. The *Diary* concludes with Amy declaring the day and its chicken buffet an astounding success and philosophizing that "the biggest day of your life" is "every day thereafter," not the pledge to love someone, but the act of fulfilling that pledge: echoing the Carpenter's tune and popular first-dance number, Amy tells us, "It's only just begun" (294). Yet, like the bridal magazines and wedding planner its protagonist criticizes, *Diary of a Mad Bride* is itself a wedding primer. In part a self-help book for nervous or overwhelmed brides-to-be, it is a product that—intentionally or not—fuels the flames of the industry it satirizes. Not surprisingly, it has been presented as a bridal shower gag gift and has been profiled along with Kinsella's and Matthews's novels as an "engaging read" by *Modern Bride* magazine.

As it is popular fiction, chick lit's social implications are not progressive but rather two steps forward, one step back. In its exploration of the protagonist's subjective journey, chick lit does not depict the character's wedding as what has been frequently called the crowning experience of female life. Examples of successful long-term marriages are scarce; heroines are often the children of divorce. Because protagonists have typically gone through several, if not numerous, relationships and their dissolution, those who marry at the plot's close do so soberly, that is, with awareness that happily-ever-after is neither a given nor effort-free. Chick lit, observes Imelda Whelehan, "provides . . . the post-feminist narrative of heterosex and romance for those who feel they're too savvy to be duped by the most conventional romance narrative" ("High Anxiety" 7). Chick lit does not critique marriage per se but shows skepticism toward the traditional HEA. At the same time, a feminist consciousness about the commodification of romance does not overrule the protagonist's yen for a well-appointed wedding. Depictions of marital dissatisfaction and the aftermath of divorce impart a sociologically realistic commentary on the tenuousness of the marital bond and the romantic wedding's failure to assure long-term fulfillment.

More often than not, however, wedlock still signifies a developmental endpoint of sorts; dating is teleological in intent. While chick lit foregrounds how modern courtship seldom leads in a clear, direct line to the altar, the genre does reveal that romance is still a significant yearning of career women. That is, chick lit as a temper of postfeminism seems to express the fact that feminism's gains in the professional arena have not abated the desire for romance. The disdain the critic may feel toward the chick lit author can be attributed to the fact that these beneficiaries of the women's movement, often educated at first-rank institutions, have relatively conventional desires.[16] Older feminists must take seriously young women's desire for marriage and participation in commodity and media culture, as well as the pleasures of femininity romance affords through the recognition of sexual difference, if it is to speak especially to a younger generation of women.

Final Measurements

The chick lit protagonist strives to carve out personal happiness within the dominant social order that has bequeathed both professional opportunity and partner search challenges. While she may pause to criticize the system, she is not an activist. The novels make a strong case for investing in friendship and not forgetting your friends after finding a partner, as chick lit participates in radical feminism's questioning of the nuclear family as a model social unit and complicates liberal feminism's ideal of independence and autonomous choice. Chick lit should not be considered "antifeminist" but a selective, half-utopian amalgamation of earlier feminist tenets. This quality, as some feminist cultural studies critics have observed, crosses over to other women-centered media forms concurrent with chick lit. For example, in their essay "Having it *Ally:* Popular Television (Post)Feminism" (2002), the title of which alludes to postfeminism's problematizing of the ideal of "having it all," Rachel Moseley and Jacinda Read argue that postfeminism is characterized not by negation or rejection but instead by a "repeated articulation of new spaces in which previously discretely held positions—feminist and feminine, professional and personal—are held together" (246). As a form of postfeminism, chick lit does not operate through renunciation (giving up the pleasures of adornment and heterosexual romance) but struggles to reconcile "our feminist desires with our feminine desires" (238).

At the same time, chick lit's humor and its saturation with designer names work to deflect its mixed social messages. It is as if its generic amalgamation muddles its ultimate stance on the status of the single woman. Anxieties about body image—a recurrent feature of the genre, as discussed in chapters 2 and 4—are usually assuaged or resolved by the conclusion, regardless of whether it involves a marriage or betrothal. Michelle Cunnah's *32AA* (2003) culminates with the protagonist's acceptance of her diminutive breast size. The protagonist, the daughter of a prominent cosmetic surgeon, arrives at the realization that just as she doesn't need bigger breasts to please a lover, neither does she have to alter her personality to accommodate another, a mistake of a previous relationship. While the trope of a gay male friend may seem progressive, the novel's representations of gay men are stereotypical. He is sexually voracious, fashion savvy, and physically graceful; if not a great dancer, then he is at least a discerning shopping companion. The gay man works as a guide to classy consumption for the straight woman but then is made to move out of the picture. In some instances he moves from trusted confidante to AIDS victim: works like Alex Witchel's *Me Times Three* (2002) and Rita Ciresi's *Pink Slip* (1999) intertwine the heroine's adventures with the sidekick's announcement of his HIV status, his illness, and demise. This subplot reads as an attempt to compensate for the attention the protagonist focuses on husband hunting and socializing. It might modify the romance's pattern of the heroine's sacrificial death, with a gay man serving as a surrogate. It allows the specter of sexually transmitted disease to enter the novel's discourse, as references to STDs and STIs from heterosexual behavior are negligible. Instead of adding scope and gravity to the chick lit novel, the intermittent references to AIDS come off as token gestures of social awareness. The contrast of fates ironically makes the protagonist seem more self-absorbed.

When not commended for their style by the heroine, gay men are sometimes depicted negatively through straight men who cast them as figures of clinical aberration. As the central male character of Lisa Jewell's international best-seller *Thirty-Nothing* (2000) walks around a train station with the scrawny terrier of a former sweetheart, who unexpectedly stows her belongings at his apartment and then contemplates returning to her husband, the character thinks that he "probably looked like a sad homosexual" carrying "an Alexander McQueen clutch-bag," the simile joining gay men's association with designer fashion to depression and clinical aberration (307). The paranoid humor reoccurs as he, ticketless and oxygen-depleted from chasing a romantic interest, hypothesizes that a perturbed ticket collector is tired of "breathless homosexuals" (308). Neutral representations of gay males are virtually absent, and with minimal exceptions, the stylish gay male is the only acceptable figure outside heterosexuality.

Chick lit offers a compulsively readable commentary on modern social institutions and rituals and the psychology of female consumption. Yet, more often than not, chick lit's defamiliarization is just that, or more pre-cisely, a dynamic of critique met with retraction or counterexample. For instance, in the opening pages of *Diary of a Mad Mom-to-Be* the protago-nist expresses a compulsory motherhood-type critique of married friends and elderly strangers' attempts to push the recently married couple toward procreation. The protagonist, undecided about wanting children and in "no rush to breed" on page 16, ten pages later issues an ultimatum to her husband as her thirty-one years suddenly seem geriatric: "I felt like Rip Van Winkle waking up from a decades-long sleep only to discover that I was OLD" (25). Though rendered speechless when an acquaintance asks if she'd want to go on a date with an Indian American car-service driver, the protagonist of Daswani's *For Matrimonial Purposes* exhibits an uncommon sensitivity for cross-cultural cost analysis. Her family pays one matchmaker 25,000 rupees, which the narrator compares to "the price of a small Louis Vuitton bag—and more than enough, certainly, for him to live on for the next six months" (28); in an effort to reconcile her lifestyle as a jet-setting New York fashion publicist with her traditionally conservative Mumbai upbringing, she seeks psychotherapy, pointing out that the rate of $100 an hour is approximately the monthly income of the general manager of her father's jewelry company (137). Nevertheless, this impressive East-meets-West debut novel concludes with the protagonist's wedding, which "resembled a movie set so elaborate that it made a Spielberg production look like a kindergarten nativity play" (275). I suspect the simile is neither hyperbolic nor ironic.

Too often questions or critiques of power systems are contained within marriage or whining without self-motivated agency. Laura Weisberger's *The Devil Wears Prada*, Barnes and Noble's top-selling chick lit title of 2004, is a case in point. *Devil* was inspired by the author's stint as *Vogue* editor in chief Anna Wintour's assistant after her graduation from Cornell. In a nutshell, protagonist Andrea Sachs lands a position at the fictional fashion magazine *Runway* after graduating from Brown. Despite her boss's global reputation for being demonically difficult, assisting editor in chief Miranda Priestly is a job that a million girls would die for.[17] And the novel tells us this many, many times. She accepts the position with the idea that a one-year commitment and a job recommendation will open doors at the *New Yorker*, where she really wants to write. Eleven months into the stint and hours after her boss discusses promotion, offering even to assist her in obtaining employment at Condé Nast, she loses her cool at an important fashion show, uttering a banal "fuck you" twice before being terminated. Her verbal rebellion comes off as a jejune temper tantrum. Though the novel critiques the fashion industry's pressures on its representatives to conform to weights as low as its runway models, it offers no positive alternatives. The closing scenes find Andrea, formerly a 115-pound five foot nine, eating a Burger King lunch after a doughnut breakfast, a diet hardly worth emulating. The acceptance of some fictional pieces into *Seventeen* is certainly a start for her writing career, but we wonder if she just traded one publication for another, especially as *Seventeen*'s target audience diverges considerably from the *New Yorker*'s. *Runway*'s fashion freebies bring in $38,000 when she sells them to an upscale consignment shop to subsidize her writing. She keeps, though, a pair of Manolos and a Diane Von Furstenburg wrap dress to send to a Hispanic high school senior in Newark who had written a letter of admiration months earlier asking if Miranda could send her something for Fourth of July weekend. Let alone that the girl doesn't mention her dress or shoe size, Andrea's reasoning—"This girl should know—just once—how it feels to own one beautiful thing. And, more importantly, to think there's someone out there who actually cares"— reads as a token multicultural charity gesture and of dubious value (358). Here, as in too much of the genre, "beauty" is not only defined in material terms but also is difficult to dissociate from values of high fashion, namely, exclusivity and expense.

While saturated in representations of the media industry, the genre's depiction of city residents outside of this sector is narrow. One would not know from watching *Sex and the City* that most people in New York use public transportation or that homeless people live in the city. The type of outreach presented in *The Devil Wears Prada* hardly seems a viable solution: Andrea uses company expense accounts to hand out Starbucks coffee and snacks to a band of Fifty-seventh Street regulars daily. The twenty-four-dollar expense each workday is more a self-confessed "passive-aggressive swipe at the company" than an altruistic gesture, especially as some of the beneficiaries, she surmises, don't appear to be homeless (139). In Tyne O'Connell's Hollywood-set *The Sex Was Great But . . .* (2004), celebrity makeover host Holly Klein's snatched purse is rescued by the male hero, Leo, while panhandling with his friend. Narration contrasts the two worlds, minutes apart yet lifestyle light-years away. Leo undergoes a phys-

ical makeover and brings about positive character changes in the protagonist, once voted in a glossy magazine's reader poll "Most Shallow Female
Celebrity." Nevertheless, the princess-and-pauper resolution lacks credibility, with the glamour makeover's cosmetic erasure of homelessness ultimately uniting the pair. Marian Keyes's *Sushi for Beginners* examines urban
homelessness, the social issue offering some equilibrium to the principal
setting of a women's style magazine's glossy world. A gal Friday succeeds
in arranging employment for a young homeless man who takes residence in
the perimeter of her apartment building, but to its credit the novel refrains
from drawing optimistic predictions for the rest of Dublin's poor.[18]

Chick lit has created a sisterhood clearly visible in the genre's online
communities and, at the turn of the twenty-first century, opened unprecedented opportunity to new women writers. While chick lit offers an effective remedy to the strident aspects of second-wave Anglo-American feminism, its lack of engagement with politics—equal pay concerns, the health
system, reproductive rights, child-care support—seems a shortcoming,
especially given its readership's large audience of young adults and college students. With minimal exceptions we have still to see protagonists
in male-dominated occupational fields, and female-populated helping pro-
fessions like social work and early-childhood and secondary education—
historically associated with single women—have yet to be represented.[19]
If chick lit is to expand further, authors such as Weiner speculate, it will
need to feature plots that include the long-term care of chronically ill or
debilitated parents ("Is Chick Lit Chic?"). While protagonists' media-
related jobs often make for exciting plots and working-girl glamour, their
creators would benefit by questioning more the media they produce, especially as many were or remain media professionals. As numerous major
publishers have established formal space for the genre, chick lit need not
fear it will lose support networks if it adds more scope with the trade-off
of less glamour to its repertoire. At the same time, the genre needs to retain
its sassy voice, its vacillations between whining and optimism, in order to
remain a distinctive market niche. If chick lit becomes too serious, it will
compromise its establishment as a subset of women's general fiction and
humorous literature.

High readability is both part of the formula and an impediment to
evaluating chick lit as literary. The critic may be disappointed in finding
many chick lit novels a mediocre execution of a time-honored theme: the

coming of age of an aspiring writer. The protagonist's subjective tug-of-war between conventional heterosexuality and autonomy has a corollary in chick lit's relationship to the literary: as if still ambivalent toward the woman writer's deliberate strivings for monetary gain, it oscillates between the easy transparency of entertainment reading and more intricate generic innovation.

Epilogue

And modern literature, with all its imperfections,
has the same hold on us and the same fascination.
It is like a relation whom we snub and scarify daily,
but, after all, cannot do without. It has the same
endearing quality of being that which we are, that
which we have made, that in which we live, instead
of being something, however august, alien to
ourselves and beheld from the outside.
    —Virginia Woolf, "How It Strikes a Contemporary,"
    The Common Reader: First Series

ONCE A Princetonian scoff for the literary works
of distinguished Anglo-American women writers, chick lit has evolved—
or, for some, degenerated—into an international media-consumer phenomenon. It is published by more than thirty presses and has a cast of
leading writers.[1] Genre-defining chick lit texts are being reincarnated into
other media forms: *Bridget Jones's Diary* is in the initial stages of development as a musical stage production, with the London world premiere
estimated as early 2011. Fielding, who has been working on the musical for

several months, has written some of the lyrics (likely a parody of Fielding's parody), the *Daily Mail* reported in May 2009, with Working Title,
the London-based company behind the Bridget films, at the heart of the
project. In July 2009, Working Title confirmed that a third movie is in the
early stages of production. *Sex and the City 2* was released in May 2010.
Though still dominated by Caucasian authors with Caucasian protagonists, the genre has had new Latina, African American, Indian American,
and Asian American women authors graft traits of the chick lit formula
with narratives of immigration, identity negotiations of first-generation
children, and inner-city struggle.[2]

At the same time, the market is much more difficult to break into, especially for first-time authors. "The strong will survive," observes Louise
Burke, executive vice president and publisher of Pocket Books, who oversees the imprint Downtown Press: "Now we've come back to reality, and
it's limited, and there are many, many more people publishing into it"
(qtd. in Danford, "Category"). Opining on chick lit's tight market, Marilyn Weigel in June 2007 commented that "the chick/lady lit voice is still
very desirable to editors, but . . . the author's platform has to be a big one
and/or the plot very high concept." Romance Divas, an online romance
writer's resource forum, sponsored in June 2009 a roundtable chat titled
"What Happens When Chick Lit Grows Up?" in which registered members could pose questions to six novelists. One of them, Blossom Kan, who
with her cousin Michelle Yu, authored *China Dolls* (2007), a debut novel
that weaves together the stories and close friendship of three career women
in Manhattan, perceives "a definite focus more on career (non-fashion-
related) or unique circumstances that manage to constitute a 'hook' that
we haven't seen before." For Kan, chick lit still lives, but she advises new
authors "to steer clear of the clothes/wedding contexts." Lois Winston, an
award-winning author of chick lit and an associate with the Ashley Gray-
son Literary Agency who was interviewed in May 2009 via e-mail for this
study, maintains that in order for a chick lit novel by anyone but the A-list
authors of the genre to sell, it has to be "incredibly unique." It appears
editors shudder at the words "chick lit," and many authors have taken to
calling their books "humorous women's fiction" rather than negatively
prejudicing editors against their work.

At one point I hypothesized that the recession and the war in Iraq would
make some aspects of the chick lit universe seem obnoxious, and that while

chick lit's serial dating and free spending share the supposed libertinism of President Clinton's second term, the political climate between 2004 and 2008, the years when chick lit's popularity began to taper off, might have directly correlated with a tighter market for authors. Market saturation appears, though, to be the primary cause of chick lit's kiss-of-death stigma for debut (or even midlist) novelists. Title cutbacks, according to Heather Foy, a senior PR manager for Harlequin enterprises, stem from the fact that "the market was flooded with so many titles that it was very difficult to get the attention of readers." Winston assesses the situation as a not uncommon case of what happens in commerce when a product becomes popular:

> Publishers saw an emerging market and flooded it, which caused the market to start drying up even before the last raindrop fell. There [were] just too many of the same pink polka dot widgets at basically the same price. And just how many pink polka dot widgets does any one consumer need? So then the manufacturers of the pink polka dot widgets decided the fad was over and stopped manufacturing pink polka dot widgets altogether. Having little foresight or imagination about widgets, since these decisions are usually made by the blinder-wearing widget counters who don't understand the subtleties and potential of widgets, they had no idea that there was still a widget-buying public out there, clamoring for widgets. They just wanted different widgets from the pink polka dot ones.

Another best-selling chick lit novelist, Jenny Gardiner, whose humorous women's fiction manuscript for *Sleeping with Ward Cleaver* (2008) won the American Title III contest, sponsored by Dorchester Publishing and *Romantic Times* magazine, and who is the recipient of numerous other distinctions in that genre, concurs with Winston. The industry jumped on the bandwagon when chick lit began to gain attention in the late 1990s, and in consequence, Gardiner surmises, glutted the market with "not only just more of the same, but more of the same with vastly inferior quality." When sales of chick lit began, not surprisingly, to drop, "unfortunately the message the industry took away from this is that chick lit is dead and the nails are hammered on that coffin." Gardiner notes that one effect of these title cutbacks on authors is that it puts those who prefer to write in a strong first-person voice at a disadvantage for getting contracted; that type of narration raises a red flag to agents who see it as a hallmark of chick lit. Inez

Kelley, one of the guest authors for the roundtable, notes, though, that the control the agents and editors have over what texts are classified as chick lit is not absolute. If an author avoids describing a manuscript as chick lit, a publisher may be more open to the initial read, but once the manuscript is sold, bookstores determine where to shelve the book.

Madeline Hunter, a *New York Times* best-selling novelist of historical romances with over 6 million books in print, connects the tidal wave and decline of chick lit with a more paratextual component: shoddy book manufacturing. Commenting on the physical quality of the books, the two-time RITA winner in an e-mail exchange in October 2009 states frankly, "First, the covers were drab and cheap. Second, the paper was cheap, and not at all what one expects from quality trade paperbacks. Actually, most of these books were no better than mass market in production qualities, and worse with covers. In other words, in terms of printing I suspect some of those cost less per unit to produce than mass-market books." Hunter speculated that the appeal to publishers was the ability or intention to move a large audience into the more profitable trade-size books and the opportunity to scale back these trade books to cheaper materials, because it was assumed this audience had come to them from mass market, not hardcover, and would not care about the difference in paper quality from typical trade books. As to the effect of these initiatives, Hunter concedes, "At some point, though, one has to wonder if some of the readers did not look at the product and conclude it was too much money for that package (in addition to any conclusions about the content)."

Market saturation and fiercer competition between publishers are not full deterrents. New offshoots of the chick lit formula have proven lucrative, as MaryJanice Davidson has been credited with starting the genre of paranormal chick lit. Her best-selling Undead series (2004–) is a fixture in paranormal fiction's current ubiquity. (Ten to fifteen years ago it was next to impossible for an author to sell a paranormal romance, according to Winston.) At the time of my writing this epilogue (June 2009), this genre has supplanted chick lit as the "hottest" trend in fiction, with Stephenie Meyer's Twilight quartet (2004–2008) and its film adaptations (2008, 2009, 2010) of a popularity comparable to J. K. Rowling's Harry Potter series among the young adult population; the four Twilight books were the best-selling novels of 2008 on the *USA Today* Best-Selling Books list. The Buffy the Vampire Slayer phenomenon, with its film, TV series, comics, and video games, worked to preface the Carpathian vampires of number one *New York Times* best-selling author Christine Feehan, whose Dark series (1999–) has garnered multiple Paranormal Excellence Awards for Romantic Literature. Joining the paranormal craze with that of Austen fan fiction, offshoots substantially spurred by chick lit as discussed in chapter 2, Seth Grahame-Smith's best-selling *"Pride and Prejudice" and Zombies* (2009) presents an "expanded edition" of *Pride and Prejudice,* in which 85 percent of the original text has been preserved but fused with "ultraviolent zombie mayhem." For publishers, paranormal may soon be next season's overstock: Winston states that publishers are now clamoring for steampunk. The term, coined by novelist K. W. Jeter in the 1980s as a tongue-in-cheek variant of cyberpuk, denotes a subgenre of fantasy and speculative fiction. Works are set in an era or world where steam power is still widely used—usually the nineteenth century and often Victorian-era England—but with prominent elements of either sci fi or fantasy such as fictional technological inventions like those found in the works of H. G. Wells and Jules Verne or real technological developments like the computer occurring at an earlier date. Chick lit authors may migrate into this up-and-coming mass-market trend: Kate MacAlister, a *New York Times* best-selling author of chick lit–inspired vampire novels such as *Sex and the Single Vampire* (2004) and *A Girl's Guide to Vampires* (2003), has a steampunk series forthcoming in 2010.

Initially intended to impart comic relief to single professional women, chick lit's humor and lighthearted quality work to deflect attention from the wounded economy, high unemployment rates, and the health-care crisis. The number of chick lit titles published exploded from 2002 to 2004, as the industry hypothesized correctly that fiction readers would be attracted to a respite from the world news' pervasive grimness and onslaught of natural disasters. Yet, the minor exception of "widow lit" notwithstanding, the events of 9/11 arguably helped solidify chick lit, despite its notably antiromantic elements, as a bubble of bourgeois escape.[3] With the exception of the transnational novels of Kavita Daswani, chick lit, at least that published within the time frame of my study, does not more than superficially reflect, if at all, on its Western, urbocentric privilege. The message of its earlier social function, upheavals in Anglo-American marriage and education patterns, is now well acknowledged, yet chick lit, like a protagonist who can't get over a breakup, too often keeps telling the same story.

Its repetitious covers and quasi-identical titles (not one but two mommy lit texts dubbed *From Here to Maternity,* for example) seemed time warped. In the case of American chick lit or the notable number of UK texts set in New York, the novels' adventurous joie de vivre is more reminiscent of New York's late 1990s. The protagonist's promotions and ability to raise herself out of debt are more in keeping with the late 1990s bull market and record low unemployment of that time than the depressive economy of the new millennium's early years. Chick lit's one moment of real gravity—the death of a gay male friend to AIDS—while by no means dated, seems more part of the cultural conversation of the 1990s. While Fielding's first chick lit novel aimed to parody aspects of postmodern culture, the events of September 11, and chick lit's continued hyperfocus on upper-middle-class and middle-class domestic woes, hastened the genre's classification as entertainment reading, if not self-caricature.

Chick lit's minimal representations of bodily violence against women coexist uncritically in the face of the Taliban and other misogynist regimes. The lifestyle of chick lit protagonists—presuming an unquestioned right to premarital or nonprocreative sex, the ability to spend freely and to dress in a flattering, if not alluring manner—is a large part of what the Taliban is trying to suppress in Muslim women, with chick lit to some extent the flipside, or opposing paradigm, to the Taliban's regime of sexual control. The events of 9/11 and their aftermath raise the question of whether the terms *postfeminism* and *postfeminist* can continue to be used responsibly outside the context of white Anglo-American metropolitan feminism. Chick lit, especially Fielding's *Olivia Joules,* reveals to the feminist critic that this strand of postfeminism assumes a position of privilege, and one profoundly domestic, with references to world leaders and political figures not part of chick lit's lexicon. Its earlier attempts at social satire have come to be upstaged by a nonironic merger of romantic love with postmodern values and an absence of reflexivity on the utopian quality of this venture. Chick lit's success as a genre lies in its seductive bricolage of approximate dichotomies: independence and a husband, the writing life and married cohabitation, fine accessories and entry-level income.

Conversely, it is not fully fair to judge chick lit as a template for some twenty-first-century transnational feminist how-to guide. By 2002, chick lit established itself as formula fiction whose lightheartedness and humor were central to its market niche. A year later, the original formula's evolution into distinct subsets may have widened the possibility for different protagonists but retained chick lit's central affective functions. Authors can have lows in their stories, but, as RDI editor Margaret Marbury concedes, "No one reads chick lit to get depressed" ("Hour with"). More than a humorous or lightly sarcastic tone, what continues to define chick lit in its permutations is a focus on a female protagonist's journey; while there may be a hero (or maybe even more than one potential hero), there doesn't have to be. For Amanda Brice, "What Happens When Chick Lit Grows Up?" panel moderator, attorney, and published author of romantic comedy, mysteries, and teen romance, "Her journey might involve a romance, or the romance might be a reward for completing her journey. But the journey is never the romance itself."

In the future, readers may see significant changes to the chick lit formula while it retains this constant in crossover genres. Alisa Valdes-Rodriguez, one of the guest authors on the "What Happens When Chick Lit Grows Up?" panel, commented that the shift in American presidents has influenced the content of her novels:

> I think that during the Bush II years chick lit was dominated by the mood of the era—rampant materialism, selfish disregard for consequences of foolish actions, a sort of Alberto Gonzalezian view of the world as one endless cocktail party. Unless and until chick lit (and its editors) moves away from this passé mode of thinking (shoes! handbags! fashion!) it will be outmoded. The end of the Bush era has opened more doors for me stylistically. Before Obama, the expectation in publishing was that "girls" were shallow and wanted to read about shopping. That is no longer the case.

Her novel *The Husband Habit* (2009) features a talented female chef who accidentally keeps falling for married men who omit telling her they are married until it is too late. While ostensibly following a plotline keeping roughly with traditional chick lit formula, the novel has neither overt sex nor references to fashion, the latter Valdes-Rodriguez was relieved her editor didn't make her sprinkle throughout the manuscript. She confesses, "I never liked writing about shoes. I live in Asics and Target sweats. It's about time we all started being real."

While dubbed the "Godmother of Chica Lit" by *Time* in 2005, the author has, interestingly, for the first time in her novels purposely avoided ethnic or racial identity for any of the characters. *The Husband Habit* is the first book set in her beloved hometown of Albuquerque, a setting Valdes-Rodriguez hopes will allow her to pursue a new direction in her fiction career—that is, to remake herself as "a regional writer, a New Mexican writer." The transition might be savvy given that Janet Reid of FinePrint Literary Management, one of Manhattan's high-profile agents, expressed on her blog in May 2009 that she is eagerly looking for "cowgirl lit," a new, perhaps Cormac McCarthy–inspired variant with Kennedy Foster's *All Roads Lead Me Back to You* (2009) the inaugural title.

Chick lit has not failed as a genre or passed its shelf life. Though pronouncements of chick lit as "dead" have become a refrain in journalism on the genre, claims of this sort often express the critic's frustration with chick lit's continued sales and backhandedly acknowledge the genre's longevity.[4] As journalists repeatedly pronounce chick lit "dead," it is fitting that the university, recognizing it as a subgenre, is starting to incorporate chick lit into the classroom. Instructors teach not only *Bridget Jones's Diary* but courses that frame this fiction within wider literary traditions. Iryce Baron at the University of Illinois at Urbana-Champaign has taught since 2001 an overview course on chick lit titled "Women in the Literary Imagination." Lynn Houston teaches a course with "Chick-Lit" in the title at California State University, Chico. Caroline Smith, an assistant professor at The George Washington University, instructs a course titled "Chick Lit: Writing about Women's 'Literature,'" which foregrounds the baggage of the genre's backstory. In fall of 2006, Harvard University's Women, Gender, and Sexuality program offered a new course called "The Romance: From Jane Austen to Chick Lit." Chick lit has been identified by Ferriss and Young (2006) as an accessible "starting point for intergenerational discussion of feminism," one evidenced in the topic of Brenda Bethman's Texas A&M University junior-level honors seminar "Flirting with the 'F-Word': Chick Lit, Feminism, and Postfeminism."

I have tried to preserve the exhilaration with which I first encountered these novels and their authors' fresh voices. I began this study when I was on the verge of twenty-nine; it ended as I was nearing thirty-five. I protracted finishing this book because it was, at the risk of taking myself unduly seriously, a formal ending to a fairly exuberant youth. It would be disingenuous not to concede that the transition from grad student aficionado to full-time college English teacher aroused frustration with chick lit. With this professional transition—one, yes, roughly concomitant with the move from highlights to demi-permanent color to full-coverage gray—I simply did not have the time I used to for reading novels in whose realist-fantasy-comic hybrid I found a time out, the bright covers and jokes of the novels offsetting the grim medical scenarios of my father's failing health. I remained attracted to the external femininity of the texts, written by women my own age, but frankly saw little of that in the Ivy League, my dark waist-length hair a visual aberration; a high voice didn't help. I never showed up to work wearing Jimmy Choos, Manolos, or Christian Louboutins, none of which I even own—it was more like Ferragamo flats, and that was only after my student loans were paid; yet I would sometimes receive comments from otherwise excellent male colleagues, untenured, tenured, tenure-denied, who would introduce me to other members of the university with remarks about my shoes implying, the way I took it at least, a sneering synecdoche for my research. My advisor was (correctly) worried about my prospects on the job market and encouraged me to publish pieces from another project to offset the noncanonical focus of the project. This is just to say that the gum-popping connotations of the chick lit label affect both the perception of the primary texts and the producers of its secondary literature. It was a deliberate choice not to harmonize any vocal schizophrenia in these pages. I ask that any tonal aberrations stand as an authentic statement of enthusiasm's transmutation into investigative form.

Despite its Pollyanna-like commitment to an individuated happy ending, we must not dismiss chick lit's influence on several major narrative traditions. Chick lit's humor belies its ambitious amalgamation of literary and popular forms, regardless of whether the ultimate product betrays solipsism or limited literary ability. Chick lit has monumentally changed the representation of single women in fiction. The genre has imparted not figures of deliberate scorn, pity, or derision but a cast of funny, usually capable women not looking to settle. It no longer exclusively represents young, never-married, childless women but encompasses wifehood, motherhood, widowhood, divorce, middle age, and menopause. While presently a taboo word for marketing a work of fiction with a female protagonist, chick lit transformed the dominant romantic formula of the Harlequin. The voice and that archetype of original protagonists survive vigorously today in other genres, particularly young-adult novels, mysteries, and speculative fiction.

Notes

Introduction

1. Men have not felt entirely unthreatened by chick lit's growth and sales volume. In October 2003, David Elliot and Brad Thompson mobilized a campaign against chick lit by establishing a British publishing company exclusively for men's and boys' books. Demanding a greater representation of "male lit," Elliot and Thompson argue that authors such as Helen Fielding have received too much attention. The development of buccaneering tales that instruct boys about chivalry and stoicism will combat, they contend, this pink menace ("Publishers"). The company, Spitfire Books, will publish boys' books under the imprint title "Young Spitfire." This nomenclature denotes images of fighter aircraft, yet ironically encodes emasculation: *spitfire*, used famously by Samuel Richardson's Mr. B in reference to Pamela, is often an appellation for feisty and boldfaced heroines.

2. See for example journalist Hanne Blank's *Baltimore City Paper* big books feature "Don't Hate Me Because I'm Cute," which references Eliot's essay to argue for the vapidity of the chick lit genre. Blank bemoans the fact that silly novels by lady novelists are back in vogue, appearing on top-seller lists "like candy-colored mushrooms in the front lawn of literature," but she acknowledges that pejoratives targeted at women writing to the female reader are a sexist commonplace in literary history.

3. This quote, and the novels of Kavita Daswani, were first brought to my attention by Pamela Butler and Jigna Desai in their pioneering article, "Manolos, Marriage, and Mantras: Chick-Lit Criticism and Transnational Feminism" (2008), an introduction to South Asian chick lit novels published in English.

4. In February 2003, the Association for Research in Popular Fictions (ARPF) hosted a colloquium on chick lit. ARPF's official journal, the Liverpool John Moores University–based *Diegesis*, devoted its Winter 2004 issue to the colloquium's proceedings. In July 2005, the first dissertation on chick lit was com-

pleted by Patrizia Sevieri of Milan. In October of that same year, the pioneering casebook *Chick Lit: The New Woman's Fiction* was released by Routledge. Edited by Suzanne Ferriss and Mallory Young, its fourteen essays survey the chick lit genre's origins and influences as well as its subsets. These essays work in synergy with the volume *Reading "Sex and the City"* (2004), edited by Kim Akass and Janet McCabe, which devotes its primary attention to the HBO series through close readings of episodes and personal essays on the series' sartorial influence. In 2006, the National Women's Studies Association featured a panel on the genre at its annual convention. Caroline J. Smith can be credited with the first monograph on the chick lit, *Cosmopolitan Culture and Consumerism in Chick Lit* (2008), a revision of her dissertation. This study focuses particularly on chick lit's dialogue with popular women's magazines, dating guides, and domestic advice manuals, pairing, in each chapter, chick lit texts with women's advice literature to which they respond.

5. This series is more accurately classified as "teen glitz lit"—that is, fiction featuring young adults set in a competitive, American upper class (in this case, Manhattan's Upper East Side) or overtly moneyed milieu. While the Gossip Girl series has been claimed as chick lit, "glitz lit" is a tag for today's glamour novel, a subgenre discussed in chapter 2.

6. *Elements of Style* (2006), a satirical New York novel by the late Wendy Wasserstein, alludes to *The Nanny Diaries* (2002) by Emma McLaughlin and Nicola Kraus as well as *Bergdorf Blondes* (2004) by Sykes (110). The title of the manual *See Jane Write: A Girl's Guide to Writing Chick Lit* (2006) by Sarah Mlynowski and Farrin Jacobs alludes to Melissa Senate's *See Jane Date* (2001) and Bank's *The Girls' Guide to Hunting and Fishing* (1999), fictions whose fresh voice and frank depiction of the dating gauntlet generated imitations.   .

7. In her dissertation, "*Cosmopolitan* Culture and Consumerism in Contemporary Women's Popular Fiction" (2005), Caroline Smith notes that Kim Cattrall, one of the stars of *Sex and the City*, appeared on the cover of the February 2002 issue of the British magazine *Red* and recalls on a January 2003 visit to London seeing a billboard for season 4 of the HBO series (7). There is also transatlantic overlap on the point of scholarship: Kim Akass and Janet McCabe, editors of *Reading "Sex and the City"* (2004), are British academics.

1. Postmodernism's Last Romance

1. Founded in 1980, Romance Writers of America is a professional trade association of more than nine thousand published and aspiring romance authors.

2. I do not mean to suggest that before the 1970s there was an absence of popular romance fiction, but instead that Woodiwiss's and Rogers's novels were pivotal

in the romance novel boom and revived historicals after a relative absence of more than twenty years (Ramsdell 8).

3. In a Yahoo! Chick Lit listserv post Shanna Swendson describes the genre as stories "essentially about one woman's life, but ultimately about all women's lives because we write about Everywoman," maintaining that at least one aspect of these women-narrated novels resonates with the reader's experience ("Relevance of Chick Lit," 1 Dec. 2003). "Jane's struggles are everywoman's" is cited as praise for Melissa Senate's *See Jane Date* in its front matter.

4. Despite the canonical status of picaresque texts featuring female protagonists, such as *Moll Flanders* (1722) and López de Ubeda's *La pícara Justina* (1605), the picaresque is largely conceived of as a male-centered form with the *pícara* usually either a prostitute or confidence artist who employs her charms to deceive her way into the hearts and pocketbooks of wealthy noblemen.

5. The RITA Awards, named for Rita Clay Estrada, are the most acclaimed awards for romance fiction.

6. For an inversion of this plot, see Laura Wolf's *Diary of a Mad Mom-to-Be* (2003), in which the protagonist's divorced mother-in-law chooses her pooch over an allergic suitor.

7. While a strong first-person voice may be a characteristic of chick lit, today it raises a red flag with editors, especially in the case of first-time novelists. While Harlequin continues to publish fiction written in the first person under its MIRA line, Jenny Gardiner, whose five works of humorous women's fiction have received numerous industry awards and distinctions, contends that if writers "come to the table with first person and a strong voice, then expect an editor to think long and hard before committing to it, and don't hold your breath either, because nine times out of ten they'll pass on it" (e-mail to the author, 1 May 2009).

8. In part responding to market trends, Christian chick lit capitalizes on the increasing sales of Christian-oriented titles as sales in Christian fiction have doubled in the past decade (Donahue). In 2005, RWA reported that Christian romance sales in Christian bookstores had risen 25 percent a year since 2001 (Cote 10).

9. In a reading of this cartoon, Juliette Wells suggests that it might deliberately echo the opening scene of *Jane Eyre* (1847) in its depiction of a woman in a window seat with a book (47). In Brontë's novel, a boorish male interrupts the young woman's reading; she throws her book at him, with the knowledge that she will be reprimanded for her audacity. The cartoon depicts a middle-aged couple with a hyperactive son, but the father's attitude toward genres creates a parallel with Brontë's intruder.

10. The novel's status as distinct from romance, argues Margaret Doody in *The True History of the Novel* (1996), is an "incessant assertion" in English-speaking critical discourse (1). See also Hunter (25, 360n7). The split between novels and

romance, Hunter speculates, is not as pronounced in continental narratives as it is in the English tradition in part because of Protestant cultural features that forced a sharper break.

11. However, Elaine Showalter, professor emerita and instructor of the course from the mid- to late 1980s, in personal communication could not confirm the term's usage. Showalter stated that while the students might have referred to the course as such, they did not, understandably, directly inform her. Showalter has publicly stated she admires the work of best-selling authors Sophie Kinsella, Marian Keyes, and Princeton graduate Jennifer Weiner.

12. Ironically, almost twelve years after his snarky *New Yorker* editorial a paean to the chick flick genre by Wolcott appeared in *Vanity Fair.* Wolcott describes this medium as "a post-feminist construction cushioned by affluence and aired out with sexual liberty" ("The Right Fluff").

13. *Lucky* magazine is a periodical devoted to women's shopping culture. Lucky Chick's marketing slogan "products for a lucky lifestyle" may allude to the publication.

14. In January 2008, this Yahoo! discussion list changed its title to "Fiction That Sells," indicting the establishment of the genre as commercial fiction.

15. Created by Marshall Herskovitz and Ed Zwick, the ABC program *thirtysomething* (1987–1991) received an Emmy for best dramatic series in 1988.

16. Personal consumption, however, does not underlie all meet-the-author events or the genre's paratexts. Proceeds from the fundraising anthology *Girls Night In* (RDI, 2004) benefit War Child, an international relief and development organization aimed at helping children affected by war conflict. Each of the twenty-one authors, many best-selling, contributed for free. That year Downtown Press published its trade paperback anthology *American Girls about Town,* whose seventeen stories benefit the UK children's charity Barnardo's and the American Make-A-Wish Foundation. The anthology format reflects chick lit's establishment as a genre.

17. The description is Weiner's response to the question "What is chick lit?" posed at the New York City chapter of the Women's National Book Association panel "Is Chick Lit Chic?" held January 15, 2004.

For a chick lit novel that earned notoriety for its illegal use of amalgamation, see Kaavya Viswanathan's *How Opal Mehta Got Kissed, Got Wild, and Got a Life* (2006). Viswanathan (b. 1987), a Harvard undergraduate, plagiarized from the works of chick lit novelists Meg Cabot and Sophie Kinsella, the best-selling young-adult author Megan McCafferty, as well as Salman Rushdie. Little, Brown and Company initially stood behind Viswanathan, who claimed in a statement issued by her publisher that her literary identity theft was "completely unintentional and unconscious," but ultimately recalled all copies of the novel and canceled Viswanathan's UK publicity tour.

18. Ellen Fein and Sherrie Schneider's unanticipated blockbuster spawned at least twenty-seven translations, nationwide support groups, signature lipstick and jewelry, as well as offshoot editions *The Rules II* and *The Rules for Marriage*.

19. See Alisa Valdes-Rodriguez's *The Dirty Girls Social Club* (2003) for another example of chick lit's strong ties with the success story. The first Latina chick lit novel, *The Dirty Girls Social Club* received a record $475,000 advance for a debut novel from either a Latina or a native New Mexican writer. The international best-seller tells the story of six Latina female professionals who met at Boston University as freshmen. Ten years later, their Buena Sucia (literally, Good Dirty Girl) Social Club convenes regularly twice a year. The ending presents one character who, while in a committed relationship with a reformed drug dealer, has a story published in a literary journal and wins a scholarship to UMASS Boston's Latin American Studies program. Another, a divorced magazine publisher, is not only engaged to a software millionaire but also purchases a brownstone she decorates in a "Yankee chic" style. One sucia produces a hit Spanish rock album and becomes an Aztec-inspired singing sensation. Another establishes a successful interior design business after being abandoned by her abusive husband, who flees after the final meeting. Target expresses interest in carrying a line of her houseware designs, while one character produces the pilot episode of what the Cuban-born Martha Stewart hopes will be a series called "Casas Americas."

2. *Bridget Jones's Diary* and the Production of a Popular Austen

1. In 2005, *Pride and Prejudice* beat *Jane Eyre* in a survey of the seven-hundred-strong members of the Romantic Novelists' Association, with Austen's *Persuasion* ranking seventh ("Austen Tops Romantic Novel Poll").

2. Butler and Desai's article, though a pioneering and rigorous contribution to chick lit criticism, samples only three novels, including two by the same author.

3. See Whelehan's chapter "Crashing of the Superwoman: The 1980s" in *The Feminist Bestseller* (2005) and Deborah Philips's chapter "Shopping as Work: The Sex and Shopping Novel of the 1980s" in *Writing Romance: Women's Fiction, 1945–2005* (2006) for analyses of best-selling bonkbusters' narrative patterns.

4. Quotation appeared in an April 2005 online interview with Deanna Carlyle. http://www.deannacarlyle.com/interviews/s-mlynowski.htm.

5. Chick lit, according to novelist Shanna Swendson, "takes that 'everywoman' reality and throws it into some wish-fulfillment fantasy" ("Re: Research Study").

6. The sequel's film adaptation, in contrast, concludes with Bridget's parents renewing their vows and Bridget engaged. The initial shots of the wedding lead the viewer to believe the ceremony is Mark and Bridget's, as if the film will finally mimic *Pride and Prejudice*'s close.

7. For *BBC Magazine* journalist Rebecca Moy, the revived *Independent* column elicited the sense of inhabiting a time warp, with readers of the online editions wondering why they should pay one pound to read the "diary of a drunken fool," given today's "blogcentric" media world. Its continuation met with a mixed reception of enthusiasm, disappointment, and indifference.

8. Sharon Maguire, a close friend of Fielding, was the model for the character Shazzer in the novel. The *Bridget Jones's Diary* director acknowledges that she did coin the term "emotional fuckwit" and has been prone to drunken rants about the men in her life (Whelehan 12).

9. Though a memoir, Karyn Bosnak's *Save Karyn: One Shopaholic's Journey to Debt and Back* (2003) integrates the chick lit formula with the post-9/11 economy. Bosnak, a TV producer, becomes unemployed when the newly launched *Ananda Lewis Show* is preempted by news for two weeks after the attacks. When it starts airing again, ratings are lackluster because daytime TV viewers are tuning into world news stations. Unable to pay $20,000 in credit card debt largely from designer apparel purchases, Bosnak receives international media coverage as one of the first and most successful Internet panhandlers. Responses to her panhandling Web site, which launched the summer after 9/11, dovetail with responses to the chick lit genre: some members of the online community find the site's daily humor upbeat, while others cry narcissism, self-indulgence, and myopic social concern.

10. The four episodes portrayed nine weeks of ten modern-day Britons trying to meet mates while living under the conditions and customs of Regency-era England. For instance, the participants live at a country estate for a house party, similar to those hosted at the height of the period; the owner of the manor and chaperons devise ways to bring their charges together as well as keep them apart. The eligible women wear corsets and rub lemons under their armpits, while the men are put through riding games to showcase their prowess or lack thereof.

11. See Natalie Tyler's interview with celebrated romance novelist Jennifer Crusie for an example of Austen claimed as the mother of modern romance (Tyler, *Friendly* 240–41).

12. Burris is not the first to focus on Georgiana's story, as Julia Barrett's *Presumption: An Entertainment* (1993) takes this *Pride and Prejudice* secondary character as its protagonist.

13. See Tyler (275–77) for an annotated bibliography of Austen novel offshoots.

14. See Wiltshire (7–10) for an earlier discussion of Jane Austen as a cultural commodity and the associations of her brand name.

15. See also *Us* magazine's review of *Bride and Prejudice*, which refers to the film's source text as a "chick lit classic."

16. See Buckley (18) and Abel et al. (5–14) for an outline of the bildungsroman plot and its attributes.

17. Until the rise of feminist criticism in the 1970s, the bildungsroman was generally regarded as the novel of the development of a young man in the style of Goethe's *Wilhelm Meister*. Second-wave feminist scholarship began to identify a new or at least revised form, the female bildungsroman with distinct patterns and myths. See Fuderer's *The Female Bildungsroman in English: An Annotated Bibliography of Criticism* (1990) for a succinct overview of narrative patterns of women-centered coming-of-age novels.

3. *Sex and the City* and the New York Novel

1. *Goodnight Nobody* (2005) by Jennifer Weiner alludes to the sequel of *Bridget Jones*, that is *Bridget Jones: The Edge of Reason* (1999) (141). Weiner's protagonist alludes to British chick lit as a genre as she confides that for a flight she purchased from a duty-free shop "two paperback novels with candy pink covers, comically bewildered British heroines, and the promise of a happy ending by page 375" (173).

2. The reception of Bushnell's *New York Observer* column, described as a "weekly blabathon" by one reviewer, reveals that chick lit's denigration is not confined to novels ("Too Sexy for This Book").

3. *SATC* is the official acronym for the TV series.

4. See Jim Smith (261–62) for a comparison sheet between the characters of the Bushnell's collection and that of the series.

5. Quotations from HBO's *SATC* are parenthetically referenced by season number, episode number, and episode title, respectively; the episode title is omitted if referenced within the sentence.

6. Written by *Sex and the City* consultant Greg Behrendt and story editor Liz Tuccillo, *He's Just Not That into You*'s ten case-study lessons co-opt Carrie's and the girls' dating misconceptions to educate women on how to detect lackluster interest and stop rationalizing a dead-end relationship.

7. This figure is substantially larger than the estimate of 300 customers a week (i.e., 15,600 people yearly) reported in *TV Guide* in 2004 (Hochman 34).

8. See Virginia Postrel's study *The Substance of Style: How the Rise of Aesthetic Value Is Remaking Commerce, Culture, and Consciousness* (2003) for evidence of the rising importance of surface images in Anglo-American identity. Her term "the aesthetic imperative," a parallel concept to my idea of "compulsory style," suggests that while aesthetics may not trump consumer issues such as cost and performance, aesthetic pleasure is increasingly likely to be among our top criteria, regardless of how mundane the product (7).

9. To note an analogous real-life case, the Philadelphia wedding planner Mark Kingsdorf, who runs The Queen of Hearts Wedding Consultants, alleges to have found an increased market around men who want a romantic way to propose but need guidance and assuagement of their anxiety. The process usually begins with an hour-long interview for Kingsdorf, possessed with what he playfully dubs an "all-around clear eye for the straight guy," to learn about the client and his soon-to-be fiancée in order to proceed with proposal strategy and logistics (Melamed 116).

10. I do not mean to imply that such models are new but that they are increasingly prominent. According to the psychologist and martial choice theoretician Bernard Murstein, the "exchange model of interpersonal transactions," articulated by the sociologists Thibaut and Kelley (1959), Homans (1961), and Blau (1964), applies some elementary economic concepts—rewards, costs, assets, liabilities—to maintain that individuals attempt to make social interaction as profitable as possible (108–9).

11. Wendy Straker's series-inspired career guide *Sexy Jobs in the City: How to Find Your Dream Job Using the Rules of Dating* (2003) offers an inverted application of this thematic, connecting media-sector job hunting to dating savvy.

12. In her analysis of the early history of the "commodification of romance," Eva Illouz (1997) draws on a diverse sample of texts from 1900 to the 1930s to investigate not only the role the cultural motive of romance played in the construction of consumer mass markets, but also how romantic ritual incorporated economic practices of the market (11, 25).

13. John Molloy's *Why Men Marry Some Women and Not Others: The Fascinating Research That Can Land You the Man of Your Dreams* (2003) details relationship stage schedules, offering quantitative benchmarks to measure whether a courtship is progressing on schedule. Malloy, an image consultant and *New York Times* best-selling author of the *Dress for Success* series, purports to offer dating dos and don'ts that insure an "up to 60 percent" increase in the likelihood of marriage when modeled correctly. Featured guidelines specify that the shift from casual to monogamous dating should occur between one to four months and that twenty-two months of dating marks a watershed moment as the statistical trend line for receiving a proposal begins to drop off.

14. Samantha's perspective on heteroexchange seems to have grown narrower from her appraisal of the sexes as "equal opportunity exploiters" in season 1. Here, though, her assertion echoes those of sought-after dating coaches such as Myreah Moore, who advocates a "Pair and Spare" philosophy of dating at least three men at once.

15. See also Illouz, who maintains that romantic love both links and condenses the contradictions in late capitalist culture: romance has become entwined not

only with "the pleasures, images, and dreams of the sphere of consumption" but also with "the economic rationality of entrepreneurial capitalism" (11, 188).

16. Shortly after its finale, *SATC* opened its costume closet to the general public. The *Sex and the City* Wardrobe Sale took place on March 12, 2004, to become part of the series' lore and a historical event in Manhattan shopping culture. Held at INA, a designer retail boutique on Prince Street, the sale drew hundreds of locals as well as out-of-state fans, with lines stretching around the block and down to the next corner, at Elizabeth Street, for most of the day. The online store was also flooded with orders from fans eager to buy a piece of fashion history. Prices ranged from $20 to $5,000 for a black sequined Chanel minidress. Many of the show's signature outfits had already been claimed by cast members, while other couture pieces were auctioned for the actresses' favorite charities. Since INA was where most of the pieces were originally purchased by the show's fashion stylist, Patricia Field, HBO accountants turned to the boutique to resell the remaining wardrobe contents.

17. The series continues to inspire the fashion sector. In 2004, Sarah Jessica Parker appeared in Gap commercials and print ads in the apparel company's longest-running endorsement deal. Kim Cattrall the same year starred in Liz Claiborne's Spark Seduction fragrance line print campaign: the actress's sultry confidence reflects the essence of the fragrance, said Claiborne Cosmetics president Art Spiro of the decision to cast Cattrall. Both Parker and Kristin Davis remain frequently photographed style icons, with Bushnell, who served in 2005 as a judge on the reality TV series *Wickedly Perfect*, featured in Manhattan society and fashion-world photojournalism.

18. For those unfamiliar with the series, "tea bagging" refers to the practice of engulfing the scrotum with the mouth during oral sex. The sentence's reference to urination alludes to wetting directly on a partner, sometimes termed "water sports," during heterosexual intercourse.

19. See Anna Godbersen's *The Luxe* (2007) for a best-selling young-adult historical fiction not squarely within the chick lit genre that nevertheless co-opts Wharton as an "upscale" allusion. Set in fin de siècle New York, its epigraph from *The Age of Innocence* about old New York's fear of scandal and "scenes" foreshadows the novel's blurring of duplicity and decorum, propriety and falsity. Its cover, featuring gold calligraphy script and a young model in a couture pink strapless ball gown, attempts, as does it title, to seduce prospective readers by evoking the surface grandeur of Wharton's Gilded Age.

20. For a more recent figure, see Essig (18), who reports that average credit card debt rose from $518 in 1980 to $8,650 as of January 2009.

21. From approximately 1999 to 2001, Fraser corresponded with an interviewed more than 150 single women across Canada. While attempting to cover a broad

range of ages, economic and personal circumstances, sexual orientations, and ethnic and religious backgrounds, Fraser focuses chiefly on women over thirty, arguing that younger women are "not yet defining themselves as single" (3).

22. Unless otherwise noted, all biographical information about Bushnell is taken from two interviews conducted with the author in May 2007.

23. While the *Los Angeles Times* commended the film for not leaving "its characters frozen in amber after a fairy tale ending" but "allow[ing] life to go on, happily and unconventionally," the *New York Times* deemed it "vulgar, shrill, deeply shallow," the *New York Observer*'s Rex Reed panned it as "irritating, glossy, trite, superficial and boring," and the *New York Post* judged it as compromised by "lethally slow pacing and utterly predictable plot."

24. The scenes featuring the women in the four-star Mexican resort were shot in Malibu.

25. *Sisterhood Is Powerful* is the title of Robin Morgan's classic anthology (1970) of writings from the women's liberation movement.

26. On February 15, 2000, Fox featured its infamous special *Who Wants to Marry a Multi-Millionaire?* drawing a total of 22.8 million viewers and a third of all female viewers aged eighteen to thirty-four (Paul 44–45).

27. In Jackie Rose's *Marrying Up* (2005), for instance, the protagonist breaks things off with a San Francisco millionaire to unite with a less affluent neighbor.

4. The Legacy of Working-Girl Fiction

1. My colleague Peter Stallybrass has suggested in conversation that chick lit's roots can be traced back to Samuel Richardson's *Pamela; Or, Virtue Rewarded* (1740). The titular protagonist shares several characteristics with the chick lit heroine: she not only falls in love with her boss but also possesses a keen interest in clothing (her job is to care for her mistress's son's fine linen). The mismatch between the volumes of writing Pamela produces in her closet and her status as a full-time maid has been a common critical observation. The absence of scenes depicting Pamela in service makes her station appear more bourgeois than her actual economic status; we are hard pressed to consider her working class because of her knowledge of Shakespeare, classical mythology, and religious allegory. In this light, she offers an ancestor to the middle-class chick lit protagonist who performs entry-level service, often for a worldlier boss who becomes the love interest.

To be sure, *Pamela*'s operating structure—delay, according to Barbara Fuchs, being its "great engine of narrative interest"—differs from most of chick lit, as the latter may present multiple sexual encounters, unfold a long-term relationship's dissolution, or commence with the morning after (113). Yet, because *Pamela* is narrated in letters nearly all of which are written by Pamela, the epistolary novel often approaches the monologue form, and consequently, its male protagonist is underdeveloped. *Pamela*'s impressionistic present-tense narration predates the breathless style of much of chick lit in its technique of "writing to the moment," what Richardson termed his "new Manner of Writing" (Brody 20). While Richardson intended his first novel foremost as a disguised conduct book, the heroine-centered text's vivacity and earnest yet unpolished prose (its colloquial diction was criticized by some of Richardson's contemporaries) often upstage its function of moral instruction. These factors, in conjunction with the heroine's successful manipulation of class status, may point to *Pamela* as the earliest British ancestor to the chick lit genre.

2. A small number of male writers, including B. D. Gardner (*A Year of Samantha* [2003]) and the late E. Lynn Harris (*A Love of My Own* [2003]), have authored chick lit novels.

3. *Kitty Foyle* (1939) by Christopher Morley, for instance, chronicles the protagonist's Philadelphia lower-middle-class childhood to her rise as a top cosmetic industry developer in the early 1930s. The protagonist rebukes the insistence of her Main Line boyfriend (and former boss) that she return to college, with his implication that a liberal arts degree will polish Kitty enough for marriage into his prominent family. She deems honest labor in the beauty industry preferable to being a "Paper Doll" married suburban socialite. The first-person account, adapted into a popular movie starring Ginger Rogers, articulates partner choice dilemmas chick lit revisits, as Kitty in conversation with a girlfriend deliberates the "WCG" (White Collar Girl) conflict: "Yes, Molly says, a Pooh-bear on the bedspread isn't enough. If they try to escape by marrying a good provider maybe he's got no brains or he don't talk her language. If they marry a man who's smart he may be more interested in his work than he is in her. How are you going to find a man that's both dumb enough and sweet enough?" (334). The novel's humor, urban setting, and girlfriend-shared confidences dovetail with chick lit, especially as its closing line, "Hello Darling," leaves off with Kitty in a new relationship. As it is set mostly in the Depression years, scenes of nightlife are relatively absent; Kitty is too busying working to recap dates. Considerable portions of the novel retell scenes from childhood and emphasize the close relationship with her late father—her mother dies when she is a girl. Hence, we have the orphan trope but with sections devoted to a life stage not given much coverage in chick lit.

4. I am indebted to Elaine Hoffman Baruch for this term. In her survey of nineteenth-century Anglo-American fiction classics, Baruch observes that both male and female *Bildungsheld* venture out into the world on their own, yet the ultimate aim of the heroine's development is not life within her larger community (as it is for the male) but marriage with the suitor of her choice. Though these novels validate the search for self, because the heroine's growth remains closely tied to marriage, they remain imperfect or abortive coming-of-age stories (357).

In French *manqué* (the past participle of the verb *manquer*, to miss) is sometimes applied to someone who has failed to gain professional status—such as *un médecin manqué* (a failed doctor), whereas, in English, it need not have that pejorative implication.

5. The opening ceremonies for the Empire State Building took place six months before Baldwin's novel appeared (Hapke 264).

6. See Marian Keyes's best-selling *Lucy Sullivan Is Getting Married* (1999) for a chick lit novel that explores clinical depression in tandem with lighthearted subjects. In Poland, chick lit often features the specter of suicide (Donadio).

7. Stanger and Mandell derive their data from a U.S. singles map published by the *Boston Globe* and studies published by *Forbes*.

8. Predating *The Group* by five years, *The Best of Everything*'s character Gregg Adams may have offered the prototype for Kay Strong. Both, unlucky in love with a playwright, incur a fatal fall of ambiguous cause.

9. The June/July 2005 issue of *Shop Etc.* described *The Best of Everything* as "the original chick lit novel" in a feature titled "The Beach Read" (Hrabi).

10. All quotations are taken from Jong's interview with Jacobson.

11. See also Whitehead, *Why There Are No Good Men Left* (49), for instances of the appellation *Jane*.

12. See Guerrero for an insightful comparison between *Waiting to Exhale* and *Bridget Jones's Diary*.

13. For instances of lesbian characters in chick lit, see Jennifer Weiner's *Good in Bed*, which includes a mother who came out as a lesbian in midlife, and *The Dirty Girls Social Club* by Alisa Valdes-Rodriguez, which explores homophobia in the media through a character who, after attempting to relocate with her lover to Colombia, returns because of the country's antigay policies.

5. Theorizing Postfeminist Fictions of Development

1. Deborah Philips includes a chapter titled "Resentful Daughters: The Postfeminist Novel?" on the topic in *Writing Romance: Women's Fiction, 1945–2005*, but only mentions the term *postfeminism* once, concluding that this group of novels—ranging from chick lit (*Elegance* [2003] by Kathleen Tessaro) to literary fiction (the Booker Prize–nominated *Astonishing Splashes of Colour* [2003] by Clare Morrall)—dismisses feminism as wholly irrelevant, with femininity expressed in these texts "not as a matter of assertion or equality but of consumption" (141).

2. One origin story uncovered by Yaszek ascribes the first use of the term to the 1920s popular press, which used it to celebrate the passage of the Nineteenth Amendment and, the logic follows, the natural conclusion of feminism itself.

3. Quotation from roundtable discussion of the Women's National Book Association, New York City, "Is Chick Lit Chic?" panel held January 15, 2004.

4. Personal communication with author via e-mail, 16 Nov. 2004.

5. Qtd. in Postrel (27).

6. Ibid.

7. I do not wish to argue that second-wave feminism is entirely without media associations of glamour. See Scott (268) on how popular women's magazines claimed feminist leader Gloria Steinem as a fashionista and celebrity beauty.

8. The widowed mother of the thirtysomething protagonist in Karen Templeton's *Loose Screws* (2002) is depicted as a naturally beautiful, strong, capable woman. Though the protagonist comes to see some of her character strengths as inherited from this parent, the mother's feminist-socialist activism is not entirely without negative associations: a Columbia University professor, she gives away a disproportionate amount of her income to support the homeless, transients, battered women's shelters, and other causes, with the protagonist recalling how many of her childhood meals in consequence were of inexpensive, processed food like Twinkies and boxed macaroni and cheese. The jilted daughter sells her two-carat Tiffany engagement ring and leads us to believe that she donates the sum to the battered women's shelter her mother supports, but this gesture's credibility is tenuous given that a few months earlier she not only was laid off with no severance pay but shortly thereafter had most of her possessions destroyed in a fire, the double whammy leaving the newly singleton nearly broke (280).

9. Personal communication with author via email, 19 Sept. 2003.

10. See Mead (24–27) for a discussion of the particulars of the Condé Nast Bridal Group study. In her memoir, *A More Perfect Union: How I Survived the Happiest Day of My Life* (2006), Hana Schank states that the wedding industry grosses approximately $70 billion a year, the profits of the entire U.S. food processing industry (7); this figure's source, though, is without a reference.

11. In an example of chick lit's synergistic relationship with the media and wedding industry, Style's reality TV series *Whose Wedding Is It Anyway?* followed seven wedding planners as they directed their clients to the altar. Premiering in September 2004, its title appropriated from Margaret Bower's 1992 play of the same name, while preceding Melissa Senate's RDI novel released that December.

12. See my review essay "Consuming Heteroscripts: The Modern Wedding in the American Imaginary" (2004) for a survey of cultural studies projects on the wedding industry in America and England as well as on the history of this ritual in American law and literature.

13. For the Melissa Rivers–John Endicott wedding, decorators transformed the Terrace Room of the Plaza Hotel into the Hermitage, the Russian palace featured in *Doctor Zhivago*, by erecting a dramatically lit birch-tree forest covered in thousands of white roses and twinkling lights to simulate snow.

14. My term "heteroscripts" is derived from human sexuality sociologists John H. Gagnon and William Simon's theory of scripts and scripting to explain

sexual behavioral phenomenon. Introduced in the 1970s, their concept of "scripts" encompasses two dimensions: first, the external or interpersonal, in which the script functions as the organization of mutually shared conventions; second, the internal, motivational elements that produce arousal or at least a commitment to the activity (20).

15. Mead observes how the American Wedding Study's tally of the amount spent by Americans on getting married increases, and for a New York City bride, these figures may be easily twice the national reported average: from about $22,000 in 2003 to more than $26,000 in 2005 to, in 2006, a grand total of $27,852 (*One Perfect Day*, 24, 27).

16. A notable number of chick lit novelists are graduates from top-tier post-secondary educational institutions. Caren Lissner, Sarah Dunn, and Leanne Shear hold bachelor's degrees from the University of Pennsylvania; Jennifer Weiner holds one from Princeton. Jennifer O'Connell earned a BA from Smith and an MBA from the University of Chicago, while Alisa Valdes-Rodriguez holds a BA from the Berklee College of Music and an MA in journalism from Columbia University.

17. The trope of the tyrannical boss or unscrupulous employer appears in a number of the genre's best-selling works. See, for instance, *The Nanny Diaries* (2002) by Emma McLaughlin and Nicola Kraus.

18. Templeton's *Loose Screws* (2002) contains a nod to how gentrification of the Upper West Side in the early 1980s resulted in a displacement of boarders in its single-room-occupancy hotels, but this observation occupies less than one of the novel's 331 pages (67).

19. See Kate Harrison's *The Starter Marriage* (2005) for a chick lit novel that features a public primary school teacher.

Epilogue

1. In the United Kingdom, chick lit authors Helen Fielding, Sophie Kinsella, Marian Keyes, Jenny Colgan, Lisa Jewell, Adele Parks, Carole Matthews, and Jane Green have each produced several international best-sellers. In the United States, Jennifer Weiner, Melissa Bank, Melissa Senate, and Lauren Weisberger are best-known authors in the genre. In its popular mystery subset, leading authors include Susan McBride and Janet Evanovich, creators, respectively, of Avon's Debutante Dropout series and St. Martin's Stephanie Plum novels. In its Christian subset, the works of Kristin Billerbeck, Robin Jones Gunn, Penny Culliford, and Neta Jackson have received significant media attention, inspiring Harlequin's launch in 2004 of its Steeple Hill Café imprint, which combines elements from its RDI line with that of its Steeple Hill "inspirational" romances.

2. See Donadio for a brief survey of how original chick lit novels have emerged

from countries such as India, Italy, Finland and the Scandinavian nations, and Hungary.

3. Five days after 9/11, American lawyer Emily Giffin, now a leading chick lit novelist, quit her job and moved to London to begin work on *Something Borrowed* (2004).

4. Janet Maslin begins a *New York Times* review of *Literacy and Longing in L.A.* (2006) by Jennifer Kaufman and Karen Mack by contending that chick lit "appears to be in its death throes." Maslin then offers a warm review of the novel, which she describes as "a fusion of bibliomania with romantic comedy." Though Maslin finds chick lit's "obligatory yadda-yadda about Prada" tiresome, she acknowledges the genre's widespread popularity.

Bibliography

Abel, Elizabeth, Marianne Hirsch, and Elizabeth Langland, eds. *The Voyage In: Fictions of Female Development*. Hanover, NH: UP of New England, 1983.

Aidan, Pamela. Fitzwilliam Darcy, Gentleman ser. Coeur d'Alene, ID: Wytherngate, 2003–2006.

Ahern, Cecelia. *P.S. I Love You*. New York: Hyperion, 2004.

Akass, Kim, and Janet McCabe. "Welcome to the Age of Un-Innocence." Introduction. *Reading "Sex and the City."* Ed. Akass and McCabe. London: Tauris, 2004. 1–14.

Allison. "Girl Time! Great Chick Lit and Movies." Amazon.com list. Accessed 20 May 2009. http://www.amazon.com/Girl-Time-Great-Chick-Movies/lm/R1DIPTXXRDUT9E.

Aston, Elizabeth. *The Exploits and Adventures of Miss Alethea Darcy*. New York: Touchstone, 2005.

———. *Mr. Darcy's Daughters*. New York: Touchstone, 2003.

———. *The Second Mrs. Darcy*. New York: Touchstone, 2007.

———. *The True Darcy Spirit*. New York: Touchstone, 2006.

Atwood, Margaret. *The Edible Woman*. 1970. New York: Anchor, 1998.

"Austen Tops Romantic Novel Poll." *BBC News*, 11 Feb. 2005. http://news.bbc.co.uk/1/hi/entertainment/arts/4256613.stm.

Austen, Jane, and Seth Grahame-Smith. *"Pride and Prejudice" and Zombies: The Classic Regency Romance—Now with Ultraviolent Zombie Mayhem!* Philadelphia: Quirk, 2009.

Aylmer, Janet. *Darcy's Story*. 1996. New York: Harper, 2006.

Baird, Julia, with Jessica Bennett and Karen Springen. "Girls Gone Mild." *Newsweek*, 26 May 2008: 46–49.

Baker, Ernest A. *The History of the English Novel*. Vol. 3. London: Witherby, 1929.

Baldwin, Faith. *Skyscraper*. 1931. New York: Feminist, 2003.

Bank, Melissa. *The Girls' Guide to Hunting and Fishing.* New York: Viking, 1999.

Baratz-Logsted, Laura, ed. *This Is Chick-Lit.* Dallas: BenBella, 2006.

Barrett, Julia. *Presumption: An Entertainment.* New York: Evans, 1993.

Barrientos, Tanya. "Sassy, Kicky 'Chick Lit' Is the Hottest Trend in Publishing." *Philadelphia Inquirer,* 28 May 2003. http://www.ledgerenquirer.com/mld/ledgerenquirer/entertainment/5960564.html.

Baruch, Elaine Hoffman. "The Feminine *Bildungsroman:* Education through Marriage." *Massachusetts Review* 22.2 (Summer 1981): 335–57.

Baumgardner, Jennifer, and Amy Richards. *Manifesta: Young Women, Feminism, and the Future.* New York: Farrar Straus & Giroux, 2000.

Baym, Nina. *Women's Fiction.* Ithaca: Cornell UP, 1977.

Bebris, Carrie. Mr. and Mrs. Darcy Mysteries ser. New York: Tor, 2004– .

———. *North by Northanger, or, The Shades of Pemberley.* New York: Tor, 2006.

Beer, Gillian. *The Romance.* London: Methuen, 1970.

Behrendt, Greg, and Liz Tuccillo. *"He's Just Not That into You": The No-Excuses Truth to Understanding Guys.* New York: Simon Spotlight Entertainment, 2004.

Belkin, Lisa. "The Opt-Out Revolution." *New York Times Magazine,* 26 Oct. 2003: 42–47, 58, 85–86.

Bellafante, Gina. "Back to the City, for More than Just Sex." *New York Times,* 4 May 2008. http://www.nytimes.com/2008/05/04/movies/moviesspecial/04bell.html?_r=1.

Belle, Jennifer. "Don't Call This Belle a Chick." Interview with Jeff Baker. *Oregonian* [Portland], 25 May 2007. http://www.oregonlive.com/entertainment/oregonian/index.ssf?/base/entertainment/1179539722245250.xml&coll=7.

Benedict, Barbara M. "Sensibility by the Numbers: Austen's Work as Regency Popular Fiction." *Janeites: Austen's Disciples and Devotees.* Ed. Deidre Lynch. Princeton, NJ: Princeton UP, 2000.

Berdoll, Linda. *Mr. Darcy Takes a Wife: "Pride and Prejudice" Continues.* 1999. Louisville, CO: Landmark, 2004.

Berlant, Lauren. *The Female Complaint: The Unfinished Business of Sentimentality in American Culture.* Durham, NC: Duke UP, 2008.

Betterton, Don. *Alma Mater: Unusual Stories and Little-Known Facts from America's College Campuses.* Princeton, NJ: Peterson's Guides, 1988.

Birchall, Diana. *Mrs. Darcy's Dilemma.* Bexhill, East Sussex, UK: Egerton, 2004.

Bird, Sarah. *The Boyfriend School.* New York: Doubleday, 1989.

Blank, Hanne. "Don't Hate Me Because I'm Cute." *Baltimore City Paper,* 10–16 Sept. 2003. http://www.citypaper.com/2003–09–10/bigbooks2.html.

Blau, Peter M. *Exchange and Power in Social Life.* New York: Wiley, 1964.

Bond, Stephanie. "Jungle Beat." *Romance Writers Report,* Jan. 2005: 40–41.

Bosnak, Karyn. *Save Karyn: One Shopaholic's Journey to Debt and Back.* New York: Perennial, 2003.

Bower, Margaret. *Whose Wedding Is It Anyway? A Play.* London: French, 1992.

Boyd, Malia, and Adrian Glover. "Chick Trips." *Budget Travel* July/Aug. 2004: 84–91.

Brettell, Karen. "*Sex and the City* Tour Goes for $24,000 in New York." ABCNews .com. 2 Apr. 2008. http://abcnews.go.com/Entertainment/BusinessTravel/ story?id=4574424&page=1.

Bride and Prejudice, dir. Gurinder Chadha. Review. *Us,* 28 Feb. 2005: 102.

Bright, Susie. *Sexual State of the Union.* New York: Simon & Schuster, 1997.

Brinton, Sybil. *Old Friends and New Fancies.* 1913. Naperville, IL: Sourcebooks Landmark, 2007.

Brock, J. Daniel. Publisher's Letter to *Elegant Bride* Subscribers. 10 Dec. 2002.

Brody, Elizabeth Bergen. *Samuel Richardson.* Boston: Twayne, 1987.

Brooks, Ann. *Postfeminisms: Feminism, Cultural Theory, and Cultural Forms.* London: Routledge, 1997.

Brown, Helen Gurley. *Sex and the Single Girl.* 1962. Fort Lee, NJ: Barricade, 2003.

Brownstein, Rachel M. *Becoming a Heroine: Reading about Women in Novels.* New York: Columbia UP, 1994.

Buckley, Jerome. *Season of Youth: The Bildungsroman from Dickens to Golding.* Cambridge: Harvard UP, 1974.

Burris, Skylar Hamilton. *Conviction: A Sequel to Jane Austen's "Pride and Prejudice."* College Station, TX: Virtualbookworm.com, 2004.

Bushnell, Candace. Amazon.com interview with Leah Weathersby. 2008. http:// www.amazon.com/One-Fifth-Avenue-Candace-Bushnell/dp/1401301614/ ref=tmm_hrd_title_0.

———. *The Carrie Diaries.* New York: Balzer & Bray, 2010.

———. Interviews with the author. New York. May 2007.

———. *Four Blondes.* New York: Atlantic Monthly Press, 2000.

———. *Lipstick Jungle.* New York: Hyperion, 2005.

———. *One Fifth Avenue.* New York: Voice, 2008.

———. *Sex and the City.* 1996. New York: Warner, 2001.

———. *Trading Up.* New York: Hyperion, 2003.

Butler, Pamela, and Jigna Desai. "Manolos, Marriage, and Mantras: Chick-Lit Criticism and Transnational Feminism." *Meridians: Feminism, Race, Transnationalism* 8.2 (Sept. 2008): 1–31.

Cabot, Heather. "'Chick Lit' Fuels Publishing Industry: Genre Aimed at Young Women Is Fueling Publishing Industry." ABCNews.com, 30 Aug. 2003. http: //abcnews.go.com/WNT/story?id=129475&page=1.

Cabot, Meg, et al. *Girls Night In.* New York: Red Dress Ink, 2004.

Cach, Lisa. *Dating Without Novocaine.* New York: Red Dress Ink, 2002.

Cameron, Samuel, and Alan Collins. *Playing the Love Market: Dating, Romance and the Real World.* London: Free Association, 2000.

Carlyle, Deanna. "Dead Men Don't Eat Quiche." *This Is Chick-Lit.* Ed. Laura Baratz-Logsted. Dallas: BenBella, 2006. 101–17.

————. E-mail to the author. 16 Nov. 2004.

————. "Have Dress, Will Date: Four Red Dress Authors Define a New Women's Fiction Genre." 2002. http://www.deannacarlyle.com/articles/dress.html.

Castagnoli, Francesca. *Princess: You Know Who You Are.* New York: Broadway, 2003.

Cawelti, John G. *Adventure, Mystery, and Romance: Formula Stories as Art and Popular Culture.* Chicago: U of Chicago P, 1976.

"Chick Lit Author Roundtable." Sponsored by AuthorsOnTheWeb.com, 2004. http://www.authorsontheweb.com/features/0402chicklit/chicklit.asp.

Christensen, Kate. *In the Drink.* New York: Doubleday, 1999.

Ciresi, Rita. *Pink Slip.* New York: Delacorte, 1999.

Cohen, Paula Marantz. *Jane Austen in Boca.* New York: St. Martin's, 2002.

————. *Jane Austen in Scarsdale: Love, Death, and the SATs.* New York: St. Martin's, 2006.

Colgan, Jenny. "We Know the Difference between *Foie Gras* and Hula Hoops, Beryl, but Sometimes We Just Want Hula Hoops." *Guardian,* 24 Aug. 2001. http://www.guardian.co.uk/g2/story/0,3604,541637,00.html.

"Confessions of a Shopaholic Enabler." CNN.com, 13 Oct. 2004. http://www.cnn.com/2004/SHOWBIZ/books/10/13/books.shopaholic.ap/index.html.

Cooke, Maureen Lynch. "The Great Escape: Modern Women and the Chick Lit Genre." B.A. thesis. Boston College. May 2006. Online pdf from Boston College EDT Repository. 86 pp. http://dissertations.bc.edu/cgi/viewcontent.cgi?article=1152&context=ashonors.

Corrigan, Maureen. " 'Pink' Books." Rev. of the chick lit genre. *Fresh Air.* WHYY-FM, Philadelphia. 7 July 2003.

Cosper, Darcy. "Everything I Need to Know about Romance I Learned from Jane Austen (I Just Wished I'd Taken Her Advice Sooner)." *Sex and Sensibility: 28 True Romances from the Lives of Single Women.* Ed. Genevieve Field. New York: Washington Square, 2005. 233–42.

Cote, Lyn. "Christian Inspirational Romance Market 2005." *Romance Writers Report,* Oct. 2005: 10–14.

Coventry, Francis. *An Essay on the New Species of Writing Founded by Mr. Fielding.* 1751. Ed. and introd. Alan D. McKillop. Augustan Reprint Society 95. Los Angeles: William Andrews Clark Memorial Library, University of California, 1962.

Crofts, Rachel. "Keeping Up with the Bridget Joneses." PA Wire, Future Foundation, 2 Jan. 2003. http://www.futurefoundation.net/coverage_02jan03pawire .htm.

Cruise, Jennifer, ed. *Flirting with "Pride and Prejudice": Fresh Perspectives on the Original Chick-Lit Masterpiece.* Dallas: BenBella, 2005.

Cunnah, Michelle. *32AA.* New York: Avon Trade, 2003.

Cusk, Rachel. *Saving Agnes.* 1993. New York: Picador, 2000.

Danford, Natalie. "The Chick Lit Question." *Publishers Weekly,* 20 Oct. 2003. http://publishersweekly.reviewsnews.com/article/CA330294.html.

———. "In a Category of Her Own." *Publishers Weekly,* 11 Oct. 2004. http://publishersweekly.com/article/CA470419.html.

Dariaux, Genevieve Antoine. *Elegance: A Complete Guide for Every Woman Who Wants to Be Well and Properly Dressed on All Occasions.* New York: Doubleday, 1964.

Daswani, Kavita. *For Matrimonial Purposes.* New York: Putnam, 2003.

———. *The Village Bride of Beverly Hills.* New York: Putnam, 2004.

Davis, Lennard J. *Factual Fictions: The Origins of the English Novel.* Philadelphia: University of Pennsylvania Press, 1996.

Dawkins, Jane. *Letters from Pemberley: The First Year.* Circleville, NY: Kitchen Soup, 1999.

———. *More Letters from Pemberley: 1814–1818.* Lincoln, NE: iUniverse, 2003.

Deegan, Dorothy Yost. *The Stereotype of the Single Woman in American Novels: A Social Study with Implications for the Education of Women.* 1951. New York: Octagon, 1975.

Defoe, Daniel. *Moll Flanders.* 1722. New York: Bantam, 1989.

Degtyareva, Victoria. "Bushnell Speaks on Sex, City and Shoes." *Stanford Daily,* 1 Mar. 2005. http://daily.stanford.edu/article/2005/3/1/bushnellSpeaksOn SexCityAndShoes.

Delman, Joan Ellen. *Miss de Bourgh's Adventure: A Sequel to "Pride and Prejudice."* Raleigh, NC: Lulu.com, 2005.

Donadio, Rachel. "The Chick-Lit Pandemic." *New York Times,* 19 Mar. 2006. http://select.nytimes.com/preview/2006/03/19/books/1125000707670 .html.

Donahue, Deirdre. "Publishers Put Their Faith in Churchified 'Chick Lit.'" *USA Today,* 29 Oct. 2003. http://www.usatoday.com/life/books/news/2003-10-29-church-lit_x.htm.

Doody, Margaret. *The True Story of the Novel.* New Brunswick, NJ: Rutgers UP, 1996.

Douglas, Ann. "Soft-Porn Culture." *New Republic,* 30 Aug. 1980: 25–29.

Dowd, Maureen. *Are Men Necessary? When Sexes Collide.* New York: Putnam, 2005.

———. "Heels over Hemingway." *New York Times,* 10 Feb. 2007: A15.

Dreiser, Theodore. *Sister Carrie.* 1990. Ed. Donald Pizer. 2nd edition. New York: Norton, 1991.

Dunn, Sarah. *The Big Love.* 2004. New York: Back Bay, 2005.

Dyer, Chris. *Wanderlust: A Novel of Sex and Sensibility.* New York: Plume, 2003.

Eagleson, Holly. "Be the Smartest, Sexiest Girl in Town." *Cosmopolitan,* Oct. 2008: 196–99.

Edwards, Anne-Marie. *In the Steps of Jane Austen: Walking Tours of Austen's England.* 1979. Madison, WI: Jones, 2003.

Edwards, Lee R. "Women, Energy, and *Middlemarch.*" *Massachusetts Review* 13 (1972). Rpt. in *"Middlemarch": An Authoritative Text, Backgrounds, Criticism.* Ed. Bert G. Hornback. 2nd ed. New York: Norton, 2000. 623–30.

Eliot, George. "Silly Novels by Lady Novelists." *Westminster Review,* Oct. 1856. Rpt. in *Selected Essays, Poems and Other Writings.* Ed. A. S. Byatt and Nicholas Warren. London: Penguin, 1990. 140–63.

Elliot, Stephanie. "And Another Thing—Chick Lit Not a Genre???" Online posting. Yahoo! Chick Lit Discussion Group, 9 Mar. 2005. http://groups.yahoo.com/group/ChickLit/message/27640.

Enstad, Nan. *Ladies of Labor, Girls of Adventure: Working Women, Popular Culture, and Labor Politics at the Turn of the Century.* New York: Columbia UP, 1999.

Essig, Laurie. "Ordinary Ugliness: The Hidden Cost of the Credit Crunch." *Chronicle Review,* 30 Jan. 2009: B10–11.

Ezard, John. "Bainbridge Tilts at 'Chick Lit' Cult." *Guardian,* 24 Aug. 2001. http://books.guardian.co.uk/departments/generalfiction/story/0,6000,541954,00.html.

Fairley, Juliette. *Cash in the City: Affording Manolos, Martinis, and Manicures on a Working Girl's Salary.* New York: Wiley, 2002.

"Faith Baldwin, Author of 85 Books, Is Dead at 84." *New York Times,* 20 Mar. 1978. Rpt. in *New York Times Biographical Services.* New York: New York Times Company, 1978. 283.

Fein, Ellen, and Sherrie Schneider. *The Rules: Time-Tested Secrets for Capturing the Heart of Mr. Right.* New York: Warner, 1995.

Felski, Rita. "The Novel of Self-Discovery: A Necessary Fiction?" *Southern Review* 19.2 (July 1986): 131–48.

Fenton, Kate. *Vanity and Vexation: A Novel of Pride and Prejudice.* New York: Dunne, 2004.

Ferriss, Suzanne. "Narrative and Cinematic Doubleness: *Pride and Prejudice* and *Bridget Jones's Diary.*" *Chick Lit: The New Woman's Fiction.* Ed. Ferriss and Mallory Young. New York: Routledge, 2005. 71–84.

Ferriss, Suzanne, and Mallory Young. "A Generational Divide over Chick Lit." *Chronicle of Higher Education* 52.38 (26 May 2006): B13.

————, eds. *Chick Flicks: Contemporary Women at the Movies*. New York: Rout-ledge, 2007.

————, eds. *Chick Lit: The New Woman's Fiction*. New York: Routledge, 2005.

Field, Genevieve, ed. *Sex and Sensibility: 28 True Romances from the Lives of Single Women*. New York: Washington Square, 2005.

Fielding, Helen. *Bridget Jones: The Edge of Reason*. 1999. New York: Viking, 2000.

————. *Bridget Jones's Diary*. London: Picador, 1996.

————. "Dumped Bridget, Wrote Spy Novel." Interview. *Guardian*, 7 Nov. 2003. http://books.guardian.co.uk/departments/generalfiction/story/0,6000, 1080054,00.html.

————. "Helen Fielding: The Making of Bridget Jones." Interview. iVillage .com, 1998. http://www.ivillage.com/books/print/0,,76635,00.html.

————. *Olivia Joules and the Overactive Imagination*. London: Picador, 2003.

Finnamore, Suzanne. *Otherwise Engaged*. New York: Knopf, 1999.

Foster, Kennedy. *All Roads Lead Me Back to You*. New York: Pocket, 2009.

Fowler, Karen Joy. *The Jane Austen Book Club*. New York: Putnam, 2004.

Foy, Heather. E-mail to the author [on Red Dress Ink imprint]. 14 May 2009.

Franken, Christien. "Me and Ms Jones: Love, Romance, and Motherhood in English-Language 'Single Women' Novels." *De Gids* 63.9 (2000): 729–36.

Fraser, Marian Botsford. *Solitaire: The Intimate Lives of Single Women*. Toronto: Macfarlane Walter & Ross, 2001.

Frisby, David. *Cityscapes of Modernity: Critical Explorations*. Cambridge, UK: Pol-ity, 2001.

Frye, Northrop. *Anatomy of Criticism: Four Essays*. 1957. New York: Atheneum, 1968.

————. *The Secular Scripture: A Study of the Structure of Romance*. Cambridge, MA: Harvard UP, 1976.

Fuchs, Barbara. *Romance*. New York: Routledge, 2004.

Fuderer, Laura Sue. *The Female Bildungsroman in English: An Annotated Bibliog-raphy of Criticism*. New York: MLA, 1990.

Furley, Phyllis. *The Darcys*. Bexhill, East Sussex, UK: Egerton, 2004.

Gagnon, John H., and William Simon. *Sexual Conduct: The Social Sources of Human Sexuality*. Chicago: Aldine, 1973.

Gardiner, Jenny. E-mail to the author. 1 May 2009.

Geller, Jaclyn. *Here Comes the Bride: Women, Weddings, and the Marriage Mys-tique*. New York: Four Walls Eight Windows, 2001.

Gibbons, Fiachra. "The Route to Literary Success: Be Young, Gifted, But Most of All Gorgeous." *Guardian*, 28 Mar. 2001: 3.

Glater, Jonathan. "Tuition Again Rises Faster Than Inflation." *New York Times*, 24 Oct. 2006. http://www.nytimes.com/2006/10/25/education/25tuition.htm.

Godbersen, Anna. *The Luxe*. New York: HarperCollins, 2007.

Goldberg, Michelle. "Feminism for Sale." AlterNet, 8 Jan. 2001. http://www
.alternet.org/story/10306/.

Goldsmith, Oliver. "From a Letter Written in the Character of Lien Chi Altangi,
1761." *Novel and Romance, 1700–1800: A Documentary Record*. Ed. Ioan Williams. New York: Barnes and Noble, 1970. 232–33.

Gramsci, Antonio. "Problems of Criticism." *Selected Cultural Writings*. Ed.
David Forgacs and Geoffrey Nowell-Smith. Trans. William Boelhower. London: Lawrence & Wishart, 1985. 99–102.

Grange, Amanda. *Mr. Darcy's Diary*. 2005. Naperville, IL: Sourcebooks, 2007.

Grazer, Gigi Levangie. *Maneater*. New York: Downtown, 2003.

Green, Jane. *Jemina J.: A Novel about Ugly Ducklings and Swans*. New York:
Broadway, 2000.

——. *Mr. Maybe*. London: Penguin, 1999.

Green, Katherine Soba. *The Courtship Novel, 1740–1820: A Feminized Genre*. Lex-
ington: UP of Kentucky, 1991.

Greenwald, Rachel. *Find a Husband after 35 Using What I Learned at Harvard
Business School*. New York: Ballantine, 2003.

Greer, Germaine. *The Female Eunuch*. 1970. New York: McGraw-Hill, 1971.

Grescoe, Paul. *Merchants of Venus: Inside Harlequin and the Empire of Romance*.
Vancouver: Raincoast, 1996.

Guerrero, Lisa A. "Sistahs Are Doin' It for Themselves." *Chick Lit: The New
Woman's Fiction*. Ed. Suzanne Ferriss and Mallory Young. New York: Routledge, 2005. 87–101.

Hacker, Andrew. *Mismatch: The Growing Gulf between Men and Women*. New
York: Scribner, 2003.

Halstead, Helen. *Mr. Darcy Presents His Bride*. 2005. Berkeley, CA: Ulysses, 2007.
Rpt. of *A Private Performance: A Sequel to Jane Austen's "Pride and Prejudice."*

Hapke, Laura. Afterword. *Skyscraper*. By Faith Baldwin. New York: Feminist,
2003. 251–69.

Harris, Gardiner. "If the Shoe Won't Fit, Fix the Foot? Popular Surgery Raises Concern." *New York Times*, 7 Dec. 2003. http://www.nytimes.com/2003/12/07/
health/07FOOT.html.

Harris, Lynn. *Death by Chick Lit*. New York: Berkley, 2007.

Harrison, Kate. *The Starter Marriage*. New York: NAL, 2005.

Harzewski, Stephanie. "Consuming Heteroscripts: The Modern Wedding in
the American Imaginary." *Iowa Journal of Cultural Studies* 4 (Spring 2004):
79–91.

Hastings, Chris, Beth Jones, and Stephanie Plentl. "Jane Austen to be Latest Teenage Sensation." *Sunday Telegraph*, 4 Feb. 2007. http://www.telegraph.co.uk/
news/main.jhtml?xml=/news/2007/02/04/nausteno4.xml.

Haywood, Eliza. *Anti-Pamela; or Feigned Innocence Detected*. 1742. New York: Garland, 1975.

———. *The City Jilt*. 1726. *The Masquerade Novels of Eliza Haywood*. Ed. Mary Ann Schofield. Delmar, NY: Scholars' Facsimiles and Reprints, 1986. 83–119.

"Helen Fielding's Bookshelf." *O: The Oprah Magazine*, June 2004. http://www.oprah.com/obc/omag/bookshelf/omag_books_hfielding_b.jhtml.

Henderson, Lauren. *Jane Austen's Guide to Dating*. New York: Hyperion, 2005.

Henry, Astrid. *Not My Mother's Sister: Generational Conflict and Third-Wave Feminism*. Bloomington: Indiana UP, 2004.

Hilton, Paris. *Confessions of an Heiress: A Tongue-in-Chic Peek between the Pose*. New York: Fireside, 2004.

Hochman, David. "*Sex* Secrets and Tantalizing Hints." *TV Guide* 3–9 Jan. 2004: 30–35.

Hochschild, Arlie Russell. *The Commercialization of Intimate Life: Notes from Home and Work*. Berkeley: U of California P, 2003.

Holliday, Alesia. *American Idle*. New York: Dorchester, 2004.

Holliday, Alesia, Naomi Neale, and Stephanie Rowe. *Shop 'til Yule Drop*. New York: Dorchester Love Spell, 2004.

Homans, George Caspar. *Social Behavior: Its Elementary Forms*. New York: Harcourt, Brace, 1961.

Hornby, Nick. *High Fidelity*. London: Gollancz, 1995.

"Hot Gloss." *Lucky* July 2004: 100.

"Hour with Margaret Marbury: Transcripts." 3 Oct. 2004. http://community.eharlequin.com/WebX?50@124.ArRga70pxgD.0@.3b9c257d/0.

Howells, William Dean. Rev. of *A Terrible Temptation*, by Charles Reade. *Atlantic Monthly* 28 (Sept. 1871): 383–84.

Hrabi, Dale. "The Beach Read." *Shop Etc.* June/July 2005: 166.

Hunter, J. Paul. *Before Novels: The Cultural Contexts of Eighteenth-Century English Fiction*. New York: Norton, 1990.

Hunter, Madeline. E-mail to the author. 9 Oct. 2009.

Illouz, Eva. *Consuming the Romantic Utopia: Love and the Cultural Contradictions of Capitalism*. Berkeley: U of California P, 1997.

Ingraham, Chrys. *White Weddings: Romancing Heterosexuality in Popular Culture*. New York: Routledge, 1999.

Irigaray, Luce. "Women on the Market." *This Sex Which Is Not One*. Trans. Catherine Porter. Ithaca, NY: Cornell UP, 1985. 170–91.

"Is Chick Lit Chic?" New York City chapter of the Women's National Book Association panel discussion. 15 Jan. 2004.

Israel, Betsy. *Bachelor Girl: The Secret History of Single Women in the Twentieth Century*. New York: Morrow, 2002.

Jacobs, Alexander. "I Don't: A Feminist Writer and 'Spinster by Choice' Hammers Away at the Registry of Reasons to Get Married." Rev. of *Here Comes the Bride: Women, Weddings, and the Marriage Mystique*, by Jaclyn Geller. *New York Observer*, 11 Jul 2001. http://www.jsonline.com/lifestyle/people/jul01/nowed15071101a.asp.

Jacobson, Aileen. " 'Chick Lit' Checklist; Essential Elements between the Covers: Single Women, Love, Adventure, Relationships, Careers and High Heels." *Newsday*, 11 May 2004, sec. 2: B2.

Jaffe, Rona. *The Best of Everything*. New York: Simon & Schuster, 1958.

Jameson, Fredric. *Postmodernism, or, the Cultural Logic of Late Capitalism*. Durham, NC: Duke UP, 1991.

Janowitz, Tama. *A Certain Age*. New York: Doubleday, 1999.

Jewell, Lisa. *Thirty-Nothing*. London: Penguin, 2000.

Johnson, Merri Lisa. *Jane Sexes It Up: True Confessions of Feminist Desire*. New York: Four Walls Eight Windows, 2002.

Jones, Ann Rosalind. "Mills and Boon Meets Feminism." *The Progress of Romance: The Politics of Popular Fiction*. Ed. Joan Radford. London: Routledge, 1986. 195–218.

Jong, Erica. *Fear of Flying*. New York: Holt, Rinehart & Winston, 1973.

Juska, Elisa. *Getting Over Jack Wagner*. New York: Downtown, 2003.

Kamen, Paula. *Her Way: Young Women Remake the Sexual Revolution*. New York: New York UP, 2000.

Kaplan, Deborah. "The Pride of Austen Critics: A Prejudice?" *Chronicle of Higher Education*, 11 Mar. 2005: B10–12.

Karbo, Karen. "The Parent Trap." *Tango*, Sept./Oct. 2006: 69–70.

Kaye, Susan. Frederick Wentworth, Captain ser. Coeur d'Alene, ID: Wytherngate, 2007– . 2 vols.

Keltner, Kim Wong. *The Dim Sum of All Things*. New York: Red Dress Ink, 2003.

Keyes, Marian. *Lucy Sullivan Is Getting Married*. New York: Morrow, 1999.

———. *Sushi for Beginners*. Dublin: Poolbeg, 2001.

Kinsella, Sophie. *Can You Keep a Secret?* New York: Delta, 2004.

———. *Confessions of a Shopaholic*. 2000. New York: Delta, 2001.

———. *Shopaholic and Baby*. New York: Dial Press, 2007.

———. *Shopaholic Takes Manhattan*. New York: Delta, 2002.

———. *Shopaholic Ties the Knot*. New York: Dell, 2003.

Kipnis, Laura. *Against Love: A Polemic*. New York: Pantheon, 2003.

———. *The Female Thing: Dirt, Sex, Envy, Vulnerability*. New York: Pantheon, 2006.

Kizis, Deanna. *How to Meet Cute Boys*. New York: Warner, 2003.

Krinsky, Natalie. *Chloe Does Yale*. New York: Hyperion, 2005.

La Ferla, Ruth. "They Want to Marry a Millionaire." *New York Times,* 4 Mar. 2001, sec. 9: 1.

Lakshmi, Rama. "India's Cheeky 'Chick Lit' Finds an Audience: Books Reveal Modern Women's Irreverent, Contrary Views on Ancient Cultural Mores." *Washington Post,* 23 Nov. 2007: A16.

Lang, Adele. *Confessions of a Sociopathic Social Climber: The Katya Livingston Chronicles.* 1998. New York: Dunne, 2002.

Langbauer, Laurie. *Women and Romance: The Consolations of Gender in the English Novel.* Ithaca, NY: Cornell UP, 1990.

"Learn to Write." Harlequin Web site. Accessed 19 Apr. 2010 http://www .eharlequin.com/articlepage.html?articleId=973&chapter=0.

Lee, Felicia. "Looking for Mr. Goodbucks." *New York Times,* 5 Mar. 2000, sec. 14: 1.

———. "Pioneers Are Taking Black Chick Lit into Middle Age." *New York Times,* 27 June 2005. http://www.nytimes.com/2005/06/27/books/27auth .html.

Lee, Hermione. *Edith Wharton.* New York: Knopf, 2007.

Lee, John Alan. "Ideologies of Lovestyle and Sexstyle." *Romantic Love and Sexual Behavior: Perspectives from the Social Sciences.* Ed. Victor C. de Munck. Westport, CT: Praeger, 1998. 33–76.

Lehmann, Stephanie. *Thoughts While Having Sex.* New York: Kensington, 2003.

Leibovich, Lori. "Reversal of Fortune." *Harper's Bazaar,* Aug. 2000: 190, 192–93.

Lessing, Doris. *The Golden Notebook.* London: Joseph, 1962.

Levine, Laura. *This Pen for Hire.* New York: Kensington, 2002.

Lieberman, Janice, and Bonnie Teller. *How to Shop for a Husband: A Consumer Guide to Getting a Great Buy on a Guy.* St. Martin's, 2009.

Lipscombe, Becky. "Chick-Lit Becomes Hip in Indonesia." *BBC News,* UK ed. 10 Sept. 2003. 10 Jan. 2004 http://news.bbc.co.uk/1/hi/world/asia-pacific/ 3093038.stm.

Lissner, Caren. E-mail to the author. 19 Sept. 2003.

———. *Starting from Square Two.* New York: Red Dress Ink, 2004.

"Literature, Sponsored by. . . ." *Writer,* July 2004: 8.

Lockwood, Cara. *I Do (But I Don't).* New York: Downtown, 2003.

Loftus, Mary. "Till Debt Do Us Part." *Psychology Today,* Nov./Dec. 2004: 42– 52.

Lorde, Audre. *Zami: A New Spelling of My Name.* New York: Crossings, 1982.

Lynch, Deidre, ed. *Janeites: Austen's Disciples and Devotees.* Princeton, NJ: Princeton UP, 2000.

MacAlister, Kate. *A Girl's Guide to Vampires.* New York: Love Spell, 2003.

———. *Sex and the Single Vampire.* New York: Love Spell, 2004.

Mak, G. Pearl. *Frozen Pancakes and False Eyelashes: One Imperfect Woman's Quest for Peace, Balance . . . and Maternal Mojo*. Charleston, SC: BookSurge, 2007.

Mancusi, Marianne. *A Connecticut Fashionista in King Arthur's Court*. New York: Dorchester, 2005.

Margolis, Sue. *Neurotica*. London: Headline, 1998.

Markham, Wendy. *Slightly Single*. New York: Red Dress Ink, 2002.

Marks, Pamela. "The Good Provider in Romance Novels." *Romantic Conventions*. Ed. Anne K. Kaler and Rosemary E. Johnson-Kurek. Bowling Green, OH: Bowling Green State University Popular Press, 1991. 10–22.

Marsh, Katherine. "Fabio Gets His Walking Papers: Can Harlequin Rekindle Romance in a Post-Feminist World?" *Washington Monthly*, Jan./Feb. 2002: 39–44.

Maslin, Janet. "Chick Lit that Mixes Voltaire with *Vogue*." Rev. of *Literacy and Longing in L.A.*, by Jennifer Kaufman and Karen Mack. *New York Times*, 19 June 2006. http://www.nytimes.com/2006/06/19/books/19masl.html.

———. "Older, but Keeping Up with the Bridget Joneses." Rev. of *Loop Group*, by Larry McMurtry. *New York Times*, 14 Dec. 2004. http://www.nytimes.com/2004/12/14/books/14masl.html.

Match.com Public Relations Team. "The Bridget Jones Effect: Fact or Fiction for U.S. Singles." 5 Apr. 2001. http://www.matchnewsletter.com/press/45.php.

Matthews, Carole. *For Better or Worse*. 2000. New York: Avon, 2002.

———. *The Sweetest Taboo*. New York: Avon Trade, 2004.

Maxted, Anna. *Getting Over It*. London: Arrow, 2000.

Mazza, Cris, and Jeffrey DeShell, eds. *Chick-Lit: Postfeminist Fiction*. Normal, IL: FC2, 1995.

Mazza, Cris, Jeffrey DeShell, and Elisabeth Sheffield, eds. *Chick-Lit 2: (No Chick Vics)*. Normal, IL: FC2, 1996.

McCarthy, Mary. *The Group*. New York: Harcourt, 1963.

McInerney, Jay. *Bright Lights, Big City*. New York: Vintage, 1984.

McGrath, Charles. "Pretty Words, Jane; Would That You Were Too." *New York Times*, 1 Apr. 2007. http://www.nytimes.com/2007/04/01/weekinreview/01mcgrath.html.

McKeon, Michael. *The Origins of the English Novel, 1600–1740*. Baltimore: Johns Hopkins UP, 1987.

McLaughlin, Emma, and Nicola Kraus. *Citizen Girl*. New York: Atria, 2004.

———. *The Nanny Diaries*. New York: St. Martin's, 2002.

McMillan, Terry. *Waiting to Exhale*. New York: Viking, 1992.

McMurtry, Larry. *Terms of Endearment*. New York: Simon & Schuster, 1975.

McRobbie, Angela. "Postfeminism and Popular Culture: Bridget Jones and the New Gender Regime." *Interrogating Postfeminism: Gender and the Politics of*

Popular Culture. Ed. Yvonne Tasker and Diane Negra. Durham, NC: Duke UP, 2007. 27–39.

Mead, Rebecca. "Love for Sale." Rev. of *Find a Husband after 35 Using What I Learned at Harvard Business School,* by Rachel Greenwald. *New Yorker,* 24 Nov. 2003: 104–7.

———. *One Perfect Day: The Selling of the American Wedding.* New York: Penguin, 2007.

Melamed, Samantha. "A Decent Proposal." *Bucks,* May/June 2004: 116.

Merck, Mandy. "Sexuality in the City." *Reading "Sex and the City."* Ed. Kim Akass and Janet McCabe. London: Tauris, 2004. 48–62.

Merrick, Elizabeth, ed. *This Is Not Chick Lit: Original Stories by America's Best Women Writers.* New York: Random, 2006.

Messina, Lynn. *Fashionistas.* New York: Red Dress Ink, 2003.

Miller, Karen E. Quinones. *Using What You Got.* New York: Simon & Schuster, 2003.

Miller, Laura. "The Last Word; Taking Wing." *New York Times Book Review,* 1 June 2003: 39.

Milne, Gordon. *The Sense of Society: A History of the American Novel of Manners.* Rutherford, NJ: Fairleigh Dickinson UP, 1977.

Mlynowski, Sarah. *Milkrun.* New York: Red Dress Ink, 2001.

Mlynowski, Sarah, and Farrin Jacobs. *See Jane Write: A Girl's Guide to Writing Chick Lit.* Philadelphia: Quirk, 2006.

Modleski, Tania. *Feminism without Women: Culture and Criticism in a "Postfeminist" Age.* New York: Routledge, 1991.

———. *Loving with a Vengeance: Mass-Produced Fantasies for Women.* Hamden, CT: Archon, 1982.

Molloy, John. *Why Men Marry Some Women and Not Others: The Fascinating Research That Can Land You the Man of Your Dreams.* New York: Warner, 2003.

Montemurro, Beth. "Charlotte Chooses Her Choice: Liberal Feminism on *Sex and the City.*" *Scholar and the Feminist Online* 3.1 (Fall 2004). http://www.barnard.edu/sfonline/hbo/montemurro_01.htm.

Moore, Myreah, and Jodie Gould. *Date like a Man to Get the Man You Want.* New York: HarperCollins, 2000.

Morley, Christopher. *Kitty Foyle.* Philadelphia: Lippincott, 1939.

Morgan, Robin, ed. *Sisterhood Is Powerful: An Anthology of Writings from the Women's Liberation Movement.* New York: Random, 1970.

Morrall, Clare. *Astonishing Splashes of Colour.* Birmingham, UK: Tindal Street, 2003.

Moseley, Rachel, and Jacinda Read. "Having It *Ally:* Popular Television (Post) Feminism." *Feminist Media Studies* 2.2 (2002): 231–49.

Moy, Rebecca. "Hello Again, Old Friend." *BBC News Magazine*, UK ed. 4 Aug. 2005. http://news.bbc.co.uk/1/hi/magazine/4745263.stm.

Murstein, Bernard I. *Who Will Marry Whom? Theories and Research in Marital Choice*. New York: Springer, 1976.

Napalkova, Ekaterina. "The Treadmill Book Club: Finding the Literary Value of 'Chick Lit' in Candace Bushnell's 'Nice N'Easy.' " Unpublished student essay. June 2003.

Neale, Naomi. *I Went to Vassar for This?* New York: Dorchester, 2006.

Negra, Diane. *What a Girl Wants? Fantasizing the Reclamation of Self in Postfeminism*. New York: Routledge, 2009.

Norwood, Stacey. "In Praise of Jane Austen." *Tea Time*, Nov./Dec. 2008: 32–36, 37–40.

O'Connell, Jennifer. *Bachelorette #1*. New York: New American Library, 2003.

O'Connell, Tyne. *The Sex Was Great But . . .* New York: Red Dress Ink, 2004.

"Oprah Talks to Sarah Jessica Parker." *O: The Oprah Magazine*, Mar. 2004: 186–89, 240.

Orloff, Erica. *Divas Don't Fake It*. 2000. New York: Red Dress Ink, 2003.

O'Rourke, Sally Smith. *The Man Who Loved Jane Austen*. New York: Kensington, 2006.

Papa, Ariella. *Up and Out*. Ontario: Red Dress Ink, 2003.

Parent, Gail. *Sheila Levine Is Dead and Living in New York*. New York: Putnam, 1972.

Parsons, Deborah. L. *Streetwalking the Metropolis: Women, the City, and Modernity*. Oxford: Oxford UP, 2000.

Pastan, Rachel. *This Side of Married*. New York: Viking, 2004.

Paul, Pamela. *The Starter Marriage and the Future of Matrimony*. New York: Villard, 2002.

Pearson, Alison. *I Don't Know How She Does It*. London: Chatto & Windus, 2002.

Peril, Lynn. *Pink Think: Becoming a Woman in Many Uneasy Lessons*. New York: Norton, 2002.

Philips, Deborah. *Writing Romance: Women's Fiction, 1945–2005*. London: Continuum, 2006.

Phoca, Sophia, and Rebecca Wright. *Introducing Postfeminism*. Cambridge, UK: Icon; New York: Totem, 1999.

"Plastic Appeal." *AARP Bulletin* Jan. 2007: 28.

Plath, Sylvia. *The Bell Jar*. 1963. New York: Bantam Windstom, 1972.

Pope, Alexander. *The Dunciad, Variorum. With the Prolegomena of Scriblerus*. London: Dod, 1729.

Postrel, Virginia. *The Substance of Style: How the Rise of Aesthetic Value Is Remaking Commerce, Culture, and Consciousness*. New York: HarperCollins, 2003.

Powell, Dawn. *Whither*. Boston: Small, Maynard, 1925.

Press, Andrea, and Terry Strathman. "Work, Family, and Social Class in Television Images of Women: Prime-Time Television and the Construction of Postfeminism." *Women and Language* 16.2 (1993): 7–15.

"*Pride and Prejudice* Is Top Read." *BBC News*, 1 Mar. 2007. http://news.bbc.co .uk/2/hi/entertainment/6405737.stm.

Projansky, Sarah. "Mass Magazine Cover Girls: Some Reflections of Postfeminist Girls and Postfeminism's Daughters." *Interrogating Postfeminism: Gender and the Politics of Popular Culture*. Ed. Yvonne Tasker and Diane Negra. Durham, NC: Duke UP, 2007. 40–72.

"Publishers Fight for More 'Male Lit.'" *BBC News*, 12 Oct. 2003. 25 Nov. 2003 http://news.bbc.co.uk/go/pr/fr//2/hi/entertainment/3180722.stm.

Pucci, Suzanne R., and James Thompson. *Jane Austen and Co.: Remaking the Past in Contemporary Culture*. New York: State U of New York P, 2003.

Quamme, Margaret. "'Chick-Lit' Makes Engrossing, Provocative Reply to Feminism." Rev. of *Chick-Lit: Postfeminist Fiction*, by Cris Mazza and Jeffrey DeShell. *Columbus Dispatch*, 28 Jan 1996: 6G.

Quinn, Karl. "Don't Mention *Sex and the City*." *The Age* [Melbourne, Australia] 28 Sept. 2003. http://www.theage.com.au/articles/2003/09/27/1064083206501 .html.

Rabine, Leslie W. *Reading the Romantic Heroine: Text, History, Ideology*. Ann Arbor: U of Michigan P, 1985.

Radway, Janice. *Reading the Romance: Women, Patriarchy, and Popular Literature*. Chapel Hill: U of North Carolina P, 1984.

Ramsdell, Kristin. *Happily Ever After: A Guide to Reading Interests in Romance Fiction*. Littleton, CO: Libraries Unlimited, 1987.

Reeve, Katherine. *Jane Austen in Bath: Walking Tours of the Writer's City*. New York: Little Bookroom, 2006.

Regis, Pamela. *A Natural History of the Romance Novel*. Philadelphia: U of Pennsylvania P, 2003.

Reid, Janet. "Cowgirl Lit!" Blog posting. 9 May 2010. http://jetreidliterary.blog spot.com.

renaynay. "Great 'Chick Lit' Fiction for Black Womyn." Amazon.com list. Accessed 10 Jan. 2004. http://www.amazon.com/Great-Chick-Fiction-Black-Womyn/lm/1QFP1F8LYPQQ3.

Ribon, Pamela. *Why Girls Are Weird*. New York: Downtown, 2003.

Rice, Marcelle Smith. *Dawn Powell*. New York: Twayne, 2000.

Rich, Adrienne. "Compulsory Heterosexuality and Lesbian Existence." *Signs* 5.4 (Summer 1980): 631–60. Rpt. in *Adrienne Rich's Poetry and Prose: Poems, Prose, Reviews, and Criticism*. Ed. Barbara Charlesworth Gelpi and Albert Gelpi. Rev. ed. New York: Norton, 1993. 203–24.

Rich, Joshua. "*Sex and the City:* A Big Box Office Win." *Entertainment Weekly,* 1 June 2008. http://www.ew.com/ew/article/0,,20187935_20187958_20203593,00 .html.

Roberts, Sam. "51% of Women Are Now Living without Spouse." *New York Times,* 16 Jan. 2007. http://www.nytimes.com/2007/01/16/us/16census.html.

Roiphe, Katie. "The Independent Woman (and Other Lies)." *Esquire,* Feb. 1997: 84–86.

Romance Writers of America (RWA). "Romance Literature Statistics: Overview." Accessed 22 Mar. 2009. http://www.rwanational.org/cs/the_romance_genre /romance_literature_statistics.

———. "RWA Defines the Romance Novel." c. 1999. http://www.rwanational .org/PressReleaseRWADefinesRomance.cfm.

Rose, Jackie. *Marrying Up.* New York: Red Dress Ink, 2005.

———. *Slim Chance.* Ontario: Red Dress Ink, 2003.

Rosemberg, Jasmin. *How the Other Half Hamptons.* New York: 5 Spot, 2008.

Ross, Josephine. *Jane Austen's Guide to Good Manners.* New York: Bloomsbury USA, 2006.

Rubin, Gayle. "The Traffic in Women: Notes on the 'Political Economy' of Sex." *Toward an Anthropology of Women.* Ed. Rayna R. Reiter. New York: Monthly Review Press, 1975. 157–210.

Russo, Mary. "Notes on 'Post-Feminism.'" The Politics of Theory: *Proceedings of the Essex Conference on the Sociology of Literature.* Ed. Francis Barker et al. Colchester, UK: U of Essex P, 1983. 27–37.

Salamon, Julie. "Will *Sex and the City* without the Sex Have Much Appeal?" *New York Times,* 9 June 2004. http://www.nytimes.com/2004/06/09/arts/ television/09SEX.html.

Sanders, Jennifer "Gin." *Wear More Cashmere: 151 Luxurious Ways to Pamper Your Inner Princess.* Gloucester, MA: Fair Winds, 2003.

Sanderson, Caroline. *A Rambling Fancy: In the Footsteps of Jane Austen.* London: Cadogan Guides, 2006.

Santini, Rosemarie. *Sex & Sensibility: The Adventures of a Jane Austen Addict.* New York: Saint, 2005.

Schank, Hana. *A More Perfect Union: How I Survived the Happiest Day of My Life.* New York: Atria, 2006.

Scott, Linda M. *Fresh Lipstick: Redressing Fashion and Feminism.* New York: Palgrave, 2005.

Seckler, Valerie. "Women's Wishes: Control, Security and Peace." Rev. of *What Women Really Want,* by Celinda Lake and Kellyanne Conway. *Staten Island Advance,* 5 Jan. 2006: C3.

Senate, Melissa. *See Jane Date.* New York: Red Dress Ink, 2001.

———. *Whose Wedding Is It Anyway?* New York: Red Dress Ink, 2004.

Sex and the City. Created by Darren Starr. HBO. 1998–2004.

Sex and the City. Dir. Michael Patrick King. New Line Cinema, 2008.

Shapiro, Juliette. *Excessively Diverted: The Sequel to Jane Austen's "Pride and Prejudice."* College Station, TX: Virtualbookworm.com, 2002.

Shear, Leanne, and Tracey Toomey. *The Perfect Manhattan.* New York: Broadway, 2005.

Silver, Amy. *Confessions of a Reluctant Recessionista.* London: Arrow, 2009.

Sittenfeld, Curtis. Rev. of *The Wonder Spot,* by Melissa Bank. *New York Times Book Review,* 5 June 2005. http://www.nytimes.com/2005/06/05/books/review/05SITT01.html.

Skerrett, Joanne. *She Who Shops.* New York: Strapless, 2005.

Smith, Caroline J. *Cosmopolitan Culture and Consumerism in Chick Lit.* New York: Routledge, 2008.

———. *"Cosmopolitan" Culture and Consumerism in Contemporary Women's Popular Fiction.* Diss. U of Delaware, 2005. Ann Arbor: UMI, 2005.

Smith, Jim. *The Manhattan Dating Game: An Unofficial and Unauthorized Guide to "Sex and the City."* London: Virgin, 2002.

Snitow, Ann Barr. "Mass Market Romance: Pornography for Women Is Different." *Radical History Review* Spring/Summer 1979: 141–61.

Sohn, Amy. *Run Catch Kiss: A Gratifying Novel.* New York: Simon & Schuster, 1999.

Soignée, Princess Jacqueline de. *The Princess-in-Training Manual.* New York: Red Dress Ink, 2003.

Sparrow, Rebecca. *The Girl Most Likely.* St. Lucia, Queensland: U of Queensland P, 2003.

Stanger, Patti, and Lisa Johnson Mandell. *Become Your Own Matchmaker: 8 Easy Steps for Attracting Your Perfect Mate.* New York: Atria, 2009.

Stansell, Christine. *City of Women: Sex and Class in New York, 1789–1860.* New York: Knopf, 1986.

Steiner, Wendy, ed. *Literature as Meaning: A Thematic Anthology of Literature.* New York: Longman, 2005.

———. *Pictures of Romance: Form against Context in Painting and Literature.* Chicago: U of Chicago P, 1988.

Straker, Wendy. *Sexy Jobs in the City: How to Find Your Dream Job Using the Rules of Dating.* New York: Hangover Productions, 2003.

Strohmeyer, Sarah. *The Penny Pinchers Club.* New York: Dutton, 2009.

Sutherland, John, and Deirdre Le Faye. *So You Think You Know Jane Austen? A Literary Quizbook.* Oxford: Oxford UP, 2005.

Swendson, Shanna. *Enchanted, Inc.* New York: Ballantine, 2005.

———. "Jane Austen: The Mother of All Chick Lit." Meeting of Dallas Area Romance Authors. Richardson, TX. 28 May 2005.

———. "Re: Research Study: Chick Lit as Writerly and Readerly Medium." Online posting. Yahoo! Chick Lit Discussion Group, 16 Nov. 2004. http:// groups.yahoo.com/group/ChickLit/message/24460.

———. "The Relevance of Chick Lit." Online posting. Yahoo! Chick Lit Discussion Group, 1 Dec. 2003. http://groups.yahoo.com/group/ChickLit/ message/14391.

Sykes, Plum. *Bergdorf Blondes.* New York: Miramax, 2004.

Tasker, Yvonne, and Diane Negra, eds. *Interrogating Postfeminism: Gender and the Politics of Popular Culture.* Durham, NC: Duke UP, 2007.

———. "Introduction: Feminist Politics and Postfeminist Culture." *Interrogating Postfeminism: Gender and the Politics of Popular Culture.* Durham, NC: Duke UP, 2007. 1–25.

Templeton, Karen. *Loose Screws.* New York: Red Dress Ink, 2002.

Tenzer, Livia. "Question about Women Write Pulp Series." E-mail to the author. 10 Nov. 2003.

Tenzer, Livia, and Jean Casella. Publisher's foreword. *Skyscraper.* By Faith Baldwin. New York: Feminist, 2003. v–xiv.

Tessaro, Kathleen. *Elegance.* New York: Avon Trade, 2003.

Thibaut, John W., and Harold H. Kelley. *The Social Psychology of Groups.* New York: Wiley, 1959.

Thomas, Scarlett. "The Great Chick Lit Conspiracy." *Independent,* 4 Aug. 2002. http://enjoyment.independent.co.uk/books/features/story.jsp?story= 321729.

"Too Sexy for This Book." *Philadelphia Style,* July/Aug. 2003: 54.

Townend, Annette. "Historical Overview." *Words of Love: A Complete Guide to Romance Fiction.* Ed. Eileen Fallon. New York: Garland, 1984. 3–29.

Trumbull, John. *The Progress of Dullness. Part Third, and Last: Sometimes Called, the Progress of Coquetry.* New Haven, CT: Green, 1773.

Tyler, Natalie. *The Friendly Jane Austen: A Well-Mannered Introduction to a Lady of Sense and Sensibility.* New York: Viking, 1999.

U.S. Bureau of the Census. America's Families and Living Arrangements: Population Characteristics, 2000. Prepared by Jason Fields. Current Population Reports P20–537. Washington, DC. June 2001.

Valby, Karen. Rev. of *Olivia Joules and the Overactive Imagination,* by Helen Fielding. *Entertainment Weekly,* 11 June 2004. http://www.ew.com/article/ 0,,645581,00.html.

Valdes-Rodriguez, Alisa. *The Dirty Girls Social Club.* New York: St. Martin's, 2003.

———. *The Husband Habit.* New York: St. Martin's, 2009.

Vance, Carole S., ed. *Pleasure and Danger: Exploring Female Sexuality.* Boston: Routledge & Paul, 1984.

van der Meer, Antonia. "Get Ready to Shop!" Editor's letter. *Modern Bride*, Apr./ May 2003: 20.

Van Gelder, Lawrence. "Publisher Offers Jane Austen's Work as 'Classic Romances.'" *New York Times*, 18 Jan. 2006. http://www.nytimes.com/2006/01/18/books/18austen.html.

Viswanathan, Kaavya. *How Opal Mehta Got Kissed, Got Wild, and Got a Life*. Boston: Little, Brown, 2006.

von Ziegesar, Cecily. *All I Want Is Everything*. Gossip Girl ser. New York: Little, Brown, 2003.

Walker, Rebecca. "Riding the Third Wave." Interview with Sangamithra Iyer. *Satya*, Jan. 2005. http://www.satyamag.com/jan05/walker.html.

———, ed. *To Be Real: Telling the Truth and the Changing Face of Feminism*. New York: Anchor 1995.

Warner, William B. *Licensing Entertainment: The Elevation of Novel Reading in Britain, 1684–1750*. Berkeley: U of California P, 1998.

Wasserstein, Wendy. *Elements of Style*. New York: Knopf, 2006.

Weeks, Linton. "Judged by Their Back Covers: Writing Well Helps Sell a Book, and Photographing Well Doesn't Hurt." *Washington Post*, 2 July 2001: C1.

Weigel, Margaret. "Some Anti-Bridgets." *Women's Review of Books* 20.10–11 (July 2003): 33–34.

Weigel, Marilyn. "Re: Industry: State of the Chicklit Union." Online posting. Yahoo! Chick Lit Discussion Group, 29 June 2007. http://groups.yahoo.com/group/ChickLit/message/49083.

Weinberg, Anna. "She's Come Undone." *Book*, July/Aug. 2003: 47–49.

Weiner, Jennifer. *Good in Bed*. New York: Pocket, 2001.

———. *Goodnight Nobody*. New York: Atria, 2005.

———. *In Her Shoes*. New York: Pocket, 2002.

———. *Little Earthquakes*. New York: Atria, 2004.

Weisberger, Lauren. *Chasing Harry Winston*. New York: Simon & Schuster, 2008.

———. *The Devil Wears Prada*. New York: Doubleday, 2003.

Wellman, Laurel. "Confessions of a Queen of Chick Lit." *San Francisco Chronicle*, 14 Apr. 2004. http://sfgate.com/cgi-bin/article.cgi?file=/c/a/2004/04/14/DDGM563P351.DTL.

Wells, Juliette. "Mothers of Chick Lit? Women Writers, Readers, and Literary History." *Chick Lit: The New Woman's Fiction*. Ed. Suzanne Ferriss and Mallory Young. New York: Routledge, 2005. 47–70.

Weston, Jessie. *From Ritual to Romance*. London: Cambridge UP, 1920.

Wharton, Edith. *The Custom of the Country*. 1913. Rpt. in *Edith Wharton: Five Novels, Complete and Unabridged*. New York: Barnes and Noble, 2006. 359–678.

———. *The House of Mirth: A Novel of Admonition.* 1905. Ed. Elizabeth Ammons. New York: Norton, 1990.

"What Happens When Chick Lit Grows Up?" Online women's fiction workshop sponsored by Romance Divas. 11–13 June 2009. http://forums.romancedivas .com/.

Whelehan, Imelda. *"Bridget Jones's Diary": A Reader's Guide.* New York: Continuum, 2002.

———. *The Feminist Bestseller: From "Sex and the Single Girl" to "Sex and the City."* New York: Palgrave Macmillan, 2005.

———. "High Anxiety: Feminism, Chicklit and Women in the Noughties." *Diegesis: The Journal of the Association for Research in Popular Fictions* 8 (Winter 2004): 4–10.

White, Kate. *If Looks Could Kill.* New York: Warner, 2002.

———. *Why Good Girls Don't Get Ahead—but Gutsy Girls Do.* New York: Warner, 1995.

Whitehead, Barbara Dafoe. "The Plight of the High-Status Woman." *Atlantic Monthly,* Dec. 1999. http://www.theatlantic.com/issues/99dec/9912white head2.htm.

———. *Why There Are No Good Men Left: The Romantic Plight of the New Single Woman.* New York: Broadway, 2003.

Williams, Jacqueline. *The Handbag Book of Girlie Emergencies.* 2001. San Diego: Laurel Glen, 2002.

Williams, Tia. *The Accidental Diva.* New York: Penguin, 2004.

Williamson, Lisa Ann. "30-Something: Single and Happy." *Staten Island Advance,* 2 May 2006: C1, C7.

Wilson, Kim. *Tea with Jane Austen.* Madison, WI: Jones, 2004.

Wiltshire, John. *Recreating Jane Austen.* Cambridge, UK: Cambridge UP, 2001.

Winston, Lois. E-mail to the author. 29 May 2009.

Witchel, Alex. *Me Times Three.* New York: Knopf, 2002.

Wolcott, James. "Hear Me Purr: Maureen Dowd and the Rise of Postfeminist Chick Lit." *New Yorker,* 20 May 1996: 54–59.

———. "The Right Fluff: A Guy's Guide to Chick Flicks." *Vanity Fair,* Mar. 2008. http://www.vanityfair.com/culture/features/2008/03/chickflicks200803.

Wolf, Laura. *Diary of a Mad Bride.* New York: Delta, 2002.

———. *Diary of a Mad Mom-to-Be.* New York: Delta, 2003.

Wolf, Naomi. *Fire with Fire: The New Female Power and How It Will Change the 21st Century.* New York: Random, 1993.

———. *Promiscuities: The Secret Struggle for Womanhood.* New York: Random, 1997.

Wolff, Janet. "The Invisible *Flâneuse:* Women and the Literature of Modernity." *Theory, Culture and Society* 2.3 (1985): 37–46.

Woolf, Virginia. "How It Strikes the Contemporary." 1925. *The Common Reader: First Series, Annotated Edition.* Ed. Andrew McNeillie. Orlando, FL: Harvest, 1984. 231–241.

Wright, Michelle Curry. *Miranda Blue Calling.* New York: Avon Trade, 2004.

Yardley, Cathy. *Will Write for Shoes: How to Write a Chick Lit Novel.* New York: Dunne, 2006.

Yaszek, Lisa. " 'I'll be a postfeminist in a postpatriarchy,' or, Can We Really Imagine Life after Feminism?" *Electronic Book Review,* Spring 2005. http://www .electronicbookreview.com/v3/servlet/ebr?essay_id=yaszekwp&command =view_essay.

Young, Elizabeth. *A Girl's Best Friend.* New York: Avon Trade, 2003.

Yu, Michelle, and Blosson Kan. *China Dolls.* New York: St. Martin's, 2007.

Zeitchik, Steven. "Publishers' Guide to Hunting and Fishing." *Publishers Weekly NewsLine,* 30 Sept. 2002. http://www.publishersweekly.com/article/420269-Publishers_Guide_to_Hunting_and_Fishing_.php?q=%22guide+to+hunting+and+fishing%22.

Zernike, Kate. "Just Saying No to the Dating Industry." *New York Times,* 30 Nov. 2003, Fashion & Style sec. http://www.nytimes.com/2003/11/30/fashion /30SING.html.

Zieger, Susan. "Sex and the Citizen in *Sex and the City*'s New York." *Reading "Sex and the City."* Ed. Kim Akass and Janet McCabe. London: Tauris, 2004. 96–111.

Zigman, Laura. *Animal Husbandry.* New York: Dial, 1998.

Zneimer, Lia. " 'I couldn't help but wonder . . .': Are Female Friends the New Soul Mate? Female Friendships in Bushnell's *Sex and the City* and Its HBO Adaptation." Unpublished essay. Apr. 2009.

Zolbrod, Zoe. "In Print: the Perils of Postfeminism." *Chicago Reader,* 25 Oct. 1996: 47.

Index

with fashion trends, 47–49; Harlequin romance vs., 25–26, 32–40; as implicit commentary on feminism's gains/deficiencies, 150–86; as light-read vicarious wish fulfillment, 147; Mazza and DeShell's concept of, 44–45, 148–50; novels of manners vs., 4–5, 20; postfeminism in, 8–11; problematic as label, 143–47; as postfeminist memoir, 156–59; readerly functions of, 169–73; as sociocultural commentary, 11–16, 148–86; varying analyses of, 5–11; Wolcott on, 45–46. *See also* feminism/postfeminism

Chick-Lit: Post-feminist Fiction (Mazza and DeShell), 44–45, 148–50

China Dolls (Kan and Yu), 188

Chloe Does Yale (Krinsky), 158

Christensen, Kate, 137–38

Cipolla, Fabio, 41

Ciresi, Rita, 182

Citizen Girl (McLaughlin and Kraus), 167–68

City Chic, 49

City Jilt, The (Haywood), 39

city scapes, 30–31; early working girl fiction, 126–38; *Sex and the City*'s consumerism, 90–122; urban sophisticate in proto–chick lit, 138–43; wedding farces in NYC, 174. *See also* New York City

Cixous, Hélène, 152–53

"class without money" conflict, 4

Clinton, Bill, 189

Colgan, Jenny, 173, 210n1

Collins, Alan, 39

commodity culture, 154–55, 159–65, 204n12; chick lit on women's value and values, 173–81; *Sex and the City*'s, 90–122

"Compulsory Heterosexuality and Lesbian Existence" (Rich), 11

"Confessions of a Queen of Chick Lit" (Wellman), 162

Confessions of a Reluctant Recessionista (Silver), 22

Confessions of a Shopaholic (Kinsella), 158

consciousness-raising novels, 125–30

consumerism, 197n4, 198n7, 204n12, 204n15, 208n1; central to chick lit, 11–12, 22; chick lit's ties with, 21, 46–52, 159–65; Kinsella's *Shopaholic* titles, 33, 158, 174, 202n9; men as vehicle for procuring commodities, 90–91; in *Sex and the City*, 90–122.

cosmetic surgery, 165

Cosmopolitan, 53, 68, 142–42, 157

Cosmopolitan Culture and Consumerism in Chick Lit (Smith, C.), 15–16, 157, 194, 197n4, 198n7

Cosper, Darcy, 80

cowgirl lit, 194

Crusie, Jennifer, 86–87, 202n11

Cunnah, Michelle, 181–82

Curnyn, Lynda, 50

Cusk, Rachel, 67

Custom of the Country, The (Wharton), 20

Dailey, Janet, 27

Daisy Miller (James), 4–5

Dark series, 191

Daswani, Kavita, 13, 34, 35, 157, 183, 191–92, 197n3

Dating without Novocaine (Cach), 130

Davidson, Mary Janice, 190

Davies, Andrew, 72, 78

"Dead Men Don't Eat Quiche" (Carlyle), 34

Death by Chick Lit (Harris), 17

CULTURAL FRAMES, FRAMING CULTURE

Books in this series examine both the way our culture frames our narratives
and the way our narratives produce the culture that frames them. Attempting to bridge the gap between previously disparate disciplines, and combin-
ing theoretical issues with practical applications, this series invites a broad
audience to read contemporary culture in a fresh and provocative way.

Nancy Martha West
Kodak and the Lens of Nostalgia

Raphael Sassower and Louis Cicotello
The Golden Avant-Garde: Idolatry, Commercialism, and Art

Margot Norris
Writing War in the Twentieth Century

Robin Blaetz
Visions of the Maid: Joan of Arc in American Film and Culture

Ellen Tremper
I'm No Angel: The Blonde in Fiction and Film

Naomi Mandel
*Against the Unspeakable: Complicity, the Holocaust,
and Slavery in America*

Debra Walker King
African Americans and the Culture of Pain

Jon Robert Adams
Male Armor: The Soldier-Hero in Contemporary American Culture

Rachel Hall
Wanted: The Outlaw in American Visual Culture

Stephanie L. Hawkins
*American Iconographic: "National Geographic," Global Culture,
and the Visual Imagination*

Stephanie Harzewski
Chick Lit and Postfeminism